245N

GOVERNMENT AND POLITICS
IN TRIBAL SOCIETIES

Government and Politics in Tribal Societies

I. SCHAPERA

SCHOCKEN BOOKS • NEW YORK

First SCHOCKEN edition 1967

Copyright 1956, © 1967 by C. A. Watts & Co. Ltd.

Library of Congress Catalog Card No. 67–26993

Manufactured in the United States of America

CONTENTS

PREFACE

THE lectures upon which this book is based were delivered at the University of Birmingham in the Winter Term of 1950. Their subject was 'Politics and Law in Primitive Society', and the various points of theoretical interest were illustrated by sketchy examples deliberately chosen from peoples in many different parts of the world. In preparing them for publication, I have confined discussion to the forms and functions of primitive governments, which in contrast with law are still a relatively unexplored field of study. I have also confined the range of illustrative material to four separate groups of peoples living in South Africa. This I have done in the belief that detailed and systematic comparison of even a few different types of society, all occurring in a single region, is likely to provide a more satisfactory basis for generalization than scattered and fragmentary citations of the kind originally attempted and still far too common in the literature of social anthropology. In effect the book is now a study of primitive governments in South Africa, not of 'primitive government' in general; but I hope that the more comprehensive analysis made possible by this limitation will compensate to some extent for omission of reference to the many other varieties of government described by ethnographers.

Some of the material discussed is drawn from my own fieldwork in the Bechuanaland Protectorate. But for the great bulk I have necessarily had to rely upon the writings of others. To indicate separately the source, or sometimes sources, of every single statement made would have greatly increased the size of the book without adding much of use to most readers; I have therefore restricted specific acknowledgment to direct quotations and points of special interest or importance, and for the rest would refer to the 'list of main sources' given at the end.

I wish here to express again my gratitude to the University of Birmingham for inviting me to deliver the Josiah Mason Lectures, and to Professors P. Sargant Florence, Leonard J. Russell, Charles Madge, and their colleagues, for much kindness and generous hospitality.

I. SCHAPERA

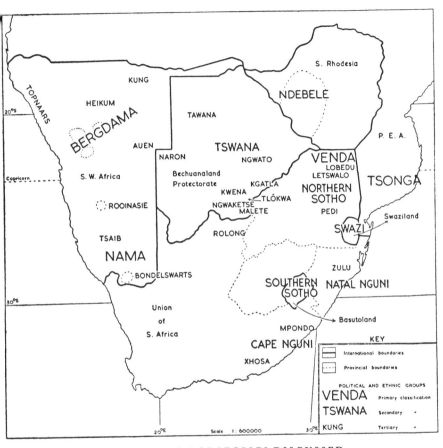

KUNG

HEIKUM

TOPNAARS

20°S

BERGDAMA

TAWANA

S. Rhodesia

NDEBELE

P. E. A.

AUEN

NARON

S. W. Africa

Capricorn

ROOINASIE

TSAIB

NAMA

BONDELSWARTS

30°S

Union
of
S. Africa

TSWANA

NGWATO

Bechuanaland
Protectorate

KGATLA

KWENA

TLÔKWA

NGWAKETSE

MALETE

ROLONG

VENDA

LOBEDU
LETSWALO

NORTHERN
SOTHO

PEDI

TSONGA

Swaziland

SWAZI

ZULU

SOUTHERN
SOTHO

NATAL NGUNI

Basutoland

MPONDO

CAPE NGUNI

XHOSA

KEY

International boundaries

Provincial boundaries

POLITICAL AND ETHNIC GROUPS

VENDA   Primary classification

TSWANA   Secondary   "

KUNG   Tertiary   "

20°E   Scale 1 : 600000   30°E

DISTRIBUTION OF PEOPLES DISCUSSED

GOVERNMENT AND POLITICS
IN TRIBAL SOCIETIES

The Political Community

I

Anthropologists have on the whole neglected the comparative study of political organization in primitive societies. Ethnographical monographs usually contain some account of how the people described manage their public affairs; most textbooks of social anthropology have a section on 'government', consisting mainly of illustrative examples chosen more or less haphazardly; many writers have speculated about the origins of chieftainship and other forms of personal authority; and, fairly recently, some detailed discussions have been published of individual political systems, notably in Africa and North America. But in contrast with what has been written about primitive kinship and marriage, economics, religion, or even law, relatively little attention has been paid to defining and comparing types of political unit in primitive societies, or to investigating such topics as the organization and use of political power, the sources and sanctions of political authority, and the relations between rulers and subjects.

It is thus not surprising that sociologists and others sometimes hold mistaken views about primitive systems of political organization. Some even deny that such systems exist. Teggart, for example, says that 'political organization is an exceptional thing, characteristic only of certain groups, and . . . all peoples whatsoever have once been or still are organized on a different basis.'[1] By political organization he evidently means state systems like those found in the modern Western world. There have been many definitions of the state, but for our present purpose that given in the *Shorter Oxford English Dictionary* will do well enough: 'a body of people occupying a defined territory and organized

---

[1] F. J. Teggart, *The Processes of History* (1918), p. 79.

under a sovereign government.'[1] In calling political organization an 'exceptional thing,' it is the territorial aspect, not the governmental, that Teggart is stressing. As he himself says,[2]

'If we compare "primitive" and "civilized" groups of men as we find them in the world to-day, almost the first point of difference that will strike the observer is that, among the former, the individual identifies himself by particularising his blood-relationships, whereas, in the latter, the individual defines his status in terms of relation to a given territory.'

The distinction here made between primitive and civilized societies was first formulated by Maine in 1861. In a famous and often-quoted passage he says:[3]

'All ancient societies regarded themselves as having proceeded from one original stock, and even laboured under an incapacity for comprehending any reason except this for their holding together in political union. The history of political ideas begins, in fact, with the assumption that kinship in blood is the sole possible ground of community in political functions; nor is there any of those subversions of feeling, which we term emphatically revolutions, so startling and so complete as the change which is accomplished when some other principle—such as that, for instance, of *local contiguity*—establishes itself for the first time as the basis of common political action. . . . The idea that a number of persons should exercise political rights in common simply because they happened to live within the same topographical limits was utterly strange and monstrous to primitive antiquity.'

Maine himself was careful to claim that his views about 'ancient societies' were correct only 'so long as they are confined to the

---

[1] Cf. J. L. Brierly, *The Law of Nations* (4th ed., 1949), p. 122: 'the essential characteristics of a state [are] an organized government, a defined territory, and such a degree of independence of control by any other state as to be capable of conducting its own international relations'.

[2] *Op. cit.*, p. 80.

[3] H. S. Maine, *Ancient Law* (Pollock's ed., 1930), pp. 144 ff.

Aryan, Semitic, and Uralian races.'[1] Other writers applied them more widely. Morgan, especially, said that 'all forms of government are reducible to two general plans.' The first, which he calls 'social organization' or 'a society (*societas*)', occurs among all savages and barbarians; it is 'founded upon gentes, phratries and tribes', and the government deals with people in their personal capacity as members of kinship groups. The second, distinguished as 'political organization', 'political society', or a 'state (*civitas*)', is characteristic of civilization; it is founded upon territory and property, and the government deals with people in their residential capacity, as inhabitants of a regional unit such as a township, county, or state.[2]

The view that political aggregates in primitive society are essentially groups of kin was echoed by many later writers, including Durkheim, Hobhouse, Vinogradoff, Hartland, and Davy. Although often criticized, notably by Lowie and Goldenweiser, and although explicitly disproved by studies published in *African Political Systems* (1940), it still prevails with some modern sociologists. As recently as 1947, for example, MacIver wrote:[3]

'Tribal government differs from all other political forms in that the territorial basis is not sharply defined. In its primary sense a tribe is a community organized on the basis of kinship . . . and usually claiming to be descended from a common ancestor. Tribal government is characteristic of simple society and is then equivalent to primitive government.'

Similar statements have been made, though rather more cautiously, by Ginsberg and Seagle.[4] Even Malinowski, who should have known better, maintains that 'The primitive state is not tyrannical to its own subjects' because, 'first and foremost, we know that a primitive tribe is always a body of people related by bonds of kinship and relationship, by clanship and age-grade'; and

[1] *Lectures on the Early History of Institutions* (1874), p. 66.
[2] L. H. Morgan, *Ancient Society* (1877), pp. 6 f., 61.
[3] R. M. MacIver, *The Web of Government* (1947), p. 158.
[4] M. Ginsberg, *Sociology* (1934), pp. 129 f.; W. Seagle, *The Quest for Law* (1941), pp. xv, 43.

he also speaks of the tribe as a group 'where practically everybody is related, really or fictitiously, to everybody else.'[1]

There are many instances in primitive society, notably among food-gatherers, where the political community does in fact consist of people all of whom are or claim to be related. The Australian aborigines are a famous example. No doubt Fortes and Evans-Pritchard had such societies in mind when they wrote:[2]

'It seems probable to us that three types of political system can be distinguished. Firstly, there are those very small societies . . . in which even the largest political unit embraces a group of people all of whom are united to one another by ties of kinship, so that political relations are coterminous with kinship relations and the political structure and kinship organization are completely fused.'

But even among food-gatherers there are some, such as the Andaman Islanders, among whom the members of a community do not all claim to be related, and people can readily remove from one community to another; and among pastoralists and cultivators, notably in Africa, political aggregates often contain people of many different ethnic stocks.

Even where all members of the community are related, moreover, kinship is not the only basis of solidarity. The territorial factor is also important—far more important, indeed, than writers such as MacIver and Seagle are willing to concede. What they seem to have overlooked is that, especially among food-gatherers, the community seldom if ever embraces the whole of a person's kin. The Australian aborigines, for example, live in small autonomous bands, each with exclusive and jealously guarded rights to a well-defined tract of land. The males and unmarried females of a band are all related to one another agnatically. But, owing to the widespread rule of local exogamy, a man's maternal relatives and affines almost always belong to some other band than his own; moreover, kinship ties are so comprehensively extended that he is

[1] B. Malinowski, *Freedom and Civilization* (1947), pp. 266, 253.
[2] M. Fortes and E. E. Evans-Pritchard (eds.), *African Political Systems* (1940), pp. 6 f.

usually held to be related 'to every person with whom he has any social dealings whatever, whether of his own or of another tribe.'[1] Nevertheless, he always distinguishes clearly between members of his own band and people living elsewhere; the latter belong to foreign communities, do not share his territorial rights and local obligations, and are sometimes even his enemies. His political associates, in other words, are not the whole of his kin, but only those particular kinsmen who belong to his own local group.

It is therefore incorrect to maintain that 'political union' is based solely on kinship in primitive societies, and on 'local contiguity' in civilized societies. Even in Australia kinship is not the only 'basis of common political action'; and even in modern Western society appeals to ties of 'common blood' have featured prominently in doctrines of racial supremacy and in laws against miscegenation. Both kinship and locality serve everywhere to link people together, and the most we can claim is that in primitive societies kinship is often much more important than among ourselves in the regulation of public life.

II

What has just been said may be illustrated in detail by reference to four different groups of peoples, all living in South Africa, whom I propose to use here as representative of 'primitive society'.[2] They are the Bushmen, Bergdama, Hottentots, and Southern Bantu. I choose them partly because some are known to me from personal observation, and the others from familiarity with the literature.[3] Each group, moreover, consists of many separate though similar political communities, and I believe that intensive comparison of such communities may yield information

[1] A. R. Radcliffe-Brown, *The Social Organization of Australian Tribes* (1931), pp. 13 f.
[2] I use the term 'primitive' in the conventional sense for peoples whose culture is non-literate; cf. *Notes and Queries on Anthropology* (6th ed., 1951), p. 28.
[3] Among Bantu, I have studied the Tswana, and paid fleeting visits to Zulu, Swazi, and Southern Sotho; I am also acquainted at first hand with Hottentots and Bushmen.

unlikely to be obtained by following the usual practice of discussing 'typical societies' chosen somewhat arbitrarily from
various parts of the world.[1] The four groups also have different
modes of subsistence, and can therefore be used to test theories
about the relationship between political structure and 'stages of
economic culture.'[2]

These peoples have all been influenced in many ways by contact both with one another and, more recently, with Europeans;
for example, they are now all subject to European governments,
and their culture sometimes differs markedly from the traditional
pattern. However, it is still possible to determine that pattern, both
from what survives and from the records of earlier observers; and,
since we are here concerned primarily with 'primitive' society,
I shall ignore recent changes except where they seem to be
relevant.

The Bushmen in their native condition are hunters and collectors, deriving their food supply entirely from the natural
resources of their environment; they have no domestic animals
except the dog, and practise no agriculture. At one time spread
over most of Southern Africa, today they are found relatively
undisturbed only in northern and western Bechuanaland and the
adjoining districts of South West Africa and Angola. The best-
known 'tribes' in this region are the Naron, Auen, Kung, and
Heikum.[3] These speak different though related languages, and in
culture constitute what is termed the North-Western division of
Bushmen. It is with them alone that I shall be dealing here. Their
numbers are not accurately known, but may be estimated at
about 8,000 in all.

The Bergdama, numbering about 29,000, live chiefly in the

[1] Schapera, 'Some notes on comparative method in Social Anthropology',
Amer. Anthrop., vol. 55 (1953), pp. 353-61; cf. Fortes and Evans-Pritchard, *op.
cit.*, p. 3.
[2] Cf. Hobhouse, Wheeler, and Ginsberg, *The Material Culture and Social Institutions of the Simpler Peoples* (1915), chap. II.
[3] For the reader's convenience I use simplified forms. In the conventional ortho-
graphy the names are *Naron* (‖*aikwe*), ‖*Kau-‖en*, !*Khu*, and *Hei-‖om*, the sym-
bols ‖ and ! representing "click" consonants.

central parts of South West Africa. They are one of the great ethnological puzzles of the country. Physically of true Negro stock, they are isolated far from others of their kind, and speak the language of the Nama Hottentots, to whom most of them were once subject. Nowadays they are mainly in European employ or settled on Mission stations. But independent communities still survive in mountain fastnesses; here the great majority live solely by hunting and collecting, though some also keep goats and grow a little tobacco.

The Hottentots are racially and linguistically allied to the Bushmen, but differ in culture. They formerly consisted of four main divisions (Cape Hottentots, Eastern Hottentots, Korana, and Nama), which varied in details of language and custom. The first three have virtually disappeared as separate entities. The only relatively intact division today are the Nama, found chiefly in the southern parts of South West Africa, and numbering altogether about 24,000. They too have changed greatly under European domination, but their traditional culture is fairly well known. In their native condition they keep cattle and sheep, and supplement their staple diet of milk by hunting and collecting.

The Bantu differ from the three other peoples in race, language, and culture. Still vigorous and flourishing, they greatly outnumber all other inhabitants of South Africa (including Europeans), and in many regions retain their old tribal system. They are usually classified into four major divisions: Nguni, Tsonga, Sotho, and Venda. The Nguni, found chiefly between the Drakensberg escarpment and the sea, from Swaziland in the north far down into the Cape Province, consist of several subdivisions; the most important the Cape Nguni (2,380,000), Natal Nguni or 'Zulu' (2,048,000), Swazi (410,000), and Transvaal Ndebele (144,000). The Tsonga (1,369,000) live mainly in Portuguese East Africa south of the Sabi River, with offshoots in the adjoining districts of the Transvaal. The Sotho, who occupy the great interior plateau north of the Orange River and west and north of the Drakensberg, are subdivided into the Southern Sotho (1,391,000), Tswana or Western Sotho (816,000), and Northern or Transvaal

Sotho (772,000.) The Venda are by far the smallest division; confined largely to the Soutpansberg district in Northern Transvaal, they number only 133,000.[1]

This classification of the Bantu is based primarily upon language, each division speaking dialects unintelligible to the others, though unmistakably of the same family. There are also many important variations in culture, which sometimes overlap the linguistic divisions. In their native condition, however, all Bantu subsist mainly upon animal husbandry and hoe-culture; they keep cattle, goats, and sheep, and raise crops of various kinds, notably sorghum and maize. Wherever possible, they also hunt and collect edible wild plants.

The four peoples differ not only in mode of subsistence, but also in the nature and size of their political communities. By a 'political community' I mean a group of people organized into a single unit managing its affairs independently of external control (except that exercised nowadays by European governments). Each community also has its own territory and an official head or 'chief'. But the criterion I wish to stress here is independence. No community is completely isolated; its members may exchange visits, trade, and intermarry, with those of other communities, and may also fight against them or as their allies. But so long as it alone decides on matters of local concern, so long as there is no dictation from outside, and so long as its decisions and actions cannot be overruled by any higher authority, it may be said to have political independence. That is the feature immediately distinguishing the modern state, for example, from such other associations as churches, trade unions, and municipalities; the latter, though all partly autonomous, are in the last resort subject to the control of the state, which on the other hand is sovereign within the territory that it occupies. When applied to primitive societies, the use of our criterion means that we are justified in treating as like units the Bergdama band and the Sotho 'nation' of Basutoland, despite their great difference in size, territorial extent, social composition,

[1] The population figures for the Bantu, based on the 1946 census, are taken from van Warmelo (1952), p. 5.

and complexity of organization. Here I disagree with Murdock, who says:[1]

'One may . . . seriously question the validity of those comparative studies of government which deal with the largest political aggregates in diverse societies, whether they be communities, organized tribes, or complex states. The Arunta band and the Inca empire, for example, are not comparable units, although it might well be profitable to compare the former with the local Peruvian *ayllu*, or the governmental institutions of the Incas with the Dahomean monarchy.'

He might as well argue that the political scientist interested in forms of the state is not justified in comparing the U.S.S.R. with Monaco, or the United States of America with the principality of Liechtenstein.

Among the Bushmen, people speaking the same language are collectively distinguished by a common name (Auen, Kung, etc.). But although usually referred to in the literature as a 'tribe', they are not united under a single government, nor do they all ever act together. Instead they are divided into separate local 'bands'. Each band, containing on the average from fifty to one hundred persons, is self-governing and independent, and warfare between bands of the same tribe is by no means unusual. It is consequently the band, and not the tribe, which constitutes what I have termed the political community. The Heikum have at least eight, and the Auen fifteen, but these figures, the only ones available, are probably incomplete.

The Bergdama, though linguistically homogeneous, are divided into eleven major groups, inhabiting different regions and bearing distinctive names. These groups, like the Bushman 'tribe', lack social cohesion. The largest political aggregate (outside modern Mission stations) is also the band, consisting of from ten to thirty persons who live together habitually in a separate area of their own. There are said to be 'hundreds' of such bands, all independent of one another.

[1] G. P. Murdock, *Social Structure* (1949), p. 86.

Hottentot political communities are much larger than those of Bergdama or Bushmen. The Nama, who all speak the same language, consist historically of two main divisions: 'Great Namaqua', some of whom have been in South West Africa for several centuries, and 'Orlams', who migrated there from the Cape Colony at the end of the eighteenth century and early in the nineteenth after adopting many features of European culture. The former, with whom alone we are here concerned, were by 1850 grouped into nine separate political communities, usually referred to locally as 'tribes'. These tribes, commonly known nowadays by Afrikaans versions of their own names, have lost much of their former cohesion and become widely scattered; today only the Rooinasie, Bondelswarts, Swartboois, and Topnaars survive as distinct entities. But towards the end of the nineteenth century all were still largely intact, with populations ranging from about 500 to 2,500 each.

Among the Bantu, each of the divisions and subdivisions named above contains many different political communities, generally also called 'tribes' in South Africa. Altogether there are probably well over a thousand separate tribes. They vary greatly in size. Some have only a few hundred members each, others several thousand, and others as many as twenty thousand or more. In Bechuanaland, for example, the principal tribes (all belonging to the Tswana subdivision of the Sotho division) are the Tlôkwa (pop. 2,300), Khurutshe (3,000), Malete (9,500), Kgatla (20,000), Ngwaketse (39,000), Tawana (39,000), Kwena (40,000), and Ngwato (101,000). By far the largest tribe, at present, are the Sotho of Basutoland (682,000), and then come the Eastern Mpondo (260,000) and the Swazi of Swaziland (204,000). In the nineteenth century there were several others of comparable size, such as the Zulu, Pedi (Northern Transvaal), and Shangana (Mozambique); but, owing mainly to civil wars and conflicts with Europeans, they have since broken apart. Many other tribes, too, have disintegrated; the great majority, however, still retain corporate existence.

III

The members of every political community in South Africa normally occupy the same territory. MacIver, it will be recalled, says that in primitive societies 'the territorial basis is not sharply defined', and, he adds, 'When the tribe is nomadic we have the extreme case of the detachment of political government from a clearly delimited territory'.[1] In view of this generalization, the relationship of South African peoples to their land requires discussion. What constitutes a community's 'territory', and do its members claim rights over land and its resources that are denied to outsiders? Moreover, one essential characteristic of the modern state is territorial sovereignty: it exercises control over all persons living in its territory, and only by moving elsewhere—not always easy in these days of passports, visas, and currency restrictions—can they withdraw from its jurisdiction. The state is therefore sometimes said to be 'a community in which membership is not voluntary, but imposed upon all individuals within a given territory'.[2] This suggests another problem that we must consider. Does the South African community embrace all the inhabitants of a given region, or can people share the use of the land and yet have no other common link than that they are co-residents?

Among both Bushmen and Bergdama, each band has corporate and exclusive rights to the land that it occupies. Its territory is clearly defined by recognized boundaries, such as river beds, sand dunes, hills, and belts of trees; occasionally, among Bushmen, band territories are also separated by broad zones of neutral land. The average Bushman band is said to have an area of 200 sq. miles or more; for Bergdama no figures are available, though other evidence suggests that their territories are much smaller. The members of a Bushman band usually trek together over their land from one water-hole to another, but during the dry season

1 *The Web of Government* (1947), p. 158.
2 W. J. Shepard, 'Government (History and Theory)', *Enc. Social Sciences,* vol. vii (1932), p. 9.

families often wander about separately for a while, either singly or in small clusters. They have no permanent camping sites, and live in crude shelters of bush easily made and lightly abandoned. The Bergdama, too, are mostly nomadic, but although individual families may break away for a few days all members of a band normally camp together; indeed, bands keeping goats often have fairly stable villages, with huts carefully made of branches and grass. The band, among both peoples, is thus a compact residential group for at least part of the year.

Normally, moreover, only its own members may live and seek food in the area that they occupy. These rights are shared equally by all, individual or family holdings being unknown, and when necessary they are defended against violation by outsiders. If neighbouring bands are friendly, there is much visiting between them, they trade, intermarry, and occasionally have joint initiation ceremonies for boys, and in case of local drought a group in distress may receive temporary hospitality from another more favourably situated. But strangers caught poaching or wandering without permission through the land are ruthlessly punished and may even be killed. Because of this hostile reaction to trespass, people seldom venture outside their own territory unless well acquainted and friendly with those into whose land they have to go. It can hardly be maintained, therefore, that the Bushman or Bergdama band does not have a 'sharply defined territorial basis.'

Among Hottentots, on the other hand, there were formerly no clear-cut tribal boundaries. The members of each tribe usually ranged with their live-stock and portable mat huts round certain fountains or other permanent water-holes, which they regarded as theirs because of habitual and continuous exploitation. Occasionally they all camped together, but seldom for long; normally they were dispersed over the country, at intervals of perhaps 20 to 50 miles, in groups of not more than 200 to 300 people, each wandering about on its own in the vicinity of a fountain to which the people regularly returned whenever grazing conditions permitted. There were no individual or family rights to land; everybody grazed and watered his cattle wherever he wished, and even the small local groups often broke apart temporarily into smaller units consisting of only a few closely-related families. Strangers trekking through the country were allowed the same privileges, and no attempt was made to exclude them. But if they intended to remain anywhere for long, they had to seek permission from the local people and pay annual tribute, usually in cattle, in token of allegiance. Failing this, there might be fighting, the usual outcome of which was that the weaker group moved somewhere else.

Most of the tribes that came from the south in the eighteenth and early nineteenth centuries initially paid such tribute to the Rooinasie, who were the first to settle in the country; but they gradually reasserted their independence and gained mastery of the land they had been allowed to occupy. The development of missionary enterprise from about 1840 onwards led also to the establishment at the most reliable fountains of permanent tribal centres, a feature hitherto unknown. In consequence, increasing regard was paid to boundaries, and by about 1860 the territory of each tribe was fairly well defined, usually by such natural features as hills and river beds. It was generally accepted, too, that all inhabitants of a tribal area were subject to the authority of the local chief, without whose permission no stranger might settle there. During the many wars of later years territorial changes were frequent, but under colonial rule (1884 onwards) each of the surviving tribes was given its own 'Reserve', usually only part of the land it had previously controlled. These Reserves, at the present time, vary in size from about 55 sq. miles (Rooinasie) to 675 (Bondelswarts). Most of the inhabitants have permanent homes either in the central village or at one of the few outlying hamlets sometimes also found, but live-stock are kept mainly at outposts shifted according to grazing and water conditions and visited periodically by the owners to supervise the resident herdsmen.

Among the Bantu also tribal boundaries were at first fairly vague. Each tribe seems to have claimed only the land actually used by its members for residence, cultivation, grazing, etc., and relatively big stretches of 'unpeopled' country sometimes divided neighbouring tribes. But the fact that when war threatened the main paths were charmed 'to peg down the country' and keep out invaders shows that boundaries of some kind were recognized; and how deeply the people were sometimes attached to their land was seen among the Southern Sotho when, 'at a time of public danger', Chief Moshesh concluded an exhortation to his men with the cry, 'Let us die for our country!' 'The whole assembly was electrified; and nothing was heard but the words, repeated a thousand times,—"Let us die for our country!"[1] However, since tribes or portions of tribes often migrated because of war, famine, or internal dissension, territorial disputes due to encroachment were common. Many tribes now occupy land originally acquired by settlement or conquest; many others, in the course of their history, were driven from several successive homes.

In general it is only within the past century and a half, and largely owing to the spread of European domination, that tribal territories have become fairly stable and precisely defined. But much of what was formerly tribal land has been appropriated for European settlement, and in some parts of the Union, and in Swaziland, the members of a single tribe now often live in discrete areas or on farms owned by Europeans. Elsewhere compact tribal territories still exist. They vary greatly in size. In Bechuanaland, for example, where there has been relatively little disturbance, the Kgatla occupy some 3,600 sq. miles, the Ngwaketse 9,000, the Kwena 15,000, the Tawana 34,500, and the Ngwato 42,000; similarly, the Sotho of Basutoland have about 11,700 sq. miles. Such large territories, however, are decidedly exceptional; the great majority of tribal territories are less than 200 sq. miles in extent, and some are very much smaller.

Each tribe claims exclusive rights to the land that it occupies. All people living there are subject to the chief, as head of the local government, and only by moving away can they escape his control. Outsiders may not settle in the territory without his permission, and he places them where he wishes; henceforth they too are his subjects, and if they disobey him they may be expelled. He also regulates the distribution and use of the land, and must ensure

[1] Casalis (1861), p. 157 f.

that every married man receives private holdings for residence and cultivation.

In contrast with our other peoples, the Bantu may be termed sedentary; their settlements are relatively stable, and their huts built to last for many years. Two main types of settlement pattern may be distinguished. The Nguni and Tsonga live in small discrete hamlets lying apart at distances of, say, a hundred yards to a mile or so. Such hamlets seldom contain more than about 20 people each, though the head-quarters of chiefs and important sub-chiefs may have as many as 100 or more. The live stock, which graze by day on the surrounding veld, are kept at night in special enclosures inside the circle of dwelling-huts, and the fields cultivated by the inhabitants are within easy walking distance. The Sotho and Venda, on the other hand, live in compact villages, often several miles apart. Most villages have from 50 to 300 inhabitants, but many are much larger; among the Tswana, especially, the capitals of some tribes have 5,000 or more inhabitants, perhaps the largest being Kanye (Ngwaketse) with 23,000. As a rule people occupy their village all the year round; their fields are close by, and their cattle graze on the common pastures in the immediate vicinity. But in Bechuanaland the arable lands of the larger settlements are often too far away to be visited daily from home; the inhabitants therefore move out for the cultivating season, when they are scattered about in small family groups each living temporarily next to its fields. The cattle, too, are kept at special grazing-posts in the open veld, sometimes many miles away, where they are herded continuously by the owner's servants or adolescent sons.

It may be said, therefore, that in South Africa each political community not only has its own territory, but occupies that territory to the exclusion of all others. The local inhabitants share rights of exploitation that are denied to outsiders except by special permission, and they act together as a unit in defence of those rights. Among Hottentots and Bantu the precise definition of tribal boundaries is a relatively recent development, but even before that tribes were territorially segregated and inter-tribal disputes over land often occurred. In view of all this, we can hardly

endorse Maine's contention that in primitive societies 'local contiguity' is never a 'basis of common political action'; it is at least
one of the factors uniting the members of a band or tribe and distinguishing them from other people. The Swazi, indeed, use the
word *live* for both 'tribe' and 'tribal territory', and the same com-
bination of meanings, with its implication that community and
land are inseparably connected, is found in other Nguni languages
and in Tsonga.

IV

The conclusion just reached does not necessarily invalidate the
whole of Maine's distinction between civilized and primitive
societies; it implies merely that political communities in South
Africa are always territorial entities with well-defined rights to
the land that they occupy. The basic question still remains: are the
members of a band or tribe all connected by ties of kinship, real or
putative, or are they on the contrary of diverse origins, making no
claim to be a single body of kin? The social composition of the
community must obviously determine what significance we at-
tach to local contiguity. If the community is essentially a kinship
group, its members may be living together just because they are
all related to one another; if it is not, their occupation of the same
territory needs another explanation.

The people belonging to a Bushman band are generally described
in the literature as a group of relatives. The exact nature of their
relationship is seldom specified; but one band of Kung, containing
31 adults (of whom 16 were males), was found to consist 'of an old
man with two sons, several grandsons both in the male and female
line, a son-in-law, and nephews and great-nephews, mostly
brother's descendants'.[1] The band is exogamous. A man when he
first marries moves to his wife's group; occasionally he stays there
for good, but normally she returns with him to his former home
after the birth of a child. These and similar indications suggest
that the band is probably a patrilocal extended family, with

[1] Bleek (1928. b), p. 109; for similar data, cf. Lebzelter (1934), pp. 19, 84.

temporary and perhaps even permanent additions of male affines and their children.

The Bergdama band is also a patrilocal extended family; it consists typically of a man and his married sons, his younger brothers and their married sons, and the wives and unmarried children of them all. As among Bushmen it is exogamous, and a newly-married couple sometimes live with the wife's people, but only until their first child has been born. In exceptional instances a band also contains one or more unrelated dependants, usually men found destitute in the veld and taken into service.

Bushmen and Bergdama may therefore be regarded as representing types of primitive society in which the political community is indeed composed exclusively or predominantly of kin. This cannot be said of the Hottentots. Here the tribe is not only proportionately much larger than the Bushman or Bergdama band, but also more varied in composition. Many of its members do claim to be related by descent in the male line from a common ancestor, the legendary founder of the tribe. But every tribe also contains people of alien stock, either descendants of refugees and captives, or themselves immigrants; some belong by origin to other Hottentot tribes, but the majority are ethnically distinct. About 1880, for example, the Tsaib tribe at Keetmanshoop consisted of 40 Tsaib, 60 Bondelswarts, 50 'Orlams', 110 'Basters' (mixed-breed Hottentots from the Cape Colony), 34 half-breeds (children of Hottentot women and White men), and about 130 Bushman and Bergdama servants; similarly, the Topnaar tribe at Sesfontein consisted in 1947 of 124 Nama (mostly Topnaars, but also some Swartboois), 262 Western Bantu (Himba, Herero, and Tjimba), 374 Bergdama, and 25 others (including Bushmen and 'Basters').[1] Such heterogeneity is due largely to the events of the past century, though (as already mentioned) Bergdama have been serfs among Nama from the earliest recorded times.

Among Bantu, the core of a tribe generally also consists of people related to the chief by descent from a common agnatic

---

[1] Vedder (1934), p. 567, quoting contemporary missionary records; van Warmelo (1951), p. 50.

ancestor. But even the smallest tribe nowadays contains families of alien origin, and in the larger tribes the royal descent group may constitute only a small proportion of the whole. Thus, in Bechuanaland, about half the Tlôkwa (pop. 2,300) are kinsmen of the chief, the others between them representing nine different alien stocks; at the other extreme, less than one per cent of the Tawana (pop. 39,000) trace agnatic descent from the founder of the tribe. Similarly the people of Basutoland, who now form a single tribe, are derived not only from what were formerly many different Sotho tribes, but partly also from Cape and Natal Nguni of varied origins, who constitute about 15 per cent of the total; among the Lobedu, a Transvaal Sotho tribe (pop. 33,000), over 90 per cent of the people differ in origin from the ruling stock, these aliens including Venda, Lemba, Tsonga, and Shona (from Rhodesia); among the Swazi of Swaziland the 162 heads of local districts include 41 of non-Swazi stock (22 'Zulu', 16 Sotho, and 3 Tsonga); and among the Mpondo 21 of the 67 clans locally represented are also of alien origin.[1]

Obviously, therefore, the tribe is by no means composed exclusively of kin. Nor is there any evidence that either Bantu or Hottentots ever practised what Maine terms 'factitious extensions of consanguinity', whereby, through adoption or some similar expedient, aliens incorporated into a tribe could *feign themselves* to be descended from the same stock as the people on whom they were engrafted.'[2] Like many other primitive peoples, it is true, both have classificatory systems of kinship terminology. But these are not of the kind found in Australia, where 'the recognition and classification of relationships is usually extended without any limit to embrace the whole society'.[3] A man applies kinship terms to almost everybody with whom he is genealogically connected by descent or marriage, and sometimes, as among the Nguni, he also uses them for people of his own and certain other clans, even if no

[1] Schapera (1952), p. 93 ff., p. 119 f.; Sheddick (1953), p. 13 ff.; Krige (1943), p. 85 ff.; Kuper (1952), p. 59 ff.; Hunter (1936), p. 58.
[2] *Ancient Law* (Pollock's ed.), pp. 147 f.
[3] Radcliffe-Brown, *Social Organization of Australian Tribes* (1931), p. 13.

genealogical tie is known to exist. But he certainly does not regard as a kinsman everybody whom he meets or even knows, and, especially in the larger tribes, the vast majority of his fellows are to him what Tswana call *batho basele*, 'other people', or *batho fêla*, 'merely people'. In some tribes, moreover, differences of ethnic origin are reflected and perpetuated in well-defined distinctions of social class.[1]

Malinowski, incidentally, maintains that only in 'higher stages of civilization' do 'we find two or several cultures living under the same authority', and the examples he gives are all taken from the recent history of Europe.[2] But cultural homogeneity, though characteristic of the Bushman or Bergdama band, is certainly not always a feature of the Hottentot or Bantu tribe. It is true that in the Zulu kingdom founded by Shaka (1816-28) 'all the tribes which made up the nation spoke dialects of the same language and had a common culture',[3] and that elsewhere, as among Tlôkwa and other small Tswana tribes, almost all aliens have by now adopted the language and customs of their rulers. But in Basutoland both Sotho and several Nguni dialects are in current daily use, each spoken by people differing from the others in certain details of culture; some Venda tribes contain unassimilated groups of Northern Sotho and Tsonga; and among the Swazi of Eastern Transvaal there are also many people whose home language is Tsonga. Still greater diversity is found in Northern Bechuanaland. The Ngwato tribe (pop. 101,000) contains, for example, about 10,000 Bushmen, 23,000 Kalaka, 1,000 Herero, 1,000 Rotse, and 700 Yeei, none of whom are Southern Bantu and all of whom differ from one another and from the ruling stock in language and customs; and the 39,000 members of the Tawana tribe include 13,000 Yeei, 6,000 Herero, 5,000 Mbukushu, 4,000 Bushmen, and 1,500 Gcereku, all of whom are also linguistically and culturally distinct.[4] Among the Hottentots, too, the Bantu members of the

1 Cf. Chapter II, p. 56.
2 *Freedom and Civilization* (1947), p. 261.
3 Gluckman (1940. a), p. 30.
4 Sheddick (1953), p. 78 ff.; van Warmelo (1935), pp. 117-21; Myburgh (1949), pp. 40, 54, 90, 102; Schapera (1952), pp. 65, 94.

Topnaar tribe speak their own language (Herero) and have their own distinctive customs.[1] In tribes composed of such diverse elements, differing sometimes even in race, political unity obviously cannot be attributed to kinship ties alone.

v

The mixed population of Hottentot and Bantu political communities raises the question: how is membership acquired? In modern Western societies, people can become nationals of a state in several different ways, including for example birth in its territory, descent (no matter where born), marriage (of women), naturalization, and transfer of territory from one state to another. But in primitive societies, according to Maine, 'political rights were attainable on no terms whatever except connection by blood, real or artificial.'[2]

The South African data show once again that he was too dogmatic. Among all four of our peoples, admittedly, membership of the political community is determined primarily by descent: a man, no matter where he is born, belongs to the same band or tribe as his father. In modern Bantu life, for example, men often leave home to work abroad. Any children born to them there, even by foreign wives, are held to be members of their own tribe, and can always return to live in its territory. But if a man is working temporarily in another tribe, say as a Government employee, the children born to him there are, like himself, regarded as aliens and do not have the same rights as local citizens. Using the conventional legal terms, we may say that Bantu recognize *jus sanguinis*, but not *jus soli*. This applies also to Bushmen and Bergdama, where the first child in a family, though usually born among its mother's people, is nevertheless a member of its father's band.

But descent is not the only method of acquiring membership.

[1] van Warmelo (1951), pp. 46, 50.
[2] *Ancient Law*, p. 148.

Among Bushmen and Bergdama, as already noted, men take their wives from other bands; among Hottentots and Bantu the tribe is not exogamous, but inter-tribal marriages do sometimes occur. The rule everywhere is that a wife moves to her husband's community, of which she then becomes a member; except among Bergdama, however, he occasionally joins her people instead. Marriage is thus a recognized method of admission to a community into which one is not born. For example, three of the ten clans among the Swartbooi Hottentots are said to be descended from foreigners who remained in the tribe after marrying local women, and among the Ngwaketse (Tswana) the ancestors of Laka and Rrantadi wards became naturalized in the same way.[1]

In pre-colonial days Bantu tribes often also acquired new members by conquest. Inter-tribal wars were common. They were usually fought to avenge insult or injury, loot cattle, or assert mastery over disputed rights to land, and in such cases the victors seldom tried to impose their rule upon the others. But, especially if there was perpetual trouble, they did sometimes annex those portions of the vanquished tribe that failed to find safety in flight. Among groups said to have been assimilated in this way were, for example, the Malebye, Mabodisa, Rokologadi, and Bididi, wards of the Kgatla, and the Sikwa and Madibana wards of the Malete.[2]

Recruitment by conquest more often occurred when a tribe deliberately pursued a policy of expansion or sought a home in some other region. The local inhabitants then had to surrender or fight, and if defeated their only alternatives were to flee or become subject to their invaders. Early in the nineteenth century several large 'kingdoms' were created in this way. The Zulu under Shaka (1816-28), the Swazi under Sobhuza I (1815-39) and Mswati II (1840-68), and the Pedi under Thulare (d. 1824) and Sekwati (1827-61) all expanded greatly by defeating and absorbing many of their neighbours; Shaka, especially, is known to have subjugated well over a hundred separate tribes. His example was

[1] Hoernlé (1925), p. 9 f.; Schapera (1952), pp. 42 f., 45.
[2] Schapera (1952), pp. 111, 112, 113, 121.

followed by other Natal Nguni chiefs, who after fleeing from him created large domains of their own: Mzilikazi (1822-68), after dominating the Central and Western Transvaal for about fifteen years and taking many Sotho captives, went on to conquer the Shona peoples of Southern Rhodesia, where he established the Ndebele kingdom, and Soshangana (1819-56) conquered many of the Tsonga tribes in Portuguese East Africa, where he established the 'Shangana' (Gaza) kingdom. In Bechuanaland the Ngwato, during the reigns of Kgari (1817-28) and Sekgoma I (1834-75), gradually extended their control in the same manner over Bushmen, Kgalagadi, Kaa, Phaleng, Tswapong, and the peoples along the Botletle River (Khurutshe, Yeei, etc.), and the Tawana, after moving to Lake Ngami (c. 1800), similarly became overlords of the local Yeei, Bushmen, and Kgalagadi, and subsequently of Mbukushu farther north; in both instances the subjugated peoples lived in small separate communities and were therefore unable to offer effective resistance to their more powerful opponents.

Warfare led also to the flight of many tribes or portions of tribes before an invading enemy or from the oppression of a conqueror. Some managed to retain their independence elsewhere, but others preferred or were forced by local conditions to seek the protection of an alien chief. The Cape Nguni tribes, for example, received large accessions of refugees from tribes uprooted by Shaka's raids into Natal; in Basutoland, Moshesh (c. 1810-70) founded the present 'Basuto nation' partly by conquest, but mainly by accepting the remnants of other tribes scattered by the widespread repercussions of the Zulu campaigns; the invasion of Portuguese East Africa by Soshangana sent many groups of Tsonga fleeing into the Eastern Transvaal, where some attached themselves to local Swazi, Venda, or Sotho, chiefs; and the Ngwato in Northern Bechuanaland were joined by large numbers of Kalanga and other peoples fleeing from the Ndebele tyranny in Southern Rhodesia.

Other immigrants, in the old days, consisted of groups seceding from a tribe because of internal disputes, for example about succession to the chieftainship. Such groups might become independent, constituting new tribes;[1] but, especially if relatively small and weak, they often sought admission to some other tribe instead. Almost every tribe now contains the descendants of offshoots from its neighbours; the Kgatla, for example, were towards the end of the nineteenth century joined by seceding groups of Tlôkwa, Malete, Kaa, and Kwena. In addition, almost every tribe from time to time received single families or persons of alien origin who had left home because of famine, injustice, dissatisfaction with local conditions, etc.

Under European rule conquest of one tribe by another has ceased to be possible, but immigration is still an important method of acquiring new members. In Bechuanaland, for example, the Tawana were joined in 1905 by several thousand Herero and Mbandieru fleeing from South West Africa after a disastrous revolt against the local German government; the Ngwato were joined in 1913 by the main body of the Khurutshe tribe, who left their home in the Tati Native Reserve owing allegedly to shortage of land; and the Kwena were joined in 1934 by about 4,000 Mmanaana-Kgatla previously living under the Ngwaketse, with whose chief they had quarrelled. Such large-scale accessions are relatively rare, but almost everywhere individual or family immigration is fairly common. It has been reinforced by the attraction into South Africa of people from the Rhodesias and beyond; they come seeking work, and some ultimately join local tribes, especially in the Transvaal and Bechuanaland, instead of returning home. All the tribes of Northern Bechuanaland, for example, now contain large numbers of immigrants from North-Western Rhodesia who have drifted in piecemeal during the course of the present century.

Hottentot tribes have also acquired members by both conquest and immigration. Unlike some of the Bantu, they did not as a rule deliberately pursue expansionist policies, and though often at war with one another sought to destroy or expel their enemies and not to annex them; some, however, did absorb Bergdama,

[1] See below, p. 27.

Bushmen, or others, whose land they had occupied. In addition, almost all were joined from time to time, especially during the nineteenth century, by refugees scattered in war, by 'Baster' and 'Orlam' immigrants from the Cape Colony, and casual immigrants of other kinds. The Topnaars at Sesfontein, for example, became overlords of Bergdama, Herero, Himba, etc., when they occupied their present home (c. 1860), and in 1882 they were joined by a group of Swartboois from the south.

Among Bushmen and Bergdama, on the other hand, there is very little immigration; as already noted, however, a Bushman occasionally joins his wife's band, and among Bergdama a band occasionally admits an isolated stranger found destitute in the veld. Among both peoples, too, only young women and children are ever taken captive in war, and bands never try to impose their rule upon neighbours whom they defeat; their mode of subsistence prevents them from living together in large numbers, and they lack the organization for controlling scattered groups.

Among Bantu, people wishing to join another tribe must first seek its chief's permission to settle in his country. Without this formality they cannot obtain land for residence and cultivation, and should they squat anywhere of their own accord they are liable to expulsion. In the old days they were usually required to pay the chief a special tribute in cattle or other commodities, which showed that they acknowledged his supremacy and bound themselves to observe the laws of his tribe. The payment of tribute was likewise expected among Hottentots. There is no record of any conditions or ceremonies governing the admission of immigrants into a Bushman or Bergdama band.

As we shall see later, both newly-conquered peoples and recent immigrants are usually subject to special restrictions before being granted the same rights as tribesmen of long standing. For the present we need merely note that among none of our peoples, especially Bantu and Hottentots, is the political community a closed group with membership determined solely and permanently by descent. It is, rather, an association into which people may be born, absorbed by conquest, or admitted as immigrants, and from which, again, they may depart voluntarily or be driven by the fortunes of war. Descent is certainly the outstanding condition of membership in the Bushman and Bergdama band, but it is not the only one, and among Bantu and Hottentots change of tribal affiliation is fairly common.

It is not only warfare and voluntary migration that are responsible for such changes. Membership of one's political community may also be forfeited by misconduct. Thus, among Bantu, people are sometimes banished for disputing the authority of the chief or for some other serious crime; the same penalty may be applied among Hottentots to 'incorrigible offenders', among Bergdama to people who have committed incest or who are notoriously 'avaricious and unsociable', and among Bushmen to habitual wrongdoers or to those found 'guilty of sexual offence'.[1] In all instances, banishment implies not only severance of social relations, but also expulsion from the territory of the community. The exiles usually seek admission to some other group, or nowadays may go to European centres of employment. Among Bantu they are sometimes permitted to return after a while, if they succeed in appeasing the chief, but they may also be excluded for ever. This reinforces the point, already made, that as a rule only those acknowledged as members of the community have the right to live in its land.

VI

The instability of political affiliation in South Africa is shown also by the fact that the number of communities keeps varying. Some disappear, and many others are created, and with each event of this kind people change their nationality.

Thus, among Bantu and Hottentots, many tribes that formerly existed have since been conquered or destroyed; their people may have survived, as captives or refugees, but the tribes themselves are no longer politically independent entities. In Basutoland, for

[1] Schapera (1938), pp. 49 f., 122 f., 124, 274; Wandres (1909), p. 607; Vedder (1923), i, p. 7, 51; Lebzelter (1934), pp. 60, 151; Brownlee (1943), p. 127.

example, the Kgwakgwa, Sia, Taung, Kgolokwe, and Tlôkwa, among others, were at one time separate communities, but now form part of the 'Basuto nation' ruled by the descendants of Moshesh; in Bechuanaland the Kaa, Phaleng, Mmanaana-Kgatla, Sikwa, Talaote, Madibana, etc., now survive only as subject groups dispersed among several different tribes (for example, there are Mmanaana-Kgatla among the Kwena, Ngwaketse, and Rolong, and Sikwa among the Malete, Kwena, and Rolong); and among Hottentots the remnants of the Grootdoode tribe, broken up by war in 1888, now belong mainly to the Bondelswarts.

On the other hand, a community may also divide from internal causes into groups that become politically independent of one another, so that instead of the original band or tribe there are now two or more. We do not know how bands originate among the Bushmen. Among Bergdama, we are told, a band may divide if its food resources prove inadequate, or if one of the older men, having several sons and a fair flock of goats, wishes to establish his own settlement.[1] This suggests that the division is usually peaceful, and due partly to economic necessity; there is nothing to indicate that it is ever the outcome of dispute.

The Nama Hottentots have a tradition that they are all descended from a common ancestor: five of their tribes were founded by brothers, and the others are later offshoots of the Rooinasie, whose founder was the eldest of the brothers. However this may be, early in the nineteenth century most of the present 'Great Namaqua' tribes were found living under the paramountcy of the Rooinasie, from whom they broke away during the rule of Chief Oasib (c. 1835-67). The usual procedure seems to have been that a group of people moved far afield in search of fresh grazing, remained away permanently, and ultimately claimed independence. The Swartboois and Tsaib are specifically said to have separated like that from the Rooinasie, and the Topnaars of Sesfontein are a similar offshoot from those at Walfish Bay.[2]

[1] Vedder (1923), i, p. 32.
[2] Hoernlé (1925), p. 5; Vedder (1934), pp. 127, 174, 457.

Among Bantu the creation of new tribes by fission is a constantly recurring feature of the political system. Disputes among members of the royal family often cause one of them to secede, and if accompanied by enough people he will usually start his own tribe. The great majority of existing tribes, in all divisions, are said to have originated in this manner; the reigning chiefs of many different tribes in each division can consequently trace their descent back to a common agnatic ancestor.

Thus, among Tswana, the Ngwaketse and Ngwato broke away separately from the Kwena early in the eighteenth century, and the Tawana subsequently seceded from the Ngwato (c. 1795); the Rolong tribe broke up (c. 1780) into four separate tribes, each headed by a son or grandson of Chief Tau (died c. 1760); and as recently as 1884 the Tlôkwa also divided under sons of Chief Matlapeng (d. 1880) into four sections, three of which still exist as separate tribes. Among Cape Nguni, the modern Gcaleka, Ngqika, Ndlambe, Dushane, Qayi, and several other tribes, are all derived through their chiefs from what was originally the single Xhosa tribe, whose senior segment is represented by the Gcaleka; the Zulu are an offshoot from the Qwabe, as are the Kuzwayo, Makhanya, and others; and among Venda the chiefs of most tribes are genealogically related through descent from Ndyambeu, under whose sons the hitherto united tribe began to break apart early in the eighteenth century. Similar examples can be cited from every other division. In almost all of them, the leader of the seceding faction was himself a member of the ruling family; there are very few recorded instances of a new tribe being founded by a commoner.

The available evidence shows that a seceding leader was often accompanied by some of his brothers and other close relatives, but that the bulk of his following was not necessarily related to him by ties of either blood or marriage. Such unrelated followers usually consisted first of people previously attached to him as personal retainers; occasionally, as among Tswana, he was reinforced by men of his own age-set; and, especially if secession was due to a dispute about the chieftainship, other followers would include those who believed in his cause or who had reason to fear or dis-like his successful rival. Even at the time of its origin, therefore, a tribe seldom if ever consisted exclusively of kin.

These illustrations show that a man may also change his political affiliation by deserting his chief and following a rival leader. To Bantu, indeed, the tribe is essentially a body of people all paying allegiance to the same chief. They certainly do not visualize it as a group of kin, nor even in terms of residence. People identify them-selves politically as subjects of such-and-such a chief, and not, as we do, as citizens of such-and-such a country. '*Ke MoKwena waga Sechele*', a man will say, 'I am a Kwena belonging to (chief) Sechele', nor will he ever use some such phrase as 'I am a Zulu-lander' or '*Civis romanus sum*'. Venda, in fact, have no specific tribal names; the members of each tribe are known simply by the name of their chief (for example, *vhaha Tshivhase*, 'Tshivhase's people'), although since every successive chief takes the same official name his followers do not change theirs with his accession. In other divisions tribes are often, though by no means always, named after some prominent ancestor of their chief (e.g. Zulu, Gcaleka, Swazi, Hurutshe). The tribal name, moreover, is retained even if the people move somewhere else. But when a group secedes and becomes a new tribe, it sometimes takes and keeps its leader's name as a distinctive label (e.g. Ngqika, Tawana, Shangana).[1]

Among Sotho, again, the chief is often addressed ceremonially by the personification of the tribal name, as MoKwena, Mo-Ngwato, etc. He also habitually refers to himself and is referred to by some such title as *kgosi yaBaHurutshe*, 'chief of the Hurutshe people', not, be it noted, as *kgosi ya LeHurutshe*, 'chief of Huru-tsheland'. And among Cape Nguni, as was stated long ago in a much-quoted passage, the distinction between crimes and civil wrongs 'is built upon the theory that all members of the tribe be-long to, and give strength to, the Chief. Any injury to the person of any member of a tribe, whether male or female, is therefore looked upon as an injury to the Chief, to whom, and to whom alone, reparation is due. So-called 'blood cases' come under the

---

[1] On Bantu tribal names, see van Warmelo (1935), pp. 6, 96, 117.

special jurisdiction of the Chief, and no reparation or damages can be claimed by the person or family injured through violence or wrong to the person. The Chief not only throws his shield over the person of every member of the tribe, but an injury to the person of anyone is a wrong to the Chief, through the 'Chief's man'. Hence it is that all cases of killing are dealt with in the Chief's court, and that compensation can by him, and by him only, be exacted in such cases. No member of the injured man's family can claim any benefit out of the blood of the Chief's man. As the Chief is alone wronged, he alone receives the fine or blood-money.'[1]

The chief, then, is in a sense the symbol of his tribe. People become and remain members of a tribe by accepting the rule of its chief, it is primarily through allegiance to the same chief that the diverse elements in a tribe give expression to their unity, and a man changes his tribal affiliation when he becomes subject to an alien chief. To Maine's two principles of political association we should therefore add a third, where the essential bond of union is neither kinship nor local contiguity, but personal attachment to a common leader. This applies not only to Bantu, but apparently also to Hottentots, though here the evidence is not so conclusive. There is nothing analogous among Bushmen or Bergdama, where kinship is the main determinant of band membership.

VII

Neither Hottentots nor Bantu support the view that political association in primitive societies is always based on kinship ties alone; judging from the way in which new tribes originate among the Bantu, we might even say that kinship often tends to divide a community instead of uniting it. Nevertheless it does feature prominently in the political life of both peoples: almost every person belongs to an extended kinship group of some kind, and this determines his rights and responsibilities to a much greater extent than among ourselves.

[1] C. G. H. Commission (1883), p. 21 f.

Hottentots, Nguni, and Tsonga are grouped into exogamous clans and lineages. A clan consists of people all claiming descent from a common agnatic ancestor, who is usually their eponym; a lineage comprises those people within a clan who are able to trace their relationship genealogically through a more recent ancestor. Membership of the clan, unlike that of the tribe, is determined solely by descent; but new clans may originate when lineages are considered sufficiently remote from the main stem to permit of intermarriage.

Hottentot clans are fairly small, and the men of each clan mostly belong to the same tribe; they formerly camped and moved about on their own with their families and other dependants, and even today still tend to live together in the same part of the tribal village. Each clan contains from one to four or five different lineages, and although all its lineages claim to be related to one another by blood the genealogical connection between them is often not known. Among Nguni and Tsonga, clans vary greatly in size, some having several thousand members each. Here also the clan was at one time a local group; many tribes, indeed, seem at first to have consisted predominantly of one clan, with but a small proportion of foreigners. Owing to warfare and migration, most clans are now dispersed over many different tribes; conversely, a single tribe may contain portions of many different clans. Within each tribe, members of the same clan are sometimes scattered about all over the country, in single families or small groups of closely related families; usually, however, they cluster together in lineages or segments of large lineages, and sometimes a sub-district or even a district may be inhabited chiefly by people of one clan. The hamlet, the smallest well-defined local unit, in any event almost always contains only a single extended or even elementary family, except at the headquarters of the chief or a sub-chief.

Sotho and Venda are divided firstly into large patrilineal totemic groups, almost all widely dispersed over many different tribes, but each with its own special taboos and other ritual usages. Among Sotho these groups are not exogamous, nor do people regard one another as kinsmen merely because they have the same totem; among Venda, however, members of the same group do claim to be related and formerly did not intermarry, though now they often do. In both divisions, the largest effective kinship unit is the lineage, usually subdivided into segments of varying span; descent is everywhere traced through the father, and among Venda and certain Transvaal Sotho, but nowhere else, the group is also exogamous. The members of a lineage are sometimes dispersed over different tribes, the outstanding example being the chiefs themselves, many of whom are closely related. But within each tribe people of the same lineage or, more commonly, the same segment of a lineage, tend to live together; it is rarely that a man's immediate neighbours do not include some of his close agnates. The relatively small villages characteristic of Venda and Southern Sotho are indeed each inhabited mainly by people of one kinship group; only in large villages such as those of the Tswana do many different groups of kin normally settle together, though even here each tends to constitute the whole or part of a 'ward' (local subdivision of the village).

Among both Hottentots and Bantu, members of the same clan or lineage have certain common ties, regardless of tribal affiliation. Except among Sotho, they may not intermarry; they are expected to be friendly and hospitable to one another; and among Bantu, but not Hottentots, they also worship their founding ancestor. Wherever they live together, they are still more intimately connected. They rely upon one another for support and protection in their disputes and other dealings with outsiders, and for help in many domestic undertakings, especially those requiring additional labour or food. Among Bantu a man's closest relatives are held jointly responsible with him for any debts or fines he has to pay; and among Hottentots, in the old days, if anybody was murdered his next of kin was obliged to avenge him, even against a fellow-tribesman.

In addition, in every local group of kin the man senior to the rest in line of birth is their acknowledged head. He arbitrates over their internal disputes, the matter being taken to an official court only if agreement cannot be reached (as a widespread Bantu proverb says, 'Outsiders should not intrude upon the affairs of the kin'), and he is the medium through whom all their public dealings with other people and the tribal authorities are conducted. If the group predominates in its area, he is usually also the official local headman, with jurisdiction over all the inhabitants; in some of the larger Bantu tribes a whole district may be governed by the head of the clan or lineage most strongly represented. Moreover, not only is his office normally hereditary, but his near relatives always share his authority; they are his recognized advisers and assistants, and during his absence or illness one of them acts as his deputy.

Among Hottentots, again, the heads of all the clans in a tribe formerly constituted its governing council, the chief taking precedence merely as head of the senior clan. There is nothing similar among the Bantu, except that in some Tswana tribes the chief sometimes consults all the ward-heads collectively; but, as among the Swazi, the heads of certain clans may have hereditary duties in the central administration of the tribe.

I mention these features here, though they will be elaborated in later chapters, because they show that kinship ties are indeed very important in public life. To this extent the stress laid upon kinship by Maine and his followers is fully justified. But they are mistaken in regarding kinship and local contiguity as irreconcilable and mutually exclusive determinants of 'common political action'. The tribe, among Bantu and Hottentots, is not a single kinship group, but a heterogeneous collection of such groups, all occupying one territory under the rule of the same chief. Among Bantu, moreover, it is divided for administrative purposes into regional units, such as districts and sub-districts, whose boundaries are determined primarily by topography and not according to kinship ties; and the head of every such unit controls all the residents of his area, whether or not they are related to him.

Among none of our peoples, too, does the political community necessarily contain all of a person's relatives. Among Bushmen and Bergdama the rule of band exogamy ensures that his maternal relatives and affines normally belong to other groups than his own, and if, as occasionally happens among Bushmen, he remains permanently with his wife's people, then his own agnatic kin will be living elsewhere. Among Hottentots inter-tribal marriages are also fairly common, so that kinship ties cut across the political boundaries; and among Bantu, as we have just seen, clans and lineages are often dispersed over several different tribes.

So far as the individual is concerned, kinship may thus be a factor linking him to people outside his own community. He sometimes visits or is visited by his relatives in other communities, and invitations usually pass between them to weddings and other ceremonies of domestic importance. Among Bushmen and Bergdama, bands connected by marriage may also help one another in times of war or drought, and among Bantu military alliances have sometimes been made between tribes whose chiefs are related by descent or through intermarriage. On the other hand, among all our peoples there has often also been fighting between communities so connected, and in such cases a man's primary loyalty is to his own community and not to his foreign kin. Kinship in itself is thus nowhere the sole 'basis of common political action'. At most, as among Bushmen and Bergdama, it is kinsmen of a particular kind, and not the whole range of kin, who belong to a band; and among Bantu and Hottentots the fundamental unit of political activity is the localized tribe with its mixed population, and not the widely dispersed body of kin who constitute a clan or a lineage.

VIII

We may now summarize the preceding discussion, and take it further. Each of our four peoples is divided politically into a number, sometimes a large number, of separate communities. Every community has a recognized territory, which normally only its own members may inhabit and exploit for subsistence; what Maine termed 'local contiguity' is therefore always one of the bonds uniting them. But communities differ in social composition. Two basic types may be distinguished. Among Bushmen and Bergdama the community is essentially a single group of kin, and membership, for males, is acquired primarily by agnatic descent. Among Hottentots and Bantu the community generally contains people of several or many stocks that do not all claim a common ancestry; these stocks sometimes differ in language and custom, and occasionally also in race. Membership is again determined primarily by descent, but it is often also acquired by immigration or in various other ways, and in the last resort it depends essentially upon allegiance to the local chief. Even here, however, kinsmen tend to be grouped into corporate units and frequently live together under hereditary leaders of their own.

The kin-based communities of Bushmen and Bergdama are very small, seldom exceeding twenty elementary families and often, especially among Bergdama, consisting of less than half a dozen; the heterogeneous communities of Hottentots and Bantu are very much larger, many Bantu tribes especially having 20,000 members or more. These differences in size are related partly to mode of subsistence, since the nature of the food supply necessarily determines how many people can live together continuously. Bushmen and most Bergdama, as hunters and collectors, depend entirely upon the natural resources of their environment. Both Hottentots and Bantu also hunt game and gather wild foods. But Hottentots, further, keep cattle and sheep, which are available at all times and normally tend to increase by reproduction. Bantu have a still more regular and abundant source of food, since they not only keep live-stock but grow various crops that can be stored for future use. They are consequently able to provide for much larger populations than Bushmen, Bergdama, or even Hottentots.

Mode of subsistence also affects patterns of settlement. Bushmen and Bergdama must wander about intermittently, following the movements of game and the growth of wild plants. The Hottentots, owing to the grazing and water needs of their live-stock, are also essentially nomadic. The Bantu in contrast tend to be sedentary, since cultivation ties them to the soil, nor need they ever go far for new land when their fields are exhausted. Environmental conditions are likewise significant in this connection. Many local varieties occur. But, on the whole, most Bantu except Western Tswana inhabit comparatively well-watered and fertile regions, which permit of fairly close settlement by farmers and provide adequate grazing for live-stock almost everywhere. The other peoples all live in arid zones characterized by low rainfall and frequent droughts, and are consequently distributed much more patchily over the land; Hottentots, for example, often have to move with their live-stock many miles from one water-hole to another. The influence of these factors is reflected in differences of population density. The average number of persons per sq. mile is about 0.25 among Bushmen, and 2.0 among Hottentots. No figures are available for Bergdama. Among the Western Tswana, whose territories extend far into the barren Kalahari Desert, the average is about 2.5; among the adjacent Eastern Tswana (of Bechuanaland), who live in somewhat more fertile areas, it is 8.5. As already mentioned, however, all Tswana concentrate in what by normal Bantu standards are very large villages; the scarcity of good water supplies is possibly one reason for this unusual mode of settlement. Among other Bantu, not only is the population more evenly dispersed over the land, but densities are much higher; for example, there are 56 persons per sq. mile in tribal areas in the Soutpansberg (North-Eastern Transvaal), 50 in Swaziland, 46 in Zululand, 58 in Basutoland, and 98 in Pondoland.

But environment and mode of subsistence do not explain all the population differences. Bushman and Bergdama bands are admittedly always very small, and Hottentot tribes, with from 500 to 2,500 members each, also do not vary markedly in size. On the other hand many Bantu tribes, despite their superior economy and better environment, are no bigger than those of the Hottentots, whereas some contain more than 100,000 people each, and even they are small in comparison with the 680,000 Sotho of Basutoland. Conspicuous differences may also occur within a single division: among the Tswana in south-eastern Bechuanaland, where both environment and mode of subsistence are virtually identical everywhere, the Kgatla number 20,000, but the Tlôkwa only 2,300; similarly, in North-Eastern

Transvaal, the 33,000 Lobedu under Mojaji are forty times as numerous as the related and immediately adjoining Lobedu under Rakwadu, and Tshivhase's Venda (pop. 30,000) are more than seventy times as numerous as those under his kinsman Khakhu. These variations are obviously not due to ecological factors alone, but require some other explanation.

The size of a community and the distribution of its population affect the problem of social control. Among Bushmen and Bergdama the band is essentially a face-to-face group; its members live together constantly or for the greater part of each year and, since they are so few, all know one another intimately. This is also largely true of the Hottentots: although more dispersed, members of a tribe meet fairly often, especially since the creation of one central village where most of them have homes; they are therefore all personally acquainted, if nothing more. Among the Bantu, however, a man's direct knowledge of his fellow-tribesmen is usually confined to those in his own neighbourhood, unless he often visits relatives or friends somewhere else. In the larger tribes, especially, the great majority are strangers to him, and many he never meets at all. Consequently the public that habitually notices him and his doings cannot possibly be as comprehensive as, say, among Bergdama, where it embraces the whole community; nor, on the other hand, is he himself likely to be conversant with the affairs of an unknown fellow-tribesman living perhaps twenty or more miles away. The permanent dispersal of the population over different settlements usually also means, except in very small tribes, that the chief cannot personally control all his subjects. The establishment and maintenance of tribal unity therefore require institutions of a kind not needed elsewhere, such as, for example, some system of delegated authority or local government.

Some Bantu, owing to their mode of settlement, also have special local problems of communication. To illustrate this we may consider the extremes. Among the Tswana, with their very large compact villages, people can be easily and speedily mobilized for collective action; since the inhabitants of each village are mostly within earshot, except when tilling their fields, a crier on the hill-tops generally suffices. But more elaborate arrangements are presumably needed by the Nguni and Tsonga, who live scattered all over the country in very many small hamlets. It should be added in this context that the Bantu have no other means of transport than ox-back, and that urgent messages must therefore be sent by runner.

The problem of social control is also affected by the composition of the community. Among Bushmen and Bergdama, not only is the band a single body of kin, but its only subdivision is the elementary family. Hottentots and still more markedly Bantu are further divided into clans and lineages, sometimes of many different stocks, and in most Bantu tribes adults are also grouped into formal age-sets.[1] Since all such groups generally have their own special interests and loyalties, often conflicting with those of other people, the tribe as a whole cannot live peacefully or function efficiently without some additional means of regulation not needed for the band. Moreover, as we have seen, 'plural societies' are fairly common among Bantu and Hottentots, and, as everywhere else in the world, they present problems of special complexity. Bushmen or Bergdama, for example, need not decide how to treat conquered peoples or large groups of immigrants, nor what policy to adopt towards tribesmen differing from the rest in language and custom.

How these and similar problems are dealt with will be discussed in the following chapters. Here I have tried to show merely that the political communities of primitive peoples vary considerably in social composition, and by no means always conform to what may be termed the 'classical' type as defined by Maine and his followers. In particular, we have seen that all political communities in South Africa are based at least partly upon 'local contiguity', and that kinship, though everywhere important, is sometimes not the only, nor even the most conspicuous, factor in political association. We have seen also that communities differ greatly in size and patterns of residence, and that the problems of maintaining order and securing collective action vary accordingly.

1 See below, p. 47 f.

The Framework of Government

I

WE have found that among all South African peoples the
political community has a definite territory of its own.
It thus satisfies one of the criteria usually regarded as characteristic
of the state. Does it also satisfy the other basic criterion, of being
'organized under a sovereign government'?

Maine and Morgan both took it for granted that all human
societies have governments. This view is held also by some others
whose conceptions of primitive society we have had occasion to
criticize, for example MacIver. But modern anthropologists
have sometimes denied that government occurs everywhere. For
example, MacLeod says of the Yurok in California that they 'ex-
hibit the picture' of a society 'actually existing without the state,
that is, in other words, without government or political organization', Radcliffe-Brown that 'there is no organized government'
among the Andaman Islanders, Redfield that 'in the most primitive societies of living men . . . political institutions are few and
simple, or even entirely absent', and Malinowski that 'political
groupings are absent' among such peoples as the Veddas and Australian aborigines.[1] These statements all refer to food-gatherers.
But even peoples such as the Tallensi, Nuer, and Bantu Kavirondo,
who combine animal husbandry with agriculture, have been
classed by Fortes and Evans-Pritchard as 'stateless societies' characterized by the absence of 'government'.[2]

[1] W. C. MacLeod, *The Origin and History of Politics* (1931), p. 23; A. R.
Radcliffe-Brown, *The Andaman Islanders* (1922), p. 44; R. Redfield, *The
Primitive World and its Transformations* (1953), p. 14; B. Malinowski, *A Scientific
Theory of Culture* (1944), pp. 61, 165.
[2] M. Fortes and E. E. Evans-Pritchard (Eds.), *African Political Systems* (1940),
p. 5.

Except for MacLeod, the writers quoted do not intend to imply that the peoples to whom they refer live in a condition of anarchy; they mean merely that such peoples lack institutional organizations, of the kind found in the modern Western state, for maintaining law and order and directing public life generally. Fortes and Evans-Pritchard, for example, define government as 'centralized authority, administrative machinery, and constituted judicial institutions',[1] and Malinowski says that 'Political organization implies always a central authority with the power to administer regarding its subjects, that is, to coordinate the activities of the component groups.'[2] Nor do those writers maintain that personal leadership and authority are non-existent. The Nuer and Tallensi are both described as having 'chiefs', and Radcliffe-Brown, after saying of the Andamanese that 'the affairs of the community are regulated entirely by the older men and women', adds that 'in each local group there was usually to be found one man . . . who by his influence could control and direct others.'[3]

I have quoted these views because they suggest that we must not expect to find in all primitive societies systems of government akin to our own. However, since it is generally agreed that government in its formal aspects always involves the direction and control of public affairs by one or more specific persons whose regular function that is,[4] we need not for the moment labour over problems of definition. It will be more useful to see first if South African communities also have acknowledged leaders and, if so, who they are and how they obtain their distinctive positions. We can then review their public activities, and see how far if at all they can enforce their decisions. Whether such persons should be identified as a 'government', and their activities as 'political', can be left for discussion at a later stage.

[1] *Loc. cit.*
[2] *Op. cit.*, p. 165.
[3] Fortes and Evans-Pritchard, *op. cit.*, pp. 255 ff., 291 ff.; Radcliffe-Brown, *op. cit.*, pp. 44 f.
[4] Cf., for example, H. J. Laski, *An Introduction to Politics* (new ed., 1951), p. 12; G. L. Field, *Governments in Modern Society* (1951), p. 20; R. M. MacIver, *The Web of Government* (1947), p. 22.

II

As in all other primitive societies, the political communities of the South African natives have no written constitutions. But the main features of their organization can be ascertained fairly easily, both from the statements of informants and by direct observation. These show that in each community there is normally one person whom all the others acknowledge as their official head, and who bears a distinctive title that may be translated as 'chief' (Heikum and Bergdama *geikhoib*, Nama *gao-aob*, Nguni *inkosi*, Tsonga *hosi*, Venda *khosi*, Sotho *kgosi* or *morêna*). Among certain Bushmen (Naron of Sandfontein), chieftainship no longer exists, but they too had chiefs within living memory; and in all other groups of North-Western Bushmen, as among the rest of our peoples, the institution still flourishes.[1]

Everywhere, moreover, once a chief has taken up office he normally holds it for the rest of his life. Among Hottentots and Bantu he may be expelled or even killed should he arouse sufficient hostility, and in a few North-Eastern Sotho tribes he is expected to commit suicide when very old; he also loses his independence, and thus ceases to be a chief, if his tribe becomes subject to another. With these exceptions, there is no prescribed or enforced limit to his tenure of office, though he may retire voluntarily because of old age or infirmity.

The chief's duties and powers will be discussed at length in later chapters, but a brief summary may be helpful here. He everywhere represents his people in their dealings with outsiders, and organizes such communal activities as war, collective labour, and certain types of ritual; he himself often also leads his men into battle. His other functions vary widely. Among Bantu they are relatively extensive: he is both legislator and judge, with power to inflict capital punishment; he claims many forms of tribute, in both labour and kind; he controls the distribution and use of

[1] Bleek (1928. a), p. 36; Schapera (1930), p. 150 (other sources on Bushmen).

land, coordinates agricultural activities, provides for the poor and needy, and rewards those who serve him well; and he performs religious and magical ceremonies on behalf of his tribe. The duties of a Hottentot chief are more limited: he too administers justice and can punish offenders by death, but he has comparatively little control over land tenure and economic life generally, and does not himself act as tribal priest or magician. The Bushman or Bergdama chief, unlike the others, has no judicial functions or organized penal powers; his main duties are to direct the migrations and subsistence activities of his people and to perform certain ceremonies for their welfare.

Among Hottentots and Bantu each local segment of a tribe also has an official head, who is subordinate to the chief. Bushmen and Bergdama lack functionaries of this kind, since a band has no territorial divisions. Hottentots have only one grade of local authority, consisting of the 'headmen' in charge of settlements outside the tribal headquarters. Among Bantu there are usually at least two separate grades: 'sub-chiefs' in charge of major divisions such as districts (or large villages among the Tswana), and, under them, 'headmen' in charge of smaller units such as sub-districts (Nguni and Tsonga), villages (Venda and many Sotho), or wards (Tswana and some Northern Sotho). The head of a major group is often also head of one or more of its subdivisions. Among Cape Nguni, for example, the chief has his own district and sub-district; among the Ngwato, similarly, the head of Kgamane ward in the village of Shoshong is also headman of the whole village (which contains two other wards) and sub-chief of the district of Shoshong (which contains eight other villages), and the head of Masokola ward in the village of Mmadinare is also headman of the whole village (which contains four other wards) and sub-chief of Mmadinare district (which contains six other villages).

The grading and number of local rulers in any Bantu tribe seem to depend largely upon its size and complexity. For example, the Tlôkwa of Bechuanaland, who all live in one village, have only four ward-heads apart from the chief; among the Ngwato there were in 1944 eight 'senior headmen' in the capital and ten 'chief's representatives' (sub-chiefs) in outlying districts, with 292 other ward-heads under them all; and in Basutoland the officially recognized organization consisted, in 1939, of 1,006 'headmen' under 316 'sub-chiefs', who in turn were under 18 'chiefs' directly subordinate to the 'paramount chief'.[1] Moreover, the number of subordinate authorities in any tribe is not constant, since new local divisions may be created to accommodate recent accessions or to provide followers for a chief's relatives and favourites, and old ones may disappear through secession or amalgamation. The Ngwaketse, for example, had 5 sub-chiefs and 133 other ward-heads in 1939; in 1948, after some changes, there were 7 sub-chiefs and 112 other ward-heads. But the pyramidal structure is essentially the same everywhere, apart from special developments found, for example, in some Nguni and Sotho tribes.[2]

III

In addition to his local subordinates where they exist, the chief everywhere has assistants of various other kinds. These may be distinguished as 'advisers', who help him to determine policy, and executive 'officers', who help him to carry out his routine tasks. The same people are often found serving in both capacities, but, especially among Bantu, the two categories may also vary in personnel. It is therefore convenient to describe them separately.

A Bantu chief may seek special advice from anybody whom he considers likely to be helpful on a certain matter. But there are also a few people, usually referred to as his 'confidential advisers', whom he consults habitually and fairly often. They seldom belong to a formally constituted body, nor need their identity be made public, though they always include some of his close agnates; they are merely persons whom he trusts and upon whose opinions he

---

[1] Bechuanaland Protectorate Government Notice No. 1 of 1944 (Ngwato); Ashton (1952), p. 186. The terms in quotation marks are those officially used by the local European Administrations.
[2] See below, p. 76 ff.

relies, and he consults them privately and informally, individually or collectively, and may vary them according to the issues involved. Such figures as are available show that in Tswana tribes they usually number from about six to twelve.

He also has a formal and much wider council, which meets as a body at his summons to discuss important questions of public policy. It generally includes all sub-chiefs and prominent headmen, with other influential persons, and is therefore representative of the tribe as a whole. Some members live permanently at his capital and others come periodically to stay there for a while, and usually the meeting consists mainly of them. But on occasions of great importance the whole body is specially convened. Among Tswana and Venda its proceedings are private, and nobody may attend unless personally invited; elsewhere the meeting is usually held in public, and in addition to the recognized members anybody else who wishes may come. There is seldom need for the full council to meet more than about once a year, and the interval may be even longer. But members present in the capital are expected also to help the chief try the cases that come to his court, and thus advise him frequently in another capacity.

Except among Sotho the council is the tribe's main deliberative assembly, and whatever is decided here binds the people as a whole. After a meeting every local authority returns to his area or, if outside members were not summoned, a message is sent informing him of any decision; in either event, he then calls together his own followers and tells them the news.

But among Sotho, and especially Tswana, almost all matters of public concern are discussed finally at a popular assembly (commonly termed *pitsô*), which ordinary tribesmen are also expected to attend. Such assemblies. summoned by the chief whenever he thinks fit, are in some tribes held very often, at times almost weekly, except when the people are busy at their fields.[1] They usually meet in the council-place (*kgotla*) adjoining the chief's

[1] Among the Ngwaketse, during the years 1910–15, there were on the average 35 meetings annually, with as many as 56 in 1915. Cf. Schapera (1947), pp. 8, 105.

residence. Normally only the men present in the capital are summoned, perhaps merely to be told of some forthcoming ceremony, to receive instructions about public labour, or to listen to other formal announcements; and if necessary the message is communicated to outlying settlements through their local rulers. But on important occasions, as when new laws are proposed or other big decisions have to be made, the whole tribe is convened; if the matter is at all critical (such as a serious internal dispute or threatened invasion), attendance may even be compulsory. A crucial meeting of this kind is sometimes held in the open veld some distance from the capital, and the men all come to it armed and ready for trouble; it is then usually also preceded or followed by a collective drive for game.

The people sit in a big semi-circle facing the chief and his senior relatives; other leading men are in front, but otherwise there is no special arrangement. The chief, who presides, briefly explains the purpose of the meeting. If it is a matter requiring discussion, some of his advisers then give a lead by stating the views that they may have reached with him beforehand in private. They are usually but not necessarily followed by other important men, after which anybody else who wishes may speak or ask questions. The chief finally sums up what has been said and announces his decision. The assembly itself, it is important to note, seldom raises topics for discussion; it merely deliberates upon the issues presented to it, and thus enables him to ascertain public opinion. The meeting normally lasts for only part of the day, but if the matter is sufficiently weighty or controversial to attract many speakers it may be spread over two days or more. It is in any event continued until a decision has been reached. There is no special system of voting, the speeches made and the general mood being sufficient to indicate the trend of opinion; but occasionally, as among the Kgatla, if the discussion reveals marked disagreement the chief may ask the men to group themselves according to their views, and the relative strength of the different parties is then clearly seen.

Tribal assemblies are also known among Nguni and Tsonga. But owing to the local pattern of settlement they are much more difficult to organize, and are therefore usually held only on great ceremonial occasions, such as the annual first-fruits festival, or before the army goes to war. Consequently they are not nearly as important in the system of government; there seldom is any public discussion of policy, except perhaps about making war, and the chief merely uses the opportunity to inform the people of decisions already reached by him and his council. It is usually at the first-fruits ceremony, for example, that he announces new laws or the creation of a new age-regiment.

Among all Bantu, however, cases at the chief's court are tried publicly, and any man is free to attend and take part. After the evidence has been heard, the matter is thrown open for general discussion. Whoever wishes may then question the persons involved, or express an opinion about the merits of the case. In this way he helps to clarify the issues and guide the court, though the verdict itself is at the discretion of the judge alone.[1]

The kinds of advisory institution just described are found also in local government. Every sub-chief and headman has his own confidential advisers, whom he consults as occasion arises and who help him to try the cases that come to his court; if at the head of a large group he may have a small formal council; and sometimes he summons all the men under him to discuss matters of common concern. Among Nguni such local assemblies are more frequent than those of the whole tribe, perhaps because they are simpler to arrange; but even among Tswana the chief, when anxious to have something considered thoroughly, may instruct his subordinates to consult their people at home, whose views they subsequently report at the full tribal meeting. Every tribesman can also attend and take part in the hearing of cases at any local court.

A Hottentot chief has two official sets of advisers. The first is a restricted council, varying with the size of the tribe from say four to twenty members, whom he consults as a body and in private on most aspects of policy. In the larger tribes some of these men also constitute the main court of justice. The council's decisions on all major issues, such as war and peace, must however be ratified

1 The system of judicial procedure is described more fully below; see p. 78 ff.

by a much larger popular assembly, specially summoned by the chief for the purpose. Local headmen have similar advisory bodies drawn from their own followers, which also meet only as business arises.

Among Bushmen and Bergdama, the chief discusses matters of public concern with all the men of his band. They normally forgather every evening round the central camp fire, where they eat together and gossip, and whenever there is need they consider what action to take. The band is so small that it rarely contains more than about twenty men, and (especially among Bergdama) usually much fewer; in consequence, perhaps, there are no special forms of advisory council, nor does it seem that the chief must consult anybody in particular before raising a matter at the camp fire.

IV

Like his advisory personnel, the executive staff of a South African chief differs considerably in composition and size from one people to another. By far the most elaborate system is found among the Bantu. This is hardly surprising, since usually the chief not only has many more subjects to govern than elsewhere, but his specific duties are also much more extensive. In carrying them out he is helped partly by the various grades of local authority already mentioned, and partly by special officers living at, or close to, his home.

One of these officers, commonly termed the 'great induna', is in effect his principal lieutenant in all his activities, and often deputizes for him if he is ill or away. The induna is the recognized intermediary between chief and tribe, and the royal spokesman on many formal and other occasions. It is normally through him that matters are referred to the chief for decision or action, and he can himself deal with those of minor concern. He interviews important messengers or visitors; receives all cases that come to the chief's court, arranges for them to be heard, and may himself act as judge; helps the chief lead the army and organize council or tribal meetings, tribal labour, and the great tribal ceremonies; and supervises the running of the chief's household. In the larger tribes there are generally several other kinds of induna, sometimes distinguished by title as well as function; thus, one or more of them may attend to the administration of justice, others are in charge of the army and also control peace-time regimental activities, and still others look after land matters, the royal herds of cattle, or the reception and entertainment of distinguished visitors. They are usually also the chief's state messengers or ambassadors on important occasions, and may further be sent to investigate and adjust serious local disputes.

Everywhere, too, the chief habitually employs one or more professional magicians as his 'tribal doctors'. They are not so much executive officers as technical experts, but they play an important part in the system of government. They protect the chief's person with charms, and help him on such ritual occasions as rainmaking, the 'doctoring' of the army, tribal initiation ceremonies, and the annual first-fruits festival; and they always work at his request and under his supervision.

Attached to the chief's court are many other men who, under the control of the indunas, do all the routine daily work connected with tribal administration. They look after the council-place, attend to visitors, prepare and distribute food at public gatherings, and herd cattle paid as fines; they also summon people to meetings or cases, carry other simple messages, and if necessary arrest criminals or enforce judgments.

Apart from such regular and constant forms of assistance, the chief occasionally employs others for special purposes. Among Tswana and most Northern Sotho, for example, he organizes large-scale undertakings through the age-sets or 'regiments' into which all adult members of his tribe are grouped. Each regiment consists of coevals, and there are separate regiments of men and of women. The chief creates a new regiment every five years or thereabouts, when all the eligible youths (aged roughly from 14 to 18) are initiated simultaneously and given a distinctive group name. He may afterwards call upon it for public service whenever he wishes. The men's regiments fight as separate units in the tribal army, and in times of peace are often employed on such tasks as rounding up stray cattle, hunting game, destroying beasts of prey, and acting as police. Work of this kind is usually given only to regiments whose members are still relatively young and active. Normally, too, the chief summons only those men who live in his capital or close by; but if need be he will also call upon the residents of outlying settlements, or instruct their local rulers to have them do whatever he wishes.

The Zulu and Swazi also use age-regiments for both military purposes and tribal labour. Among the Zulu, in the heyday of their power, each regiment on active service lived in a separate kraal of its own close to the chief's home; these kraals, controlled by resident indunas and various subordinates, often had thousands of inhabitants, and were thus a conspicuous exception to the traditional Nguni pattern of settlement. The men remained there for years until the chief formally allowed them to return home and marry, and when not at war they were used for anything else that he wanted done; they 'worked his fields, built his villages, herded his cattle, and hunted and raided for him', arrested and if required killed convicted or suspected criminals, served as messengers and porters, etc., and when not engaged on such tasks 'danced and idled away' their time.[1] The Swazi have apparently never had a standing army of this type, but some men from each regiment are usually in residence at the royal villages and available for service, either public or domestic.

The military organization of Venda and Tsonga is likewise based upon a system of age-regiments, though (as among Tswana) the members of a regiment usually live at their own homes when not at war. Among Venda (information is not available for Tsonga) such regiments sometimes also do special work for the chief in times of peace. Elsewhere, as among Cape Nguni and Southern Sotho, both the army and tribal labour are organized on a local basis. The men of each district, regardless of age, constitute

[1] Gluckman (1940. b), p. 53.

a separate division of the army, and may also be summoned as a unit to work for the chief.

Sub-chiefs and headmen of large groups may also have indunas, whose duties correspond on a minor scale to those noted for the chief's right-hand man. In addition, every local authority can employ his subjects on collective labour for public purposes, or for such tasks as taking messages or enforcing the decisions of his court.

In contrast with his Bantu counterpart, a Hottentot chief seems to have originally had no special officers at all. This is still true of the Topnaars at Sesfontein. But in other tribes certain members of the council now have distinctive titles and corresponding functions. They include, for example, the 'sub-chief', who presides over the main court of justice and also acts for the chief if he is ill or away; the 'judges' of the court; the 'magistrate' (himself also a judge), who arranges for the trial of cases; and the 'field cornets' and 'corporals', who administer outlying settlements and help lead the army at war. There are usually also several official 'messengers', but they do not belong to the council. As some of the titles indicate, these innovations were borrowed from the Dutch system of government in the Cape Colony, and they seem to have been introduced by immigrants or missionaries early in the nineteenth century. In addition, public labour is occasionally demanded from the able-bodied men generally, who also constitute the tribal army; there is no system of age-regiments like that of most Bantu.

In the very small compact communities of Bushmen and Bergdama the chief has little need of executive officers. Among Bergdama he is helped in some ritual activities by his senior wife, and by a special assistant termed the 'food-master'; this man also decides if wild fruits and other plants can safely be eaten, and takes official messages to the heads of other bands. Both here, and among Bushmen, the only other people with distinctive functions are the magicians employed in certain group ceremonies. All able-bodied men fight when the need arises, and there is no special organization for military purposes or for public labour of any kind.

v

As will have been gathered, the official business of a South African community is sometimes carried on by a variety of persons differing in status and function. Some have special responsibilities in an individual capacity, for example the chief and his main executive officers (including local rulers); others, as tribal councillors, combine joint activities with personal eminence; and still others serve merely as ordinary members of such bodies as popular assemblies or the army, in which they all have the same duties. This division of labour implies the existence of rules determining why and how anybody in particular should come to fill the position that he does. What, then, are the various requisites for office or rôle?

A cursory survey of the data shows that elsewhere in primitive society chieftainship may be attained by such diverse methods as birthright, formal election, the use of wealth, or military achievement.[1] In South Africa chieftainship everywhere is normally hereditary from father to son, though rules of succession vary in detail from one people to another. Among Bantu and Hottentots people have also become chiefs by usurpation or by seceding and creating tribes of their own. But in such instances they themselves almost invariably belonged to the local ruling line.[2]

In most groups of Bantu, the eldest son of the 'great wife' is the heir apparent. This woman is rarely the first that a chief marries, but her status is always clearly defined. Unlike his other wives, she is chosen by the royal family in consultation with the tribal councillors; she should preferably be the daughter of another chief or, as among many Sotho, her husband's maternal cross-cousin or

[1] For examples, cf. R. H. Lowie, *Social Organization* (1948), pp. 328 ff.; E. A. Hoebel, *Man in the Primitive World* (1949), pp. 382 ff.
[2] A notable exception is known for Cape Nguni, where Khwane, a councillor of the Xhosa chief Tshiwo (d. 1702), was put in charge of a mixed group of Xhosa and Hottentots, which subsequently became the Gqunukhwebe tribe with himself as chief. Cf. Soga (1930), p. 116 ff.; MacLean (1858), p. 20 ff.

other close relative; except among Venda and certain Sotho, the cattle given as her *lobola* (marriage payment) include contributions from all important members of the tribe, especially sub-chiefs and headmen; and at her wedding a distinctive ceremony is often held to indicate that she is to be 'mother of the tribe' or 'wife of the country'. Among Sotho and Venda she is usually chosen for the future chief during the lifetime and through the agency of his father. Among Nguni and Tsonga she is never married until he has already succeeded to office, and often not until he has ruled for some time; and should he die before choosing her, as sometimes happens among Swazi and other Nguni, the most nobly born of his widows with sons is usually accepted as mother of the heir.

If the great wife has no son, her younger sister or another substitute (sometimes termed her 'womb') may be taken to bear one for her; or, as among the Sotho, she may cohabit after her husband's death with his younger brother, the first son then born to her becoming the heir. Failing this, the right of succession passes to the eldest son of the wife next in rank. If the chief has no male agnatic descendants, he is succeeded by a brother or brother's son, usually the man nearest to him in line of birth.

Women are excluded everywhere except in some North-Eastern Sotho tribes (Lobedu, Kgaga, etc.). Here the chief is sometimes succeeded by a daughter, even if he has sons; among the Lobedu, especially, female chiefs seem to have become the rule. Such a woman takes no official husband, but cohabits with a specially chosen male relative, and one of her own children becomes chief after her. In her official capacity she also has many 'wives', and if she herself is barren one of them is chosen to produce the heir. This form of chieftainship, said to have originated locally among the Lobedu at the beginning of the nineteenth century, is decidedly exceptional; nowhere else among the Bantu can a woman ever become chief in her own right.

Despite the rules outlined above, the heir seldom succeeds automatically, even if his identity is unchallenged. When a chief dies, his senior relatives and other important advisers meet as soon as

possible afterwards to decide upon his successor. Among Swazi
and Venda they seem to have considerable latitude, since the heir
is seldom known publicly during the lifetime of his father (whose
death is also kept secret until they have finally made their choice);
this is likewise true of North-Eastern Sotho, and helps to explain
why a daughter can sometimes be chosen. Elsewhere they usually
follow the rule of seniority and merely confirm the heir apparent.
But if he is physically or mentally infirm, has a notoriously bad
character, or is deemed otherwise unsuitable, they may pass him
over and select one of his brothers. Such rejections are recorded in
many tribal histories, and they indicate that the filling of the chieftainship is always a matter of much concern.

Moreover, there are often disputes about the succession: a
chief's sons by different wives may quarrel for precedence even
during his lifetime, the family council may fail to reach unanimity
in its choice, or the adherents of a particular son may feel that he
has been wrongly passed over.[1] But in every such instance the
rival claimants are all sons or other close relatives of the former
chief. No man who is not a senior member of the royal lineage is
entitled to the succession; as Tswana say, 'A chief is chief because
he is born to it.'

The chosen heir begins to rule as soon as possible after his predecessor's death has been made known to the people. The occasion is generally marked by a great national gathering, at which
the new chief is publicly installed.[2] As part of the ceremony, his
uncles and other leading old men lecture him formally on the conduct henceforth expected of him,[3] and also exhort the assembled
tribesmen to obey and protect him.

But the heir cannot start ruling until he is considered old
enough, which usually means until he has been formally initiated
into the status of adult. If he is still too young when his predecessor dies—and this often happens, especially among Nguni—the

[1] See below, p. 165 ff.
[2] The Mpondo, a Cape Nguni tribe, seem to be exceptional in having no
installation ceremony (Hunter (1936), p. 384).
[3] See below, p. 137 f.

family council chooses somebody else to act as chief for the time being. This regent is usually one of his senior paternal uncles or older half-brothers. Among Tsonga there is a further condition: a chief must be followed by all his full brothers in turn, and only when the last brother dies does the heir apparent (the 'great' son of the first brother) take up office.

Among Sotho and Nguni instances are also known of a woman acting as regent for her son or younger brother. One of the most famous was Mma-Ntatisi, who early in the nineteenth century ruled the Tlôkwa of Basutoland with skill and courage during the minority of her son Sekonyela; among the Ngqika, one of the main Xhosa tribes, the mother of Chief Sandile (1840–74) was regent during his minority; and there are today female regents at the head of the Southern Sotho (Basutoland), Tawana (Bechuanaland), and several other tribes. They are usually chosen only if none of the late chief's senior male relatives is considered acceptable; but among Swazi a chief's mother is always principal regent during the minority of his heir, though her son's senior half-brother rules jointly with her.

A Hottentot chief is usually succeeded by the eldest son of his first wife, or, failing a son, by the next senior man of his line, such as a brother or brother's son. Should no agnatic kinsman be available, the chieftainship normally passes to the leading family of the clan next in rank, as happened long ago among the Swartboois; occasionally, however, the chief's uterine nephew is chosen instead, as happened among the Topnaars in 1947. As among Bantu, succession is not automatic. The new chief is appointed at a special meeting of the full tribal assembly; and although this often means merely that the people confirm the main heir, instances are known where owing to avarice or incompetence he was superseded by a more popular and able younger brother. If the heir is still young when his father dies, his senior paternal uncle becomes regent, though among the Rooinasie the office was early in the nineteenth century held for some years by a paternal aunt.

Bushmen and Bergdama are usually also described as having patrilineal succession. But some writers state that among Heikum and Eastern Kung a chief is habitually succeeded by his eldest sister's son, who does not even belong to the same band but is sent for when the occasion arises. This seems difficult to believe. Among Bergdama a sister's son may also succeed, but only if there are no sons or brothers. Actually, so far as one can judge from the evidence, the practice among both peoples seems to be that a chief's successor is generally his eldest son, if sufficiently mature and competent. But in such very small communities, where all the people are closely related, age and ability are evidently considered more important than seniority of descent; and if a chief has no suitable son or brother the most experienced and energetic man apparently takes over the leadership. There is no record of any formal appointment or installation ceremony.

The occasional lack of agnatic heirs among the non-Bantu peoples may be associated partly with the relatively small size of their ruling families. Among Bantu a chief generally has many wives (a dozen or so are by no means unusual, and some chiefs are known to have had more than fifty); it is therefore rarely that an heir need be sought outside his own family or those of his brothers. Among the other peoples few chiefs have more than two or three wives, and, especially among Bushmen and Bergdama, life is so strenuous that many children die young. Consequently the male line may sometimes become extinct, as happened among the Rooinasie (1880) and Topnaars (1947), with the result that a new chief must be sought somewhere else.

VI

The people who assist a chief vary not only in function but also in mode of recruitment. There is no professional civil service entered by public examination or after formal application and interview by an appointments committee, and there are also no mercenary soldiers; nor, except reputedly in some Hottentot tribes, is there popular election of councillors and other officers. Membership of assemblies and similar bodies is open freely to all who are suitably qualified, but people with specialized duties are either chosen individually or must be confirmed in offices that they inherit. Even the right to participate in popular assemblies is not unrestricted, since it is governed by sex and age and occasionally also by class. We thus have two sets of conditions to consider: the basic qualifications for public service of any kind, and the special qualifications for positions of responsibility.

As we should by now expect, the most elaborate system of differentiation is found among the Bantu. Here, we may note first, participation in public life is normally confined to men. It is true that women of the royal family often have special rôles. As already mentioned, a chief's mother sometimes acts as regent during his minority, and among North-Eastern Sotho the chieftainship itself may be held by a woman. Among Venda and some North-Eastern Sotho a chief may also appoint a sister or daughter as ruler of a local group, among Tsonga and most Nguni he usually places some of his wives in outlying districts as his 'eyes and ears' and by visiting them periodically can keep in direct touch with local affairs, and among Tswana and other Sotho all age-regiments of women are headed by his sisters and daughters, through whom he can summon them to work for him.

There are two other notable exceptions. Among Swazi the chief's mother has a well-defined constitutional position. Her village is the ritual capital, where the annual first-fruits ceremony and meetings of the tribal council are held; she exercises separate judicial powers, and is custodian of certain magical objects that her son uses together with her; he should seek and follow her advice before taking action in matters of importance, and she is expected to rebuke him for any breach of duty. After his death she is principal regent for his heir, and if she dies first another of his father's widows is chosen to fill her place. A similar institution exists among Venda. When a chief dies one of his sisters, specially chosen for the purpose by the royal family council at the time of his accession, assumes the rôle of leading *makhadzi* (paternal aunt) of his successor. She assists the new chief (or her own brother, if his *makhadzi* dies first) in sacrifices and other rites, must be consulted on all important matters of tribal policy, and exercises a restraining influence over his conduct, both official and private. Among both peoples every local ruler is similarly assisted by a corresponding female relative. This woman, too, always has an important say in the choice of his successor.

But all these instances of female leadership and authority are exceptional. Women in general do not hold official positions, except occasionally as regents for their sons. They are also excluded from councils and popular assemblies, they may not attend judicial hearings unless personally involved, and in tribal law are treated as minors always subject to male guardians, through whom alone, for example, they can sue or be sued at court. Their main rôle in public life is that they are sometimes called upon to work for the chief or their local ruler.

On the other hand, almost all men take part in at least some aspects of tribal activity: they can attend and speak at court cases and popular assemblies, and if required serve in the army and work for their rulers. But some, as already noted, have positions of special responsibility, and even the others vary in influence and authority. These differences are associated firstly with distinctions of class.

In most Bantu tribes there are usually at least two well-defined social classes, often distinguished by name, which we may term 'nobles' and 'commoners' respectively. The former include all people held to be of the same origin by descent as the chief. The remainder are 'commoners', though newly-conquered groups and relatively recent immigrants are sometimes classed separately as 'foreigners'. Among Western Tswana there is also a special category of 'serfs', who are attached as hereditary menials to various nobles and commoners and lack certain elementary civic rights; and a similarly marked pattern of social stratification, including a separate servile class, exists among the Ndebele of Southern Rhodesia.[1]

Often there are further distinctions. Among nobles, for example, the chief's own clan or lineage outranks all others, and sometimes this group alone is considered the true aristocracy; his sons

[1] See below, p. 128 ff.

and brothers, moreover, may be distinguished from the rest both in privileges and by a special term that may be translated as 'prince' (Zulu *umntwana*, Tswana *ngwana-kgosi* or *monna-kgosi*, Venda *mukololo*, etc.). In every local segment, again, the ruler and his kin take precedence, and immigrants usually rank lower than members by birth. Everywhere, too, the more closely a man is related to the head of his group the higher his status within it. So much importance may be attached to this social grading that, as among Kgatla and other Tswana, youths going through initiation ceremonies together are sometimes lined up in order of precedence so as to teach them just where each stands in relation to the rest.

Distinctions of the kind just mentioned feature prominently in public life. With occasional exceptions, foreigners are normally excluded from the most important posts and from the tribe's inner councils; they are not fully trusted, and are therefore often kept ignorant of what is being discussed. The chief's confidential advisers and central executive officers consist predominantly of senior nobles and a few outstanding commoners. His brothers and paternal uncles, in particular, are everywhere entitled and expected to assist him; among Sotho and Venda one of them is his official deputy and right-hand man, and some are also leaders of the age-regiments and thus have special authority over portions of the tribe as a whole. Other advisers, apart from his aunt (Venda) or mother (Swazi), include his principal indunas, maternal kinsmen (if in the tribe), and perhaps also personal friends of his own age. The indunas are usually commoners of certain families with a proved reputation for loyalty, ability, and discretion. They are sometimes chosen for the chief when he starts to rule, but normally he continues to employ those already in office, and as occasion arises replaces them by their sons or other close relatives. The great tribal 'doctors' are usually also commoners, of lineages noted as specialists in ritual. Like new indunas, they are specially chosen by the chief and his advisers.

The chief's minor assistants vary in personnel. Among Tswana they belong mostly to certain wards of commoners hereditarily attached to him as 'court servants' and residing permanently round his council-place; among other Sotho and Venda they include all the youths of his district, who live at his village until they marry; and among Nguni young men come voluntarily from all over the tribe to serve for a year or more in return for cattle. Those who distinguish themselves here by ability and faithful service may in due course be advanced to positions of responsibility.

Local rulers usually include men of all classes. Some are hereditary heads of old clans or lineages, or of groups more recently conquered or admitted. Others are descended from men placed in charge of tribal segments by former chiefs. Still others are new appointments; thus, in each generation, the eldest sons of a chief's senior wives are usually all given personal followings, and commoners who serve him well may be similarly rewarded. Sub-chiefs may with his approval provide in the same way within their districts for their own sons and favoured retainers.

Local headships, once recognized or created, normally descend from father to son; but the heir must always be confirmed by his overlord. If considered necessary, someone else may be appointed, which also happens if for any reason a man is deposed. In practice, the chief seldom interferes with the succession to minor positions. He is more apt to be concerned about districts and other large units, to the control of which he often appoints his senior brothers and sons. These men (or their heirs) may in due course be superseded by his successors' nominees, and then remain at the head only of the group originally given to them.

The extent to which nobles sometimes predominate as local rulers may be seen from the following figures. In Basutoland, 13 of the 18 'chiefs' in 1939 were descendants of Moshesh (they included two sons, two brothers' sons, and six father's brothers' sons, of the ruling 'paramount'), and 4 others were descended from two of his brothers; among the Ngwato, 3 of the 10 district sub-chiefs in 1944 were grandsons of Sekgoma I (1834-75), 4 others were descended from his grandfather Kgama I (1795-1817), and an eighth from his great-grandfather Mathiba; and among

Tshivhase's Venda 25 of the 32 leading sub-chiefs in 1940 were also nobles.

Minor local rulers tend to be more representative of the population generally. Thus, in Swaziland, the 162 district heads include 75 men of the chief's clan, 46 others of Swazi stock, and 41 of foreign extraction (Zulu, Sotho, etc.). In Bechuanaland, similarly, the 69 ward-heads of the Kwena include 33 nobles, 27 commoners, and 9 foreigners; and the 68 ward-heads of the Kgatla 22 nobles, 34 commoners, and 12 foreigners. But even here the aristocracy predominates in small tribes: of the 16 ward-heads among the Malete 11 are nobles, and the 5 ward-heads of the Tlôkwa are all of that class. The Tawana, again, have 40 ward-heads, of whom 12 are nobles, 22 commoners, and 6 foreigners; but servile peoples such as the Yeei, Mbukushu, and Bushmen, who collectively constitute about two-thirds of the total population, are all included in wards headed by either nobles or commoners; their own hereditary heads, of whom there are more than 100, have small-scale local authority only and do not belong to the tribal council.

The head of every tribal segment also rules with the aid of his close relatives. They are not only his recognized advisers and executive assistants, but if he is ill or away the most senior of them acts in his place. Among Sotho and Venda his uncles, brothers, and sons are like himself sectional leaders of the local men belonging to their respective age-regiments. In effect, therefore, the group is controlled not so much by him alone as by the whole of his family, though as holder of the office he personally has distinctive powers and privileges. His other assistants, in the larger groups, are men whom he has selected as indunas, etc., or who are attached to his court in the same way as at the capital.

The tribal council, as already noted, usually includes all sub-chiefs and prominent headmen, each of whom is normally accompanied by one or more senior assistants; the chief's confidential advisers and indunas are also members. and he may add any other men noted for shrewdness and ability. Among Sotho, any tribesman may attend popular assemblies and speak if he wishes (except that among Western Tswana serfs are always excluded). Both bodies thus usually contain representatives of all social classes; but in both of them men close to the chief or in charge of important local segments tend to command most attention, and foreigners in particular are seldom influential.

As suggested by all this, a person's rôle in public life depends largely upon his class and kinship ties. In general, the more highly placed his family is in the tribal hierarchy the greater is his authority. Thus, whenever men assemble for work or discussion, the most senior one present is, merely because of his social status, usually accepted as leader. But personal factors also count. If he is capable and popular, his decisions will be readily accepted; if on the other hand he is disliked, incompetent, or otherwise unacceptable, his attempts to exercise authority may be resented, though his social inferiors will nevertheless continue to show him formal respect.

However, the system of ranking is not rigid. As already indicated, commoners of lowly status may become influential through ability shown in public or while serving at court. Among the qualities highly esteemed in this connection are bravery in war, skill in debate, soundness of judgment, and knowledge of law and precedent. Men who combine such qualities with conspicuous loyalty and faithful service may be chosen as indunas or councillors by their local rulers; occasionally the chief himself will come to employ them in similar capacities, and by placing them in charge of other people may also give them personal jurisdiction. In almost all tribes there are headmen and even sub-chiefs whose ancestors were thus promoted from the ranks of ordinary commoners, or who themselves have been similarly honoured. A wealthy man generally also commands respect, and by placing out his cattle on loan and entertaining generously may attract personal adherents. A poor man, on the other hand, usually has little influence, unless he happens to be a local ruler or is distinguished in some other way; as the Zulu proverb says, 'The poor man's word is considered lost', or 'The voice of the poor is not audible'.

Everywhere, too, considerable importance is attached to age.

Only men who belong to an age-regiment or who have gone through some corresponding initiation ceremony after puberty are allowed to attend local or tribal assemblies; and among Zulu, Swazi, and Tsonga, the chief confers upon middle-aged men 'a new dignity and superior status' when he authorizes them to assume the waxen head-ring that is the sign of maturity. Old men are usually treated with deference, however lowly their rank, and if versed in law and the knowledge of precedents are often able to influence decisions at court cases and other public discussions. Where formal age-sets exist, and only Cape Nguni and nowadays also Southern Sotho do not have them, people of the same set are often bound together by ties of mutual obligation and comradeship lasting for life; and, as among Tswana, they tend to side with their leader if he is involved in a dispute about the chieftainship. The most devoted assistants of a chief or local ruler are usually men who passed through the initiation ceremonies together with him.

Hottentots also have a class system, which however differs from that of the Bantu. They distinguish between 'citizens', who are all of Hottentot stock, and 'servants', almost all of whom are Bergdama, Bushmen, and other aliens attached to individual households as menial retainers. Servants sometimes accompany their masters to war, but are excluded from all official posts and public assemblies; they are usually punished more severely for any offences that they commit, and there is no intermarriage between them and the ruling class. In effect, they have no say at all in the conduct of public affairs, and in this respect differ markedly from even the 'foreigners' in most Bantu tribes.

Apart from the chief himself, the principal officers are the members of the tribal council and the headmen of dependent settlements. In the old days the same men served in both capacities: the hereditary head of each clan ruled the local group formed by his own people, and all the clan-heads together constituted the tribal council. By the middle of the nineteenth century, as already noted, the council in most tribes had become a body including men with separate executive or judicial responsibilities. Some writers state that the members are elected periodically and for specific posts by the tribal assembly; according to others, they are chosen by the chief, who then submits their names to the assembly for confirmation. Possibly the practice varies from one tribe to another; the evidence for the Bondelswarts, for example, indicates that as a vacancy occurs it is filled by the chief, subject to the approval of the existing members. They usually include some of his near relatives (brothers, sons, etc.) and one representative or more of every other important lineage, and presumably therefore also the clan-heads, though this is not specifically mentioned. Every clan-head, in any case, still controls the local group formed by his own people in the main tribal settlement; outlying villages, however, are nowadays governed by members of the council specially chosen for the purpose.

The tribal assembly comprises all adult male citizens; women are excluded, and so are youths not yet married. Wealthy men and heads of lineages are said to be more influential than others. Under missionary guidance, indeed, the Swartboois in 1849 adopted a written constitution restricting membership of assembly and council to men owning more than five head of cattle and fifty sheep; I do not know if it is still in force, but it does show that distinctions of wealth were formerly significant. Regard is also paid to age. Hottentots have no formal age-sets, but people are expected to defer to their elders, and at public meetings old men usually have a decisive influence. Such men are often asked to arbitrate over personal disputes, they sometimes predominate in the council, and in the absence of the subchief the oldest member of the tribal court presides when cases are tried.

In the small kin-based communities of Bushmen and Bergdama there are no recognized social classes. Except for the distinctive rôle of the chief's wife among Bergdama, women are normally excluded from public life. On the other hand, every adult male can take part in the discussion of communal affairs round the camp fire; the influence he exercises depends partly upon such personal attributes as skill in hunting or knowledge of magic, but mainly upon age and experience, elderly men usually having the most decisive say in matters of importance. Among Bergdama youths initiated together rank as age-mates and companions for life, and should always help one another in hunting, warfare, and on other occasions of need. Nothing similar has been reported for Bushmen, nor is sufficient detail given for us to determine how important these age-groups really are in the Bergdama social system.

The 'food-master' who figures so prominently among Bergdama is a permanent official chosen by the chief, and should always be an elderly man with special knowledge of plants and their properties. His office is not hereditary, and if nobody inside the band is qualified to replace him when he dies an outsider may be imported. Any other alien adopted as a servant, as occasionally happens, lives apart and has no say in band affairs, but when old he is admitted into the main settlement and can then associate with the men at the camp fire.

VII

Our description suggests that in certain respects South African peoples all seem to have like arrangements for managing their public affairs. Everywhere there is in each community a single official head, who normally inherits his position and holds it till he dies; everywhere, too, assemblies of adult males help him to determine policy, whereas women have no comparable say in matters of general concern.

However, the similarity is very superficial, and to stress it would be completely misleading. The differences are much more numerous and important. A Bushman or Bergdama chief is essentially the head of a single extended family; its other members are with very rare exceptions all closely related to him, and there are no general class distinctions of any kind. A Hottentot chief has many more adherents, but most of them are aliens with no share in the conduct of tribal affairs. The population of a Bantu tribe is often still larger and more heterogeneous; except among Western Tswana all sections are represented in the wider assemblies, but the chief and his descent group constitute a dominant aristocracy, and commoners as a class are more influential than foreigners. Moreover, as shown more fully in the next chapter, the duties and powers of the chief vary greatly; they are, for example, far slighter among Bushmen than Bantu.

Among Bushmen and Bergdama, too, the community is so small and compact that there are no public officials except the chief himself (and the Bergdama 'foodmaster'), and no other 'agencies of government' than the informal camp council embracing all the men. Among Hottentots and Bantu the chief has special advisers and assistants (both central and local), who in the main achieve their positions either by inheritance or by special appointment. With himself they can be said to constitute 'the government', as distinguished from the rest of the population. Among Hottentots they function as the chief's council, the main court of justice, and subordinate heads of local groups with their own councils and courts. Bantu have a more elaborate system of central and regional executive officers (including sub-chiefs and headmen), two grades of advisory personnel at the higher levels, a well-defined hierarchy of courts, and in most tribes a separate military organization based upon formal age-groupings. Among both peoples the governmental system also provides for consultation between the chief and some form of popular assembly; this feature is far more characteristic of Sotho, and especially Tswana, than of any other Bantu.

It is tempting to relate such differences immediately to differences in mode of subsistence, which as already noted affect both the size and the territorial system of the community and consequently the organization required for managing its affairs. But, unlike the other peoples, the Bantu themselves differ much in certain respects, sometimes within a single division. Here too such factors as the size, ethnic composition, and settlement pattern, of the tribe may be partly responsible. In Bechuanaland, for example, the Ngwato (with 101,000 people occupying 42,000 sq. miles) have two, and in outside districts sometimes three, distinct grades of local authority, whereas only one exists among the

Tlôkwa (whose 2,300 members live in a single village within a territory only 60 sq. miles in extent); the Ngwato are also so much more heterogeneous than the Tlôkwa that they have developed a more elaborate class system, including serfs, and use special methods of governing subject groups in outlying regions. The prominent rôle of tribal assemblies among Tswana and other Sotho may similarly be ascribed to the existence of large compact villages, which makes it far easier than among Nguni and Tsonga to bring the people together frequently and speedily.

Other differences are not so readily explained. The standing army of the Zulu, female chieftainship among certain North-Eastern Sotho tribes, and servile castes among Western Tswana and Rhodesian Ndebele, are unique developments due to known features of local history and social conditions; but we have no such data to account for the general diversity in methods of succession to the chieftainship, the constitutional prominence of the chief's mother and aunt among Swazi and Venda respectively, and the absence of formal age-sets among Cape Nguni and, more recently, Southern Sotho. These are problems that will have to be considered in due course.

Nevertheless, despite the variations just noted, all Bantu tribes have certain basic features in common. These include not only a class system headed by the chief's descent group, but also a small informal body of confidential advisers and senior executive officers attached to the chief, a hierarchy of subordinate local rulers with their own advisers and other assistants, public assemblies at the local level, popular participation in court cases at all levels, and the possibility of commoners obtaining promotion through personal merit. Moreover, as shown in the following chapter, the allocation and range of official duties and powers are also essentially the same everywhere.

We now have some idea of the formal apparatus by means of which South African peoples manage their public affairs; we have also gathered incidentally a few impressions of what those affairs usually are. But it is still premature to attempt an answer to the problem with which we started: can our peoples all be said to have 'government'? The indications are that Bantu and Hottentots certainly satisfy the definition given, say, by Fortes and Evans-Pritchard, whereas Bushmen and Bergdama do not. But we need to know more about the duties and powers of chiefs and their assistants before we can assert definitely that the first two peoples are grouped into 'primitive states' and the last two into 'stateless societies', or before we venture instead to suggest some other classification of their respective polities. The relevant data are given in the following chapters.

The Activities of Tribal Governments

I

In the previous chapter I used the word 'chief' as a generic term for the recognized head of a political community. Recognition in this sense does not mean merely that the other members acknowledge him as their leader; it implies also that they expect him, as holder of the office, to perform certain duties. This he does with the aid of his advisers and other assistants, all of whom likewise have their own special tasks.

Whether all, or any, of a chief's official duties can rightly be regarded as 'political' is, as I have already suggested, a problem more conveniently discussed once we know what they are. After all, even in Western societies the activities of governments have changed considerably over the course of time; and though it may be true that 'there are certain functions that all governments always fulfill, on whatever scale',[1] the controversies of political philosophers and others about the limits of state action show that they may also do very much more. Max Weber, indeed, maintains that 'Sociologically, the state cannot be defined in terms of its ends. There is scarcely any task that some political association has not taken in hand, and there is no task that one could say has always been exclusive and peculiar to those associations which are designated as political ones: today the state, or historically, those associations which have been the predecessors of the modern state.'[2] It seems better therefore to describe all the functions of a

[1] R. M. MacIver, *The Web of Government* (1947), p. 316.
[2] *Essays in Sociology* (ed. H. H. Gerth and C. Wright Mills, 1948), p. 77.

South African chief and his subordinates, so far as they can be ascertained, than to start with a ready-made conception of what MacIver terms 'the business of government'[1] and to ignore anything that does not conform to it.

The following description is confined to the duties conventionally attached to the offices of the chief and his staff. Although such duties are not recorded in written constitutions, they have been described by many anthropologists and others, whose information was usually obtained by questioning local 'experts' on law and custom and by personal observation of rulers in action. Moreover, as we shall see, nowhere in South Africa are chiefs and other officers free to do as they wish; they are all supposed and empowered to attend to certain matters, and should neither avoid their responsibilities nor exceed their authority. What happens if they fail to act as they should, or if they try to do more than they are entitled, will be discussed in due course. For the moment we need merely note that popular reaction to their conduct, as narrated for example in tribal histories or the accounts of contemporary European observers, is yet another source of information about what is expected of them.

II

The Bantu chief in his official capacity has many duties, which if faithfully performed may take up much of his time and energy. He is commonly said to be the 'father' or 'herdsman' of his people. As such, he should care for them, watch over their interests, and seek to promote their welfare and security; indeed, the Zulu term *umbuso*, 'mode of dealing with or governing the people', means also 'making life happy for them.'[2] In working to this end, the chief relies mainly upon his confidential advisers and executive assistants, but whenever necessary he also summons and presides over meetings of the tribal council and the general assembly.

[1] *Loc. cit.*
[2] Bryant (1905), p. 60.

With them he arranges communal enterprises, takes appropriate action in case of war, famine, etc., and decides other questions of public policy. He also attends habitually at his council-place, a large circular enclosure or similar forum close to his residence, where he listens to news, petitions, and complaints, from all over the tribe, and gives orders for whatever action is required. Nothing of public importance may be done without his knowledge and consent.

His recognized duties include certain specific types of activity, which despite many variations in detail are fundamentally the same everywhere. As representative and spokesman of the tribe, he deals with its external relations. He communicates with other chiefs on matters of mutual concern, and receives and entertains them or their messengers should they come to see him. All other strangers visiting the tribe should be reported to him or to the nearest local ruler, and they may not settle or trade in his country without his consent. As among Tswana, too, none of his own people may go abroad without his permission.

The chief must also protect the rights of his subjects, provide justice for the injured and oppressed, and punish wrongdoers. He should see that local segments are satisfactorily governed by their rulers, and to ensure this should intervene to end gross abuse or incompetence. Both he and the heads of all local segments have their own courts, with power to enforce decisions and to compel the attendance of litigants and witnesses. But his is the highest court, to which appeal lies from the verdicts of all others, and normally it alone can punish such offences as sorcery and homicide. He himself is usually the judge, but in larger tribes senior princes or special indunas may act on his behalf, verdicts in the more serious cases being then referred to him for confirmation.

The law enforced in the courts consists very largely of rules handed down from one generation to another. But in all tribes the chief, with the approval of his people, may also make laws of his own; after consulting his private advisers he usually submits his proposals to the full council, and among Tswana to the popular assembly as well. In modern times, owing to the new conditions created by contact with Europeans, legislation has become fairly common, especially among Tswana and Southern Sotho; some chiefs have even compiled written collections of the laws so introduced.[1] But although Bantu everywhere say that legislation has always been a recognized function of the chief, relatively few examples are known from the early days. It may be that others have been forgotten; more probably, however, there was seldom need in those days for changes in the existing system.

Some of the early laws known to have been promulgated by chiefs modified usages relating to bride-wealth and the organization of the household (as among Tlôkwa, Mpondo, and Ngqika), or abolished circumcision and other initiation rites (as among Mpondo and Taung). Circumcision was also abandoned long ago by Zulu, but how this happened is uncertain; among Swazi it ended during the reign of Mswati (1840-68), which was a period of much fighting. Other changes seem to have been made by chiefs through executive or judicial action instead of by formal legislation; among the Zulu, for example, Shaka (1816-28) reformed the military organization by creating a standing army, among the Southern Sotho Moshesh (c. 1810-70) abolished the death penalty for sorcery and stock theft, and among the Ngwato Kgari (c. 1817-28) established a special type of feudal relationship between the chief and men given the custody of tribal cattle. Among the Ngwato, indeed, the famous Christian chief Kgama III (1875-1923) made so many changes that the people themselves nowadays distinguish between 'ancient laws' (melaô ya tlholêgô) and 'Kgama's laws' (melaô yagaKgama). These examples show that chiefs are not bound to adhere to the traditional system, but can if they wish pursue a policy of their own.

In his executive capacity the chief performs certain routine tasks of great public importance. Some affect the status of persons. For example, he periodically creates a new age-regiment (except among Cape Nguni and Southern Sotho), and thus formally admits youths into the social category of adults; and among Zulu

[1] Cf. Schapera (1943.c); Ashton (1952), p. 249 ff.

and Swazi, but apparently nowhere else, men may not marry until he gives permission to their age-group as a whole (which at one time, among Zulu, might not be before they were about forty years old).

Everywhere he also controls the distribution and use of land. This he does mainly through his sub-chiefs and headmen, all of whom manage the land within the areas that they govern. They must see that every married man receives, free of special charge, private holdings for residence and cultivation, and that the common pastures are sufficient for all. Should no more land be available locally for such purposes, the chief provides it either by rearranging area boundaries or by moving some of the people to parts less densely settled. All land not specifically allotted to local rulers remains under his immediate control, and he uses it both to satisfy new internal demands and to accommodate groups of immigrants. He or his subordinates likewise decide where people may build their homes, and which tracts are to be used for cultivation and grazing respectively.

Natural products providing food or raw materials for building, utensils, etc., can usually be exploited freely by anybody wherever he finds them. But in some instances they too are controlled by the chief. Thus, among Southern Sotho and Tswana he prohibits the cutting of thatching-grass and some useful species of trees and bushes during the early part of the rainy season, among Tswana and some Northern Sotho he also protects all trees growing in villages, among Lobedu (North-Eastern Sotho) he preserves 'large forests, a national asset, as places of the gods or as refuge in time of war',[1] among Venda certain wild fruit trees may not be cut down without his permission, and in Basutoland he reserves certain areas for winter grazing.

Very often he also regulates the calendar of agricultural and certain other activities. In most groups people may not plant or reap their crops until he has given the word, so ensuring that such work is done when conditions are considered most suitable, nor may they anywhere eat the first products of their fields until he

[1] Krige (1943), p. 182

has ceremonially inaugurated the new season of plenty. Among Tswana and some Northern Sotho he every year imposes, and in due course lifts, seasonal taboos on such activities as clearing new land for cultivation, killing or castrating bulls, and making pots. Violation of the taboos is held to injure the growing crops, but is also a penal offence. In some groups, notably Tsonga and Venda, he similarly enforces 'days of rest' after new moon, a person's death, a violent windstorm, etc.

From time to time, the chief everywhere organizes large collective hunts, which serve incidentally to provide the people with meat. As among Tswana, he may also summon age-regiments to destroy beasts of prey, or to round up stray cattle at the end of the dry season. In all groups he mobilizes tribal labour for the cultivation of his public fields, and for building or repairing his huts, council-place, and cattle-kraals. In these and various other ways he secures large-scale cooperation in tasks that often benefit the tribe as a whole.

He also mobilizes his people for defence against invading enemies or for aggression against weaker neighbours. Although, as among Cape Nguni, sub-chiefs occasionally embark on raids of their own, the tribal army is everywhere controlled by him alone, and only he can send it out on foreign expeditions. As a rule it is led on such occasions by one of his sons or brothers, or by a special induna noted for military capacity, but in some groups he himself may take command, especially against an invader. Such men as Shaka (Zulu), Mzilikazi (Ndebele), Sarili (Xhosa), Makaba II (Ngwaketse), Moshesh (Southern Sotho), and Sekwati (Pedi), were all noted warriors of the early nineteenth century who fought many campaigns, and several other Nguni and Sotho tribes have had chiefs killed in battle.

Before going to war, the army assembles at the capital, where it receives special magical treatment to 'fortify' it and is harangued by the chief. While it is away he and his 'doctors' work destructive magic against the enemy, and the people at home also observe certain taboos. If invasion is expected, he also sends men 'to fence in the country' by doctoring all paths crossing the tribal boundaries, so as to obstruct enemies who may try to enter there.

As indicated by what has just been said, the chief also has ritual functions. This aspect of his duties is more highly developed among Swazi, Venda, and North-Eastern Sotho, than in most other groups, notably Cape Nguni and Southern Sotho, but some features seem to be universal. Everywhere, for example, he organizes religious ceremonies upon the due performance of which his tribe's security and prosperity are held to depend. His dead ancestors, so it is believed, provide supernatural protection and help to the people they had once ruled, and therefore he visits their graves to pray and sacrifice to them on behalf of the tribe. This he does not only regularly on such occasions as the start of the cultivating season and the eating of the first-fruits, but also in times of war, drought, pestilence, or whenever else the diviners decide that his ancestors need to be appeased. Only he, as chief, can officiate at these ceremonies and, as we shall see, that is one of the main sanctions for his authority.

In all groups he also has horns or other vessels containing 'medicines' compounded of many different ingredients, including very often portions of a human being specially killed for the purpose; and he may further have grass rings (Zulu and Tsonga), drums (Venda and some Northern Sotho), or other sacred objects, which symbolize the unity of the tribe and to which, in some tribes, the skin, nails, hair, etc., of his predecessors are added as they die. The 'medicine', usually held for him by his principal magicians, he employs not only privately but also at the great tribal ceremonies. These include the doctoring of the army, when all the warriors are inoculated or sprinkled with mixtures to which the medicine has been added; the boys' initiation rites among Sotho, Venda, and Tsonga, when the youths are similarly doctored; and, in all groups, the annual series of ceremonies associated with the agricultural cycle. Among Nguni and Tsonga, especially, the first-fruits festival is an elaborate and picturesque ritual lasting for several days; the whole tribe gathers at the capital, the chief undergoes a magical treatment designed to 'strengthen' him, the army is doctored, and the warriors dance and sing in all their finery. In many tribes he also initiates the planting season by distributing medicated seed, which the people mix with their own seeds to promote the fertility of their crops, and sometimes, as among Zulu and Tswana, he may send medicines or doctors to important people who are seriously ill. Among Zulu, moreover, 'all skilled leeches had to teach the king their cures', among Swazi he 'is believed to have a greater knowledge of medicines than any of his subjects', and among Tswana all magicians must have his permission before they can practise for gain and occasionally, as among the Kgatla, he first has them tested and may also arrange for promising youths to be trained in the craft.[1]

Everywhere the chief is further expected to ensure that the rainfall is adequate, and his achievement in this respect may well affect his popularity. Among Tswana, Northern Sotho, and Swazi, he organizes annual rainmaking ceremonies; elsewhere he usually resorts to them only in times of drought, and at the direct request of his people. Some of them are public, and may involve the participation of special categories of persons such as immature boys and girls, hunters, or recently bereaved widows and widowers; others are performed in secret either by him or by the specialists whom he employs. He himself is often versed in the art of making rain, which is a form of magic considered highly suitable for him to know and practise. The chiefs of the Lobedu and Swazi are indeed famous throughout South Africa for their skill, and the former, especially, receives many pleas for help from rulers of more arid lands; and Sotho and Venda tribal histories show that in disputes about the succession preference was sometimes given to a son who had been taught the rainmaking magic or had acquired possession of the associated apparatus.

Most of the tasks mentioned above are performed by the chief with the aid of his advisers and officers, and although he alone can do some, his indunas, local subordinates, and magicians, are his agents in others. One important duty only he personally can fulfil. As shown more fully in the next chapter, he receives various

[1] Gluckman (1940.a), p. 31; Kuper (1952), p. 49; Schapera, unpublished field notes.

forms of tribute from his people in both labour and kind. In consequence he is always the wealthiest man in his tribe. But he does not use his wealth merely for domestic purposes. Apart from specially rewarding his officers and other assistants, he entertains people who come to visit him, and on great public occasions slaughters cattle and provides beer and porridge for all who gather at his village. He places cattle on loan with many of his subjects, supports destitute widows and orphans, sometimes sends food to sick people and newly-confined mothers, and in times of famine distributes corn from his granaries or, if the need is great, sends men to purchase supplies from his neighbours. 'The chief is the wife of the tribe', say the Tswana, i.e. he looks after the needs of his subjects, and Zulu refer to him as 'the breast of the nation', i.e. the source from which all draw sustenance; in the same context, he is often greeted as 'mother of the people' or 'mother of orphans'. One quality always expected of him is generosity, and should he fail in this respect he soon becomes unpopular.

III

Bantu local rulers have many duties similar to those of their chief. These duties are essentially the same for all grades, but subchiefs have wider jurisdiction and greater powers than headmen. In general, all headmen in a district are responsible to the local sub-chief, who in turn is responsible to the chief; in each case the higher authority hears appeals from the court decisions of his inferiors, tries cases that they cannot settle, and has overriding authority in all other matters.

With the aid of his own advisers and other assistants, every local ruler regulates the occupation and use of land in his area, and nobody may settle there or move away without his consent. His home is the administrative headquarters of the area. He judges cases involving any of his people as defendants or accused, and investigates serious crimes before referring them to his superior. He summons and presides over popular assemblies to discuss matters of general concern, organizes public labour, collective hunts, and other group enterprises, and among Southern, and some Northern, Sotho arranges periodical initiation ceremonies for boys and girls. Among Cape Nguni and Southern Sotho he commands all the able-bodied men of his area as a single division or subdivision of the tribal army; elsewhere, as among Tswana, he is leader of his own age-mates only, his other subjects being similarly commanded by his brothers and sons in their respective regiments. He prays to his ancestors on behalf of his subjects, and performs various other ceremonies to ensure good harvests, keep off misfortunes, etc. He is also expected to reward all his assistants, entertain his people generously, and care for them in times of need.

Relations between a local ruler and his subjects tend to be more intimate than those between the chief and the tribe as a whole. In small groups, especially, he knows all his people individually and is usually related to many or even most of them; he helps them in their personal troubles and mediates between them and higher authorities, is notified of all births, weddings, and deaths, and invited to beer-drinks and other feasts, and is often consulted on such matters of private concern as transactions about cattle or the employment of doctors.

Within his own area he is also the chief's local representative. He carries out the chief's general policy and special instructions, collects the tribute due to him, and is responsible for maintaining peace, order, and good government. He himself should visit the capital from time to time, not only to take part in council meetings, but also to report upon local conditions. Such visits are considered essential, for it is largely through them that the chief keeps informed of what is happening in the tribe.

Sometimes there are special arrangements at headquarters for dealing with local affairs. Among Mpondo, Zulu, and Swazi, for example, all local rulers are attached regardless of residence to one or other of a few 'royal villages'; the chief's own village, built after his accession, is one of these, and the others, founded by his predecessors, are all fairly close by. The head of every such village, who is either a senior noble or an important induna, hears appeals from the courts of his dependants, and when the army is summoned they and their men gather at his home before proceeding under his leadership to the capital. In certain Tswana tribes (e.g. Ngwato, Tawana, and Kgatla) all the component wards are similarly grouped into from three to five 'sections' cutting across district boundaries. In each section one of the ward-heads, living in the capital, is senior to the rest. Appeals from their decisions are heard by him before going if need be to the chief; he can summon the whole section to discuss matters of public concern; and in every age-regiment its members constitute a separate division headed by him or some one of his family. The effect of these arrangements is that for certain administrative purposes the whole tribe is divided into a small number of segments, each controlled by a man living in, or close to, the capital and subordinate only to the chief.

Among Western Tswana, some Northern Sotho, and Venda, there is another type of liaison between central and local authorities. Each outlying group, especially of foreigners, has a hereditary 'overseer' (termed 'mother' by North-Eastern Sotho), who lives in the capital. This man, a trusted noble or commoner, is the recognized intermediary between those people and the chief. He looks after them whenever they come to the capital, sponsors and assists them at court, may be sent to deal with local difficulties and disturbances, and among Tswana visits them periodically to collect the tribute they owe to the chief.

With the exceptions just noted, communications between the chief and the inhabitants of any outlying area normally pass through the recognized regional hierarchy. As will have been gathered, moreover, within his own group every local ruler has authority in many different fields: judicial, executive, economic, ritual, and maybe military. This wide range of activities helps to explain the facility with which groups can secede: from the smallest upwards, each is largely autonomous and can if need be exist by itself. During the many wars of the past, for example, tribes often broke apart; but owing to the all-round experience of even the most junior local authorities, it was almost always possible for the fragments to carry on with the traditional pattern of government.

IV

As we have seen, one major duty of all Bantu rulers is the administration of justice. Since this illustrates clearly the hierarchy of authorities, and also the powers of the various grades, it merits fuller description. All Bantu have a well-developed system of legal procedure. Self-help is permitted if an offender is caught in the act, sorcerers are often 'smelt out' by diviners at special séances, the chief sometimes punishes rebels without formal trial, and, as among Tswana and Swazi, breaches of regimental discipline or privilege may be dealt with internally. With these exceptions, wrongdoers are normally tried in the regular courts, the general rule being that they appear first before their own local ruler.

In practice, though not in formula, Bantu distinguish between 'civil' and 'criminal' offences. The former violate private rights connected with personal status, property, and contract, and are dealt with by compelling restitution or compensation. This applies, for example, to breach of marital or filial obligations, seduction, adultery, unpaid debts, trespass, theft, and defamation. Action in regard to such wrongs lies with the person aggrieved. Unless he chooses to ignore the matter altogether, he should first try to reach a settlement by negotiation; many civil disputes are in fact resolved by direct discussion between the people concerned, usually at a special meeting attended by their close relatives and presided over by the offender's senior agnate. If this does not succeed, the injured person lodges a formal complaint with the offender's headman, who fixes a day for hearing the case; in some groups, such as Cape Nguni and Venda, a goat or sheep is paid as fee to 'open the court'. At the trial the plaintiff states what reparation he wants, and if he wins he may be awarded the whole or only part of his claim, according to the merits of his case. Sometimes the judge simultaneously also punishes an offender who is held to have behaved very badly.

Crimes include offences against rulers in their official capacity, breaches of laws made by the chief, sorcery, incest, and often also homicide and other cases of bloodshed (elsewhere treated primarily as civil wrongs, for example among Southern and North-Eastern Sotho). Such offences can never be compounded. They must be reported to the nearest local ruler, who then sees to the arrest and trial of the accused. The most widespread and common punishment is a fine in cattle or small stock; the amount varies from a single beast to the whole of the culprit's property, according to the nature of his offence, his social status, and his previous record. Among Sotho and Tsonga corporal punishment is sometimes inflicted as an alternative, or in addition, especially upon paupers, thieves, and recalcitrants. Political offenders may be moved from their homes to areas where they will have less scope for their subversive activities, and if occupying positions of authority may be deposed. Imprisonment is unknown, and torture relatively rare except in cases of sorcery, but in some tribes habitual offenders may be deprived of their hands or ears. Serious crimes, such as sorcery, treason, and sometimes murder, are punished either by death or by banishment, both usually accompanied by confiscation of all the culprit's property. When fines are paid, one beast may be killed for the men at the court, but the others are kept by the judge. Sometimes, as in cases of bloodshed, criminals are both punished and ordered to pay compensation to the victim or his family.

All courts have jurisdiction over civil wrongs; but if the judge finds a case difficult, or if much property is involved (as in disputes about inheritance), he will usually refer it to his immediate superior. Local rulers also hear criminal cases. But the penal powers of headmen are limited to fairly small fines; hence, if the offence is at all serious, they should simply inquire into the facts and transfer the accused to a higher court. As already indicated, only the chief can deal with crimes punishable by death or banishment. Anybody objecting to the judgment of a minor court can also carry his case on appeal through all the intervening stages up to the chief. Sub-chiefs and even the chief himself, it may be added, are not only judges of appeal from the courts of their juniors, but also judges of first instance for their own local groups.

Courts have no fixed sessions, but meet as required; cases are normally tried as soon as possible, sufficient time being allowed for all concerned to assemble. The hearing is held publicly in the judge's council-place, and any man who wishes may attend. The judge and his advisers face the other people, who sit together indiscriminately, but with the litigants in front. With rare exceptions, as among Cape Nguni, witnesses do not stay away until wanted but are present throughout. Each litigant is supported by his relatives and friends, and is responsible for producing his own witnesses. If he has duly notified them and they do not appear, the judge sends messengers to fetch them; failure to obey the summons is punished unless good reason is shown, in which case the trial may be postponed if their evidence is considered essential.

The judge or his court induna briefly describes the case as reported to him. Plaintiff and defendant (or accused) then speak in turn, freely and uninterruptedly, and after making their statements are questioned closely by members of the court. The witnesses are next heard, starting with the plaintiff's, and they too are questioned in turn. When everybody concerned has spoken, the matter is thrown open for general discussion, and whoever wishes may ask further questions or venture an opinion. Sometimes the judge then clears the court or retires with his advisers before considering what verdict to give; but, as among Tswana, Northern Sotho, and Venda, he may instead decide upon it in open session. His advisers in turn review the case and say how they think it should be judged; finally he himself summarizes the evidence and the opinions expressed, discusses them, and delivers the verdict. This generally corresponds to what all or most of the others have said, but he is free to decide otherwise, though he should then explain why he dissents.

The evidence most favoured in reaching a verdict is that of eye-witnesses; circumstantial and hearsay evidence are also admitted, but carry less weight. There is no form of oath, ordeal, or divination (except sometimes in cases of sorcery). Knowledge of a person's character helps to determine the value placed upon his testimony; the extensive questioning he undergoes if his word is doubted generally suffices to show if he is telling the truth, and if found deliberately trying to mislead the court he may be punished. Such factors as provocation, negligence, or accident, the status of the persons involved, and their relationship to one another, are usually also considered in deciding what reparation to award or punishment to inflict. Where kinsmen or neighbours are at variance, for example, the court tries above all to effect a reconciliation, restoration of harmony being deemed more important than rigid adherence to the letter of the law.

If taken on appeal to a higher court, a case is there heard all over again from the very beginning. Proceedings follow the same lines as before, but the original judge must be present to state how he reached his decision; occasionally, if found to have been blatantly wrong or prejudiced, he may be reprimanded or even punished. The chief's judgment is usually final. But a man who feels that he has been unjustly treated may appeal to a senior noble or induna to intercede for him; a widespread formula used on such occasions is, 'Let the lion eat, but at least leave the bones', i.e. 'don't be too hard on him'. The sentence may then be reduced, but not necessarily. In all groups there are also recognized places of sanctuary, such as the hut of the chief's mother or the graves of his ancestors, to which men fearing death may flee if they can; their lives are then inviolate, though they may be expelled or punished in some other way, unless they succeed in escaping to another tribe.

Death sentences are usually carried out publicly soon after being pronounced; sometimes, for example, the culprit is thrown over a precipice after being clubbed on the head or stabbed with a spear. If damages are awarded or a fine imposed, reasonable time is allowed for the payment, failing which it is collected by force.[1] Should anyone lack sufficient means, his near relatives are expected, and may be compelled, to come to his aid. Every man is in any event responsible for the debts of his wives and unmarried

[1] See below, p. 103.

children, including fines or damages that they may be sentenced to pay; and sometimes, as among Venda, if someone is convicted of sorcery or treason the punishment extends to the whole of his family. Among Cape Nguni this principle of collective responsibility is exemplified also in the so-called 'spoor law': if missing cattle are traced to a certain kraal, its owners must prove that the animals have gone further, failing which they are convicted of theft.

v

The duties of a Hottentot chief and his assistants have not been recorded in much detail, but the available evidence suggests that they are not nearly as extensive as among the Bantu. With the aid of his council, which he must always consult on matters of public concern, the chief decides upon the admission of immigrants and deals with other routine foreign affairs; if necessary he sends messengers or goes personally on missions to his neighbours. In the event of war he mobilizes and commands the tribal army, and during the nineteenth century several chiefs were actually killed in battle; but decisions to make war or peace, to conclude a truce, or to enter into a military alliance, are taken not by the council but by the popular assembly, which also determines the plan of campaign. In the old days the removal of the whole tribe to another region was likewise a matter for the assembly to decide.

The chief further has certain economic and social functions. He organizes collective hunts and such cooperative tasks as digging or cleaning wells for the use of cattle, and according to several early writers is then expected to set an example by personally taking the lead. He orders the resting of pasture grounds that have been overgrazed, and his permission is required for burning the veld shortly before the first rains are due. He presides over the division of cattle and other booty taken in war. He distributes among their kin the property of persons dying childless, divides an inheritance among children after the death of both parents, and looks after desolate orphans. He should keep 'open house' for his people and help the poor with meat and milk. But he does not seem to reward his councillors and other assistants in the manner expected of a Bantu chief, though he may provide food for the former while in session. Nor does he figure at all prominently in ritual life: apart from organizing the great annual rainmaking ceremony early in summer, when the whole tribe assembles to pray and sacrifice to the Deity, he apparently has no official religious or magical duties of any kind.

In consultation with his council and the popular assembly the chief can also make laws. Most of the instances known were inspired by Europeans: in 1849, for example, the Swartboois adopted a written constitution drafted by a local missionary, and in 1850 the Rooinasie chief Oasib sought and accepted the advice of Francis Galton, then exploring South West Africa, in framing new regulations for dealing with stock theft and murder. But legislation occurred even before the arrival of missionaries; in 1779, for example, it was recorded that the reigning Rooinasie chief had 'in his own interests' recently authorized the marriage of first cousins, which was previously forbidden.[1]

Formerly the chief and his council also constituted the main court of justice. This is still true of such a tribe as the Topnaars of Sesfontein. Elsewhere cases are now usually tried by several specially chosen members of the council, the chief himself being called in only for major crimes or if difficulties are met. The court deals with both civil wrongs and such crimes as theft, assault, murder, and treason, and can punish offenders by fines, flogging, confiscation of property, banishment, or even death. Capital punishment cannot be inflicted without the personal approval of the chief, who if he wishes may substitute a milder penalty.

As among Bantu, disputes are often settled directly between the parties concerned, or they may invite one or more elderly men to act as arbiters. If this does not help, or if a penal offence has been committed, the injured person or his relatives report to the 'magistrate', who arranges for the hearing of the case. One or more goats are paid in advance to feed the judges while in session, but if they find for the plaintiff the animals are replaced by his opponent. The

[1] Vedder (1934), p. 257; Galton (1853), p. 122 f.; Wikar (1779), p. 27.

court meets whenever required, usually under a shady tree. Only those involved may attend, the general public being excluded, but either party may bring a relative or friend to serve as his advocate. Litigants and witnesses are summoned by an official messenger, and if necessary are taken to court by force. They remain in sight but out of hearing, and are called upon individually as required. After the presiding judge has outlined what he understands to be the issues involved, both parties and their witnesses are heard in turn and questioned; they are usually also allowed to cross-examine one another. The court is then cleared while the judges discuss what verdict to give. If they cannot agree, they report to the chief, whose decision is final. They also notify him of their verdicts in the more serious cases, which he is entitled to modify, and people sentenced to death have the right of appeal to him.

The trial and punishment of a murderer by the tribal court seems to be an innovation. Until some time after the middle of the nineteenth century the Hottentots practised blood vengeance. If a man was killed accidentally, his family might accept compensation in cattle. But if he was murdered or killed in a fight, his brother or son had to avenge him, even if the opportunity did not occur for many years. Neither chief nor council might intervene to prevent this, nor could they punish the avenger. The story is told of the traveller C. J. Andersson, who about 1861 shot a Hottentot in what he alleged was self-defence. He reported to the man's chief, by whom he was tried. The court decided not to punish him: 'I acquit you', the chief said to him, 'but according to our law the brother of Hartebeest [the dead man] will kill you and *must* kill you; therefore fly.'[1]

Formerly the component clans of a tribe were also more autonomous than they are now. As already mentioned, the families in each clan usually lived together and apart from the rest of the tribe. The men constituted an informal council over which the clan-head presided. They decided upon removals to new pasture grounds, organized their own hunting expeditions and other co-operative activities, and fought under their headman as a separate

1 Hahn (1883), p. 249.

unit of the tribal army. They also settled internal disputes and punished local offenders. Their decisions in such matters were not subject to control by the tribal council, which dealt only with conflicts between members of different clans and with all inter-tribal relations.

Nowadays each outlying settlement is controlled by an appointed headman who is the chief's local deputy. He has his own councillors to help him deal with the affairs of his group. Together with him they constitute a court trying civil disputes and minor crimes and able to impose corporal punishment or fines. But their judgments can be taken on appeal to the main tribal court, which also has sole jurisdiction over more serious crimes.

VI

It should by now be evident that both Bantu and Hottentots have 'government' as defined by Fortes and Evans-Pritchard: 'centralized authority, administrative machinery, and judicial institutions'. We are not as fully informed about the rôle of chiefs and their assistants among Bergdama and Bushmen, but the data show that they certainly lack some of the duties described above.

In effect the affairs of a band are among both peoples managed by its men generally. They forgather every evening round the central camp fire, and as the need arises discuss what should be done. They plan the following day's hunting, and periodically decide upon such other matters as moving camp or burning the veld to stimulate the growth of new plants; among Bergdama they occasionally also plan raids upon nearby Herero cattle-posts, or prohibit food-gathering in localities where the fruits are still green. From time to time they organize initiation ceremonies for boys, among Bergdama they consult with the women about selecting wives for young men, and among Bushmen they occasionally have to decide upon abandoning feeble old people when forced to migrate rapidly. They arrange trading and other visits to friendly neighbours, and take steps to resist aggression or to retaliate against enemies.

In all this, the chief's special function usually is to act as executive officer. He assigns their respective tasks to the hunters, divides the meat of any big game animals that they kill, leads the people and regulates each day's trek whenever they move, sends messengers to other bands and interviews those who come to him, and if not too old takes command on aggressive raids.

He also has certain ritual duties. Among Bergdama these are relatively numerous. He charms hunters to give them success, prepares medicines for use at the boys' initiation ceremonies or by parents who have lost a child, performs rainmaking magic, and in case of misfortune or when the band moves deposits offerings or prays at the grave of a dead ancestor. He also maintains the sacred fire that is held to influence the welfare of his group. This fire, round which the men usually meet, is kept burning continuously under a tree in the centre of the camp. All game killed in the chase, and each kind of berry and tuber as it ripens, is brought there and blessed before being eaten, the old men feed it with scrapings of magical roots while hunters and women are out seeking food, and before the band moves camp or settles in a new home the chief prays at it to the Deity for abundance and good fortune. If times are bad, the diviners may say that it has been polluted and is therefore no longer beneficent; the chief then orders every fire in the camp to be extinguished and with elaborate ceremonial kindles a new one, from which every family takes a brand to start its own again. Only he himself can perform this ritual, or renew the fire should it die accidentally.

In some of these activities he is helped by special assistants. Diviners advise him when to move camp or to perform certain rites. His senior wife tends the sacred fire, and whenever camp is shifted takes along some brands to set it going again; she also performs part of the ritual when hunters are being charmed. The 'food-master' sees to the tasting, preparation, and distribution, of all food brought to the fire, accompanies young men who go raiding and performs magic for their success, and 'doctors' any hunter who kills a lion.

The only Bushmen among whom the chief is said to have similar duties are the Heikum and Kung. Here he too maintains a sacred fire, at which he ceremonially tastes the meat of big game animals before it is distributed; in early summer he also inaugurates the eating of the new season's plant foods by a special rite in which he prays to the Deity on behalf of his people. Nothing of this kind has been recorded for other Bushmen. But everywhere among them professional magicians also perform rites of communal importance, such as 'doctoring' hunters for success, initiating boys into manhood, and making rain. It may be that in such cases they are directed by the chief, but our sources give insufficient detail to determine the question.

The Bergdama or Bushman chief has no legislative or judicial functions, nor are there official tribunals of any other kind. Among Bergdama, it is true, people sometimes ask elderly men to arbitrate their disputes, but such requests are not obligatory nor are the decisions necessarily accepted. Both here and among Bushmen, persons who arouse general hostility, for example by repeated acts of violence or by committing incest, may be punished by thrashing, expulsion from the band, or even death. There seems to be no formal trial; the data indicate merely that the decision to act against the offender is reached casually round the camp fire, and if necessary the younger men are then told to enforce it. Private disputes, on the other hand, are usually settled by self-help. A man who has been robbed or assaulted, whose wife has been seduced, or who has been injured in some other way, avenges himself as best he can, wounding or possibly even killing the culprit, or else resorting to poison or destructive magic. Neither the chief nor anybody else is entitled to intervene, and it is said also that blood vengeance is not practised against someone who thus kills a member of his own band. Similarly, a man may freely thrash or kill a disobedient child or unfaithful wife, or divorce her for any reason by simply sending her away.

VII

The descriptions given above show that in South Africa the

constitutional functions of chiefs and their assistants vary greatly from one people to another. This suggests that we can no more speak of 'primitive government' generally than we can of 'primitive law' or 'primitive religion' generally, except perhaps by contrast with some major characteristics of more advanced systems. Such a contrast has been attempted by MacIver. In his 'conspectus of the forms of government', he distinguishes *inter alia* what he calls 'primitive' or 'tribal' government. Its main features he defines as follows: 'The functions of government are minimal. There are few, if any, administrative officials. The duties of the chief may be casual, or vaguely defined. There may be no judicial apparatus whatever. Custom serves to regulate many things that in a less primitive system are determined by law or decree.'[1]

While broadly true of Bergdama and Bushmen, this definition can hardly be considered applicable to Bantu and Hottentots, both of whom also belong to the category of peoples that MacIver terms 'primitive'. Among Bantu, especially, the chief's duties are well-defined and numerous, affecting many aspects of tribal life; he has many administrative officers, including several grades of subordinate local authority; he presides over an organized system of judicial procedure involving a hierarchy of courts, and he can change existing practices by legislation or in other ways.

Undoubtedly even Bantu government differs very greatly from that of a modern Western state. But the differences are perhaps more marked in form than in function. It seems to be widely agreed that the primary functions of government in any modern state are to maintain law and order, administer justice, organize defence against external enemies, and conduct formal relations with other communities.[2] Everywhere in South Africa the chief also attends to foreign policy, and if need be mobilizes his people for defence or aggression, himself often taking command. But it is only among Bantu and Hottentots that he has legislative powers

[1] R. M. MacIver, *The Web of Government* (1947), p. 156.
[2] Cf. for example MacIver, *op. cit.*, p. 316; J. Salmond, *Jurisprudence*, 10th ed. (1947), p. 131; J. D. Mabbott, *The State and the Citizen* (1948), pp. 101 ff.; R. H. Soltau, *An Introduction to Politics* (1951), p. 108.

and maintains regular courts for punishing criminals and settling civil disputes. Among Bergdama and Bushmen legislation is unknown, and courts do not exist; public offenders are sometimes dealt with by collective attack, but for private wrongs, however serious, the only accepted remedy is personal retaliation. Bantu and Hottentot rulers thus perform all the primary functions of modern governments. But if we agree with MacIver and other writers that the administration of justice is a function that 'all governments always fulfill', then neither Bergdama nor Bushmen can be said to have government. Even among Bantu and Hottentots legislation is a far less conspicuous feature of governmental activity than in the modern state; in pre-European days, especially, chiefs usually pursued the same ends as their predecessors and performed tasks stereotyped by tradition, and marked changes of policy such as often accompany a change of government in Western societies seem to have been uncommon, though not altogether unknown.

Modern governments have many other functions than those mentioned above. In varying degrees, for example, they also control the production and distribution of commodities; conserve unappropriated natural resources; manage public utilities such as transport, communications, fuel, and water; and provide such other services as education, medical aid, poor relief, insurance, scientific research, and recreation. As Salmond says, 'the state has come also to organize constructively for the well-being of its members. We have moved away from the nineteenth-century idea of the police state, negative and repressive, to a new conception of the social-service state, and there is no sign that we have yet reached the end of the development.'[1]

But although 'public service' may be a relatively new function of governments in Western societies,[2] comparable tasks are also performed in South African societies, even if the situations to

[1] *Loc. cit.* Cf. H. J. Laski: 'the police-state of the nineteenth century has been transformed into the social service state of the twentieth'. (*Introduction to Politics* (1951 ed.), p. 38.)
[2] Cf. also Shepard, 'Government', *Enc. Soc. Sci.*, vol. 7, p. 9.

which they apply and the details with which they are concerned are far fewer than among ourselves. Everywhere, for example, the chief organizes and directs such collective enterprises as migrations and hunting, regulates the pursuit of certain subsistence activities, and conserves natural resources, if only by prohibiting their use at certain times or in certain places. Among Bantu and to a lesser extent Hottentots he assists needy people and in various other ways uses his wealth for the public benefit. This function, which may be likened to the poor relief and social insurance of modern states, he does not perform among Bergdama and Bushmen, where indeed he is no wealthier than the rest of his subjects; he does see, however, that game killed by the hunters is distributed among all members of the band. Among Bantu, but nowhere else, he also controls the occupation and use of land by members of the tribe, and provides people with private holdings for residence and cultivation. Except among Hottentots and some Bantu he likewise organizes initiation ceremonies, when youths are collectively admitted into the social status of adult and sometimes also receive formal instruction in rules of conduct.

In addition, among Bantu and Bergdama the chief either personally conducts or organizes many religious and magical ceremonies for the benefit of his people; he is thus in effect their high priest and leading magician. This intimate connection between rulers and ritual life is not usually a feature of modern governments, except perhaps where an established state church is maintained, and even then political authorities seldom act officially as clergymen. The chief also has ritual functions in some though not all groups of Bushmen, but among Hottentots his only comparable duty is to organize the annual rainmaking ceremony.

This rapid survey has shown that all chiefs in South Africa have some of the functions performed by more advanced governments: they conduct foreign relations and arrange defence against aggression, organize and direct collective enterprises, and provide certain social services. Many of them are also the ritual officers of their community, a duty not usually associated with government in Western states. On the other hand, among neither Bergdama nor Bushmen do they perform what is commonly held to be an essential task of all governments, the establishment and maintenance of law and order through legislation and the formal administration of justice. Bantu and Hottentot chiefs, although having many functions in common, also differ in certain respects. They make laws, administer justice, organize communal activities such as warfare and hunting, and assist needy subjects; but the Hottentot chief, unlike his Bantu counterpart, has virtually no ritual functions and relatively little control of land and other economic resources.

What has just been said suggests that the functions of a chief may be related to his people's mode of subsistence: in general, his duties are fewest and simplest among the food-gathering Bergdama and Bushmen, and most numerous and complex among Bantu cultivators and pastoralists. The suggestion will be discussed more fully later, after we have dealt with other aspects of tribal government. But it may be noted, in passing, that one would normally expect the chief to be faced with far fewer problems in the very small communities of Bergdama and Bushmen, and that legislative and judicial institutions are perhaps not so essential here as in the much larger heterogeneous and dispersed communities of Bantu and Hottentots. It should also be remembered, on the other hand, that the economic system and technology of even the Bantu are very much simpler than among ourselves; this alone, therefore, may be one reason why, for example, they have not developed public services to anything like the same extent.

South African governments differ from their advanced counterparts not only in function but also, and much more markedly, in organization. In Western states the activities of governments are usually carried on through specific agencies of many kinds. Legislative, executive, and judicial, functions are normally performed by three separate groups of persons, represented respectively by Parliament, the civil and armed services, and the courts. This 'separation of powers' is never absolute, and there is always some overlapping between one branch of government and the others. But the broad distinction is maintained, not merely for the sake of efficiency, but because it is thought to provide valuable safeguards against arbitrary action by the executive or control of the judiciary by sectional interests.

There is no such 'separation of powers' anywhere in South Africa. Among both Bantu and Hottentots the chief, with the help of his advisers and other assistants, initiates and promulgates legislation, administers justice and is himself the supreme judge, and controls the whole of the executive, even to the extent of sometimes leading the army into battle; among Bantu he is also high priest and magician of his people. Among Bergdama and Bushmen, too, the chief personally directs all the public affairs of his band; and if he does not also make laws and act as a judge, it is because those aspects of governmental activity are absent, and not because they are performed by other members of the community.

It is this concentration of all governmental functions in the hands of one person that most readily distinguishes tribal government in South Africa from its Western counterparts. Fortes and Evans-Pritchard are no doubt correct in applying the term 'primitive state' to communities like those of Bantu and Hottentots, where we find 'centralized authority, administrative machinery, and judicial institutions'. But the chief, in those communities, is not analogous to the constitutional head of a modern state. He personally controls the whole apparatus of government, and although, as among Bantu, indunas and other assistants may serve primarily as stewards, judges, or military commanders, their activities are directed or supervised by himself. The head of every subordinate local group similarly has undivided authority within his own area.

Two other features may be noted. Unlike the government of a modern state, the people who manage the affairs of a South African community are neither professional politicians nor civil servants pursuing a special vocation because of personal interests and ambitions or as a means of livelihood. Chiefs everywhere in South Africa occupy their positions and perform the associated functions because they are entitled and expected to do so by right of birth; and although, as shown in the following chapter, they receive various forms of tribute and other payment from their people, these do not constitute their sole source of income. Their official duties, especially among the non-Bantu peoples, seldom take up the whole or even greater part of their normal daily life, and may indeed require less frequent attention; and when not engaged on public business they follow the same occupations as all other people—hunting, looking after their cattle, or doing other work appropriate to their sex and age. Even among Bantu chieftainship is not necessarily a time-consuming profession. Robert Moffat, who visited the Ngwaketse in 1824, wrote of the chief then ruling: 'In the fore part of the day Makabbe is generally employed cutting skins for sewing together for mantles, and in the afternoon he is generally intoxicated.'[1] The description hardly does justice to Makaba, who was a veteran warrior feared by all the neighbouring tribes and of whom Moffat also says that he was 'pretty well versed in African politics', but it does show that the chief often has much time to spare from his duties. This is equally true of all his advisers and other assistants.

In addition, nowhere in South Africa is 'the government' something abstract or impersonal. Among Bergdama and Bushmen the chief is the head of a kinship group, all of whose members associate with him habitually; among Hottentots and Bantu every minor local ruler is similarly in direct and continuous contact with all his dependants, and even the chief himself is as a rule freely accessible at his council-place to any of his subjects. This personal relationship, so different from the pattern characteristic of the bureaucracy in Western societies, is of very great importance in tribal politics. It means that most rulers are regarded and approached not as strangers occupying official posts, but as individuals with whom one is either intimately connected or at least well acquainted; it means also that they cannot separate their public from their private lives to anything like the same extent as the average modern civil servant, since in both capacities they may have to deal with the same people.

1 Schapera (Ed.) (1951), p. 137.

The Privileges and Powers
of Office

I

THE persons who constitute the government of a modern Western state have special powers and privileges. Like most professional workers they are paid for their services; some also gain status and prestige from their official position, and those who perform their duties well may receive such rewards as titles or other honours. But, above all, they can compel obedience of the laws that they make or administer; in the last resort they, and only they, can use physical force (represented by army and police) to repress internal conflicts, maintain law and order, and punish offenders. Other people too can sometimes apply forcible sanctions, for example parents in dealing with children, but in such cases their powers are specifically controlled by the state.

The right and ability to resort to force have often been regarded as constituting the distinctive criterion of political organization. For example, Max Weber says: 'Ultimately, one can define the modern state sociologically only in terms of the specific *means* peculiar to it, as to every political association, namely, the use of physical force'; and MacIver maintains that 'The state is distinguished from all other associations by its exclusive investment with the final power of coercion.'[1] Similar statements have been made by many other political scientists and sociologists.

Anthropologists too have sometimes stressed the same feature. Radcliffe-Brown, for example, says that 'In studying political

Weber, *Essays in Sociology* (ed. Gerth and Mills, 1948), pp. 77 f.; MacIver and Page, *Society* (1949), p. 456.

organization, we have to deal with the maintenance or establishment of social order, within a territorial framework, by the organized exercise of coercive authority through the use, or the possibility of use, of physical force', and Malinowski that 'Political organization implies always a central authority with the power to administer regarding its subjects, that is, to coordinate the activities of the component groups; and when we say power, we presuppose the use of force, spiritual and physical alike.'[1] But Lowie, who also regards 'the exercise of force as the criterion of a full-fledged political organization', remarks that 'A simple society may be differentiated so as to foreshadow government, yet the coercive element may be lacking', and Fortes and Evans-Pritchard emphasize that whereas in 'primitive states' the chief has the command of organized force, in 'stateless societies' force is not the monopoly of any particular person or class.[2]

The statements just quoted suggest two possible alternatives: either not all primitive societies have 'political organization', or else political organization should not be defined in terms of coercive power alone. At this stage I wish merely to indicate the existence of the problem. Which of the two views is the more helpful in comparative studies is best reserved for discussion until after we have learned what are in fact the powers of South African chiefs and their staffs. For the moment I am concerned only with the powers that they are entitled to exercise, and with the sanctions by which these are maintained; whether they are always actually able to exercise such powers, and what happens in case of abuse or attempted abuse, will be dealt with in the following chapter. The relevant information is again far more abundant for Bantu than for any of the other peoples, but although essential details for the latter are often missing, or else very sketchy, enough has been recorded to provide material for discussion.

[1] Radcliffe-Brown, in *African Political Systems* (ed. Fortes and Evans-Pritchard, 1940), p. xiv; Malinowski, *Scientific Theory of Culture* (1944), p. 165.
[2] R. H. Lowie, 'Some aspects of political organization among American aborigines', *J. R. Anthrop. Inst.*, vol. 78 (1948), p. 11; Fortes and Evans-Pritchard, *op. cit.*, p. 14.

II

A Bantu chief has in his own tribe a position of outstanding privilege and authority. First, he is entitled to obedience and service from his subjects. He may send people where and on what errands he wishes, summon them to attend court cases or tribal meetings, mobilize them for public work or for war, move them from their homes and settle them where he pleases, and order them to do anything else in the public interest. He may also call upon them to build or repair his own huts and cattle-kraals, clear land for, and work in, his wives' fields, and supply him with timber, thatching-grass, water, firewood, etc.

Local rulers usually have similar rights over their own followers, but the chief's commands always come first. In addition, as we have seen, he alone may convene national council meetings or popular assemblies, promulgate legislation, arrange tribal ceremonies, create new age-regiments, send the army to war, judge certain offences, and sentence people to death or banishment. Occasionally, in large Nguni tribes and among the Sotho of Basutoland, important sub-chiefs remote from headquarters may impose capital punishment or 'doctor' their own warriors, but such special powers are rare and exercised only with the consent of the chief. He and his family also take precedence in such rites as eating the first-fruits, and this prerogative is so jealously guarded that its breach is punished as treason. Other offences against him are usually treated more severely than when the victim is a commoner; thus, if his wife or daughter is seduced the penalty may be death, and insults to him or one of his family are fined very heavily.

The chief has first choice of land for his home and fields, and occasionally reserves special areas as grazing for his cattle. But like all other members of the tribe he normally has private rights only to as much land as he requires for the use of his household; the existence of large royal estates occupied on conditions of special service or tribute by villeins or other personal dependants is not characteristic of the Bantu generally. There are also certain insignia of rank, such as leopardskin cloaks, ivory or copper bracelets, and particular kinds of bead necklace, which only he and members of his family may wear; otherwise their everyday costume is not specially distinctive. Sometimes he has other unique privileges. Where descent groups are exogamous (as among Nguni, Tsonga, and Venda), he can marry kinswomen of categories forbidden to commoners, though he does not have to make official 'incestuous' marriages of the kind reported for certain rulers elsewhere; and in some Nguni and Sotho tribes he can arbitrarily take any unmarried girl to wife, though (except among Swazi) he must then give the usual *lobola* to her people.

His exalted status is reflected in the ceremonial surrounding him. He is normally addressed by his official title (*inkosi*, etc.), or by the name of his tribe, clan, or totem; people often greet him or punctuate his remarks by such flattering terms as 'lion', 'great wild beast', 'lord of the soil', 'beautiful one', 'devourer of people'; and he alone, among Nguni and Tsonga, is entitled to the royal salute *bayede*!, 'Hail, your Majesty' (literally, 'bring them, i.e. the enemies, for us to destroy'). His personal name is everywhere used to give emphasis to oaths; but among Zulu and Tsonga, though not elsewhere, both it and any other word with one or more of its syllables are otherwise taboo.[1] Among Venda he and whatever pertains to him are sometimes described in a special vocabulary known only to habitués of his capital; thus, 'His door or hut is called the "crocodile", his beer-pot is the "shade", his salt is "sand", his dogs are "messengers"; if he is asleep, he is "breathing", and if he is eating he "works" '.[2]

Sometimes he is treated with very marked respect. Among Venda, for example, people approaching him pat hands continuously and murmur his praises, and when close by go down on their knees and bow; whenever he appears in public he is greeted

---

[1] In Zululand, for example, the word *impande*, 'root', was owing to its similarity to the name of Chief uMpande discarded and replaced by the synonym *ingxabo* (Bryant (1905), pp. 484, 217).

[2] Stayt (1931), p. 202.

by a chorus of fulsome adulation and everybody present makes humble obeisance; and court etiquette demands that those seeking an audience should be kept waiting a long time and that they always converse with him indirectly through an induna or someone else. Similar deference is shown to the chief among Zulu, Swazi, Tsonga, and some Northern Sotho. Elsewhere he is usually far more accessible and often mixes freely and informally with his people; among the Mpondo, for example, men coming to his village on business sit in the council-place and chat with him, joke in his presence, and 'pester him for tobacco'.[1] But even here he demands respect and punishes anybody presuming to be too familiar or behaving improperly in his presence. Whenever he leaves home he should be accompanied by special attendants, and on visiting places outside the capital he is generally received with great public ceremony and enthusiasm.

His installation and often also his marriage to his great wife are occasions of public rejoicing, when people assemble at his home to feast, sing, and dance. His death is sometimes announced immediately, but (as among Swazi, Tsonga, Venda, and North-Eastern Sotho) may be kept secret for many months pending the choice of a successor. As soon as it is made known, his subjects all shave their heads and observe other prescribed mourning usages; as part of the ritual, the army is specially doctored 'to cleanse the weapons'. He is buried either in his own cattle-kraal or, as among Venda and some others, in a sacred grove; among Cape Nguni, in the old days, only he and members of his family were buried, the bodies of commoners being taken out and left in the veld to be devoured by wild animals. In most groups one or more of his body-servants are also killed and buried with him, 'to be his mat' or 'to carry his sandals'. His grave is afterwards guarded for some time and, as already noted, may become both a place of tribal worship and a sanctuary for people in fear of execution.

His deeds are extolled in lengthy eulogies (Nguni *izibongo*, Tswana *mabôkô*, etc.), composed during his lifetime by men who recite them in his honour at public gatherings; and these 'praises',

[1] Hunter (1936), p. 396.

handed down from one generation to another, often embody almost all that is remembered of him. Tribal history itself, as preserved in oral tradition, is usually little more than the annals of the royal family, and the royal line of descent is invariably traced farther back than that of any commoner.

The chief's household is the largest and most elaborate in the tribe. He usually has many more wives than other men (some chiefs have over fifty), and many public officers and domestic servants are directly attached to him. Among Sotho and Venda they all live together with him in his village; among Nguni and Tsonga they are often distributed over the tribal territory in several kraals, each inhabited by one wife or more with their children and other dependants. But his huts, furniture, and food, are similar to those of his subjects, and his wives and daughters sometimes work at home and in the fields like all other women. Except for utensils of better make, ornaments and cloaks of greater value, and more frequent and abundant supplies of meat and beer, there are no special luxuries in which he can indulge.

Most of the resources that he uses to maintain his household, reward his assistants, and fulfill his other tribal obligations, come directly from his subjects. They not only work for him in the various ways already mentioned, but also pay him tribute in kind. Almost everywhere one or more very large fields are specially cultivated for him every year by individual districts or other local segments; in Bechuanaland, for example, there are 19 such fields among the Kgatla, 12 among the Kwena, and 26 among the Ngwaketse. They do not belong to him personally, but are attached to his office, and are therefore cultivated for whoever happens to be chief at the moment. He provides the seed and takes the crops, but the people do all the work, under the leadership of their respective sub-chiefs or headmen; and it is by arranging for the collective planting, weeding, and reaping, of the fields at suitable times that he regulates the cycle of agricultural activity.[1] In most groups every woman also gives him a basketful of her own grain; its presentation is a ceremonial affair organized by the local rulers,

[1] See above, p. 71 f.

and some of the grain is made into beer, which the people assemble to drink as part of the harvest thanksgiving. Often those living in his village or near by likewise send him beer or meat whenever they brew or slaughter.

Everywhere he also receives certain hunting spoils. These normally include the skins of all animals killed at communal hunts organized by himself, and the brisket or other special joint of every big game animal, the skins of all lions and leopards, one tusk of every elephant, and some feathers of every ostrich, killed at any other time by any of his subjects. Among Tswana the tusk due to him is the one that first strikes the ground, or lies next to it, when an elephant is slain; to give him the other is equivalent to denying his paramountcy over the land, and meets with severe punishment if the offence is discovered. In outlying areas successful hunters bring such tribute to their local ruler, who transmits it to the chief. Failure to do so is considered a sign of revolt, and tribal histories show that seceding leaders often announce their claim to independence by retaining for themselves tribute received from their followers.

The chief's main source of wealth is cattle. As a rule he has by far the greatest number in the tribe. Some he inherits from his father or gets as *lobola* for his daughters and other female dependants (and usually many more cattle are given for a chief's daughter than for a commoner's). Others are presented to him by household-heads on his accession (and among Cape Nguni and Tswana also when as a youth he goes through the initiation ceremonies), and the *lobola* for his great wife is often subscribed in the same way.[1] All cattle looted in war are brought to him, and although he distributes some among the successful raiders or to other men whom he wishes to favour he always keeps many for himself. He receives others from people wishing to settle or trade in his country, and from subjects seeking favours or specially grateful to him. Except among Venda cattle are given to him as 'death dues' from the estate of every household-head or other person of note, among Sotho and Venda parents pay him an ox, sheep, or goat, for every

[1] See above, p. 51.

child attending initiation ceremonies. and among Sotho stray cattle are brought to him by the finders and if not claimed within a certain time by their owners are held to belong to him. Everywhere he is also entitled to the fines imposed in his court, and in the rare event of an estate having no male heir he takes both it and the *lobola* given for any daughters.

Although distinctly unusual, one other form of tribute needs special mention. Among the Zulu, every large household is required to send a grown-up girl to the chief. The girls generally live as domestic servants in his villages; some, however, may become his concubines or even his wives, and others he gives to favourites or marries off for the sake of their *lobola*. A somewhat similar institution is found among the Lobedu. No other tribe seems to have anything like it, though in all groups chiefs occasionally receive women from colleagues or subjects to cement an alliance, say, or to secure some special favour.

The chief sometimes makes other demands upon the property of his subjects. In times of emergency, for example, as when an indemnity in live-stock must be paid after defeat in war, he may impose a nation-wide levy to which every household must contribute if it can; and when travelling in the veld he may without first seeking the owner's consent kill any animal for food, a right likewise enjoyed by his messengers on official duty. Among Nguni he occasionally tours his territory for the specific purpose of receiving gifts from the head of every household that he visits; and a Venda proverb says, 'You cannot appear before the lion without a piece of firewood in your hand', i.e. you cannot visit a chief without bringing along a present.[1] Among Venda he may further seize not only the property of men condemned to death, but even their wives and children, unless relatives are willing and able to pay ransom.

Because of all the goods and services that he receives, the chief is always the richest man in his tribe. In 1932, for example, the chief of the Kgatla owned about 5,500 head of cattle, one-seventh of the total tribal holding; he was also receiving annually about 1,200 bags

[1] van Warmelo (1937), p. 275.

of Kafir corn from his tribute fields, 30 head of cattle in stray stock, and from 20 to 40 head of cattle in court fines. Similarly, among the Swazi, where only a few men own as much as 'several hundred' head of cattle, the chief was estimated in 1936 to have about 4,000 head.[1]

But the tribute is paid to the chief in his official and not in his personal capacity (for example, it goes to a regent during the minority of an heir), and, as already mentioned, he should use his wealth not only for domestic but also for various public purposes. Sometimes, as among Swazi, Venda, and Tswana, such things as agricultural tribute, looted or stray cattle, court fines, and death dues are regarded as essentially 'tribal property'; the chief should not divide them among members of his family, or use them for other private purposes, but must reserve them for official needs; and after his death they are vested in his successor, and do not form part of his personal estate. Normally, however, his public revenue is not separated from such private income as the produce of his wives' fields or *lobola* for his daughters. Whatever comes to him, regardless of the source, is his to do with as he pleases—and so far as the people in general are concerned, that always includes being hospitable and helping them in times of need.

III

The many and often great privileges of the Bantu chief are reinforced by much power. We have already seen that in his judicial capacity he settles disputes and can impose punishments ranging from a small fine to banishment or death; we have seen also that he has certain prerogatives whose breach is a penal offence. In addition, he claims prompt obedience from his subjects; as Tsonga say, 'The chief's trumpet never refuses to blow', i.e. his words are always orders, and they must always be obeyed. Failure to do so is punished, and disloyalty or revolt is a major crime. In some Tswana tribes, indeed, at his installation he is ceremonially handed

[1] Schapera (1943.a), p. 219, and unpublished field notes; Kuper (1947), p. 151.

a spear, an axe, and a club, and told that now he has 'power to kill or to let live'. Moreover, except in some domestic situations (as when a husband or parent thrashes an erring wife or child), and except in self-defence or under special provocation (as when a murderer, adulterer, or cattle-thief is taken red-handed), it is normally illegal for anyone but him or his assistants acting officially to use force against other people or their property.

Unlike the government of a modern state, the chief does not have a constituted body of police. He uses any of his court servants to summon or arrest people for trial, administer punishments, and enforce his other decisions. Should additional men be required, he calls upon such standing reserves as the members of an age-regiment (Tswana) or the warriors stationed at his villages (Zulu and Swazi). If, for example, anyone fails to pay a fine, messengers are sent to seize the animals, with one or more others as penalty; in case of resistance, an armed detachment is directed to bring in all the offender's cattle, and perhaps also to burn his huts and kill him if need be. Some of the animals are given to those taking part in the raid, which is said to be one reason why they are usually willing to serve in this capacity.

The chief seldom employs force except as part of the judicial process. But he occasionally dispenses with formal trial. Thus, if people openly refuse to obey him, or if he suspects them of plotting against him or of planning to leave the tribe without his consent, he may inflict summary justice by sending men to kill them or to 'eat them up', i.e. to destroy their homes and confiscate all their property. The fact that wealth among Bantu consists mainly of live-stock, which are also a basic source of food, makes such confiscation both easy in practice and a very effective form of punishment. Among Nguni, people accused of sorcery are usually also not tried in the normal way; once 'smelt out' by diviners at a public séance authorized by the chief, they are deemed guilty and are dealt with immediately. Instances are likewise known in many tribes of men being arbitrarily killed or despoiled for no apparent reason except the chief's whim; but these are generally acknowledged to represent an abuse of power, and not its legitimate exercise.

The chief's judicial powers, it may be added, are not precisely defined. Although there are standard kinds of penalty for most civil and criminal offences, he may be lenient or severe as he pleases; and his decisions, unlike those of other judges, cannot be taken on appeal to a higher authority. The discretion he is thus able to exercise is a useful instrument of policy: he may deal generously with his favourites or partisans, and in similar circumstances impose heavy fines upon, or award minimal damages to, his critics or men whom he dislikes. This in itself discourages opposition, for without acting at all unconstitutionally he can always discriminate against his enemies should they appear before him at court.

The chief does not depend solely upon his command of physical force, nor do people obey him merely because they fear direct punishment. His hold over the tribe is supported by several other factors. His office itself is sometimes held to be of divine origin and virtually coeval with man. A Zulu myth, for example, relates that Unkulunkulu (the High God) created man, food, fire, and marriage, and then said: 'Let there be black chiefs; and the chief be known by his people, and it be said, "That is the chief; assemble all of you and go to your chief"'.[1] The fact that chiefs have 'always' existed, that from time immemorial they have formed part of the social system, undoubtedly helps to secure for them the honour and obedience that are traditionally their due.

Moreover, not only is the chief's office a venerable institution but he himself holds it by right of birth. Occasionally his claim to legitimacy may be specially validated, for example by his being the son of the 'great wife' whose *lobola* was paid by the tribe, by his possessing certain sacred relics inherited from his predecessor, or, as among Venda and North-Eastern Sotho, by a ritual test whereby the gods show at the time of his accession that he is indeed the true heir. Whatever the details, normally no one but a senior prince can ever succeed to the chieftainship. His birthright sustains his authority: the heads of all other descent groups in the

[1] Callaway (1870), p. 57.

tribe likewise inherit their positions, and consequently they tend, if only for selfish reasons, to support a social system upon which their own powers and privileges so largely depend.

Bantu themselves often stress the importance of chieftainship in the maintenance of law and order. One hesitates to say that they have a theory of 'government by consent', but they certainly regard chiefs as indispensable. As Casalis wrote long ago about the Southern Sotho, 'The natives cannot conceive of a community, however limited it may be, that can order its own affairs, and do without a superior; or, to speak in their own language, a *head*.'[1] Tsonga say that a tribe without a chief 'has lost its reason, it is dead, it is like a woman without a husband, there is no one to make laws or call the army together';[2] and a widespread proverb affirms that 'In a country without chiefs, people devour one another', i.e. without authority there is no peace. The knowledge and expectation that the chief will administer justice and punish wrongdoers are important factors, not only in social relations generally, but also in the popular attitude to his office; and although revolts against individual chiefs have occurred fairly often, in not a single instance was attempt made to replace chieftainship by some other kind of government.

The people depend upon the chief for certain other benefits that only he can confer. As we have seen, he conducts many ceremonies on their behalf, including the worship of his ancestors on occasions of national importance. His rôle of tribal priest helps to explain the respect shown to him. If his subjects obey him, so it is held, they and the land will be blessed; if they trouble him unreasonably, their welfare will suffer. Drought, disease, loss of cattle, military defeat, in fact any public misfortune, may be attributed by diviners to the 'sore hearts' of him and his ancestors, angered or aggrieved by disloyalty and disobedience. The Kwena chief Motswasele II ruled so badly that in 1821 he was publicly assassinated; 'after his death', said a speaker at a tribal assembly in 1926, 'his spirit rose and troubled the Kwena, he spoiled the tribe

1 Casalis (1861), p. 214.
2 Junod (1927), i, p. 382.

by scattering it through civil war.'[1] It is thus not altogether in-appropriate to say, as Casalis and some other writers do, that his people have an 'almost superstitious' regard for him; in the words of a Tswana proverb, 'The chief is a little god, one should not speak ill of him.'

Loyalty to the chief is therefore a virtue highly stressed. From childhood upwards people are taught to show him due respect. At initiation ceremonies among Sotho and Cape Nguni, youths are explicitly admonished to honour, obey, and support him, and similar advice is given by old men to the assembled tribe at the time of his installation. The distinctive ceremonial relating to him, and the precedence he takes on all ritual occasions, further empha-size his unique position.

He thus becomes the focus of attitudes and values that in the long run contribute to his control of the tribe as much as does the coercive power that he can exercise. Nor is this due merely to his being head of the government. As we have seen, he is also the only obvious symbol of the tribe's unity and exclusiveness. Bantu have no flags, anthems, or similar emblems of national solidarity, and it is primarily through their respective chiefs that people distin-guish one tribe from another. Patriotism to them does not entail saluting 'the star-spangled banner', or fervently maintaining that 'There'll always be an England'; it is epitomized instead in the opening words of a well-known Tswana war chant, '*Tlotlang kgosi e kgolo, banna,*' 'Honour the great chief, you men.'

The deep regard in which the chief is sometimes held is shown by the story of some Ngwane (Natal Nguni) men, who with the orphan heir were fleeing from enemies. They became momen-tarily separated, and after he had found refuge with a friend he sent a messenger to look for his followers. The messenger shouted for two of them by name, but although they heard him they re-fused to answer. When another of the party asked why, they re-plied: 'We were afraid that these might be Swazis, we thought perhaps they might have killed the prince, and now they had come to slay us also.' To which he rejoined, 'And had they killed

[1] Bechuanaland Protectorate Government Records (Mafeking).

you, what would that have mattered, once your chief was lost to you?'[1]

The identification of chief and tribe does not necessarily mean that he is a 'sacred king' like the rulers of some other primitive societies. It is true that among Swazi, Venda, and North-Eastern Sotho, he is the central figure of an elaborate system of ritual, and has to observe many personal taboos and other special usages. Among the Lobedu, for example, the queen 'should lead a secluded life, being seen by and giving audience to royal relatives and the nobility only', and she may not leave her country or cross its boundaries. She should also 'have no physical defect', and it is said that 'her death dislocates the rhythm of nature, bringing drought and famine, the abrogation of law and order'. But although she is expected when very old to commit suicide by taking poison (a usage also found among such other North-Eastern Sotho tribes as the Kgaga and Thabina), her death is not required because 'failure of physical powers' might 'upset the regularity of nature'; it is, rather, 'a symbol of her divinity, for it proves that she is not heir to the weaknesses of ordinary man.' Among Venda, too, the chief is 'regarded as semi-divine during the greater part of his life', and 'towards the end of it, or sometimes long before, he actually confers godhead upon himself, when after abjuring all contact with women, and putting away his wives, he performs a solemn solitary dance (*u pembela*) which makes him in very truth a god (*Mudzimu*).' But only of the Swazi are we specifically told that the national welfare is mystically related to the chief's own physical vigour, and will suffer if he becomes ill or is in mourning; his death, moreover, 'is considered to be a direct attack upon the nation, and vengeance is essential.'[2]

Such conceptions are unknown elsewhere, notably among Tswana, Southern Sotho, and Cape Nguni. But in all divisions the chief is specially 'doctored' at the time of his installation and on various occasions afterwards. This treatment, which corresponds

[1] van Warmelo (1938), p. 96.
[2] Krige (E. J.) (1938), pp. 270 f.; Krige (J. D. and E. J.) (1954), pp.63 f.; Lestrade (1930), p. 312; Kuper (1947), pp. 85 ff.

to the private doctoring that almost every person in the tribe likewise undergoes, is intended not merely to protect him from personal harm, but also to give him the power of dominating his subjects. Among most Nguni, especially, the main feature of the great annual first-fruits ceremony is the ritual 'strengthening' of the chief; and here he is said to have such an overwhelming 'personality' or 'shadow' (*isitunzi*) that ordinary people do in fact fear to approach him too closely. Sotho do not stress his magical aura to nearly the same extent, but among them too the personal 'medicines' that he uses are held to make him awe-inspiring and irresistible; and I have heard it said of an irresponsible and much-criticized young chief in Bechuanaland that his failure to command popular respect was due partly to his relying upon 'doctors' who did not know the right magic for men of his position.

Normally, therefore, the chief's power is strengthened by the belief that he has 'strong medicines' in him and at his command. He can also use more conventional methods of maintaining and extending his hold over the tribe. One of these, already noted, is to place his relatives in charge of major segments: his brothers, sons, and other close agnates are often among the most important of local rulers, and among Sotho and Venda the leaders of age-regiments are all members of his family. He himself is often allied to influential subordinates by marriage or blood; he takes wives from the families of men with large followings, and marries off his own sisters and daughters to others (thus becoming 'maternal uncle' of their heirs and successors). Through such kinship and affinal ties, which at all levels of Bantu society entail special obligations of mutual aid, he is able to control his tribe more effectively than if all its divisions were administered for him by people to whom he is merely an alien overlord.

His command of wealth is another important buttress of power. We have already seen that he should be what Tswana term *motswadintlê*, 'the source of good things'. By satisfying this expectation, he gains the affection and loyalty of his subjects. As a widespread proverb says, 'A person, like a dog, is coaxed by the hand', i.e. if you are kind to people, they will like you and come to you.

Among Zulu, similarly, 'Whenever a kindness is shown any one, the receiver will express his gratitude to the giver by saying, *inkosi*, or *uyinkosi*, i.e. you are a chief; or, whenever one asks or entreats another to show an act of kindness and mercy, he does it by reminding or telling him simply, *uyinkosi*.'[1]

His assistants, in particular, look to him for reward; among Nguni, indeed, it is primarily to acquire cattle that young men come to serve at his court. Neither they nor other officers receive anything comparable to the regular salaries of modern Government employees. But he houses, feeds, and clothes his domestic servants, and occasionally gives them a heifer or helps them pay *lobola* for a wife; he gives cattle and other valuables, maybe also wives, to his advisers, indunas, and tribal magicians; and slaughters cattle or provides other food for men frequenting his council-place, serving in the army, or summoned to cultivate his fields and do other tribal work. He usually gives a heifer or some other reward to every man killing a lion or leopard and bringing the skin to him, distributes among those taking part the meat of game killed at a tribal hunt, and cooks for the men at his court or sends to paupers and invalids the big-game joints delivered to him as tribute. He places many of his cattle on loan with deserving subjects, who live on the milk, eat animals that die, and periodically receive a heifer or two for themselves. Men who find special favour he appoints to local rulerships or employs in other responsible capacities, from which they derive not only prestige but usually also much material benefit.

His officers thus depend upon him for wealth and position. Whatever powers and privileges they possess they enjoy as his representatives and by his grace, and it is only through him that they can advance in the social scale. So long as they serve him well and faithfully, they continue to benefit; should they incur his displeasure, he can withhold his favour or dispense with their services. This is as true of important sub-chiefs as of the meanest commoner; all of them are in varying degrees bound to him personally by self-interest.

[1] Döhne (1857), p. 171.

What has just been said is well illustrated by the Ngwato and Tawana, among whom there exists an apparently unique type of relationship between the chief and some of his officers. In these two Tswana tribes, each herd of royal cattle is under the care of a selected commoner (termed *motlhanka*, 'retainer', or *mosimane wa kgosi*, 'the chief's boy'). The office is normally inherited from father to son. But as the cattle increase, both naturally and through income from the various sources already mentioned, the chief creates additional herds, which he entrusts to other men who have served him well. Each of these men then usually becomes the head of a new ward, whose other members include his close agnates and the menials who live with and actually tend the cattle out in the veld. Of the 112 wards located in the Ngwato capital (1940), 35 are headed by such retainers, and 17 of the 40 Tawana ward-heads belong to the same category.

Each retainer must periodically supply the chief with meat and milk (whence the cattle under his care are termed *kgamêlô*, 'milk-pail'), and with his followers must do any other work specially required of him. In return, he uses the cattle for his own benefit; for example, he takes their milk, slaughters a beast whenever he wishes, pays *lobola* for his sons' wives out of them, and exchanges them for other commodities. He is also the 'owner' of all Bushmen and other servile peoples inhabiting the region where the cattle are kept. Some of them do the menial work in his own household, and others herd the cattle; and he claims from them all such hunting spoils as ivory, ostrich feathers, and skins, which he delivers to the chief, who then gives him a share for himself.

On the other hand, whatever the retainer acquires independently by his own efforts is also regarded as *kgamêlô*, and hence as belonging ultimately to the chief. So long as he serves faithfully and is loyal—and that means to whoever happens to be chief at the moment—he is normally secure in the enjoyment of his property, and after his death the same rights pass to his heir; but should he ever show signs of disaffection the chief can effectively, and lawfully, ruin him by taking back the *kgamêlô*, i.e. by confiscating everything that he possesses. That is the feature distinguishing the *kgamêlô* system from similar holdings of cattle in other tribes; among the latter, the chief (or whoever else owns the cattle) is entitled to recover only the animals actually placed on loan, together with their natural increase, and has no legal claim to the rest of the holder's property. Retainers thus depend directly upon the chief for whatever they have, and in consequence are virtually bound to remain loyal to him. Nobles, it may be added, are never entrusted with *kgamêlô*, though the chief may and should provide for them in other ways.

Bantu chiefs are well aware of the power that they derive from their wealth, and try therefore to ensure that nobody else is in a position to rival them. As the Venda proverb says, 'A commoner may not have anything so fine as to astonish the chief.' Any man who becomes too prosperous tends to be regarded as a source of danger; even if his birth does not qualify him for the chieftainship itself, his wealth will enable him to attract a following that may be of great help to a potential usurper. Hence, as among Nguni, the chief may induce diviners to 'smell out' the man as a sorcerer, say after a death or illness in the royal family, and without further ado he is 'eaten up' and so ceases to be a menace; 'from being a great man, with plenty of property and many friends, he suddenly finds himself alone, and with people ready to kill him.'[1]

With the backing of both physical force and the various other sanctions mentioned, the chief can normally secure submission to his will. Among Swazi he summons even his most important subordinates 'with the imperious command, "*Ngemandla*" ("With all power")';[2] and among Kgatla I once heard the chief at a tribal meeting abruptly quell adverse comment on an unpopular edict by announcing firmly, '*Ke bua ka thata ya borêna, ke apere nkwê*', 'I speak with the power of chieftainship, as wearer of the leopard-skin'. *Le roy le veult*! This does not mean that he is an absolute sovereign always able to do as he wishes, or that he never encounters opposition. But the mere fact that he is chief usually ensures that, so long as he does not behave outrageously, his people will

[1] Shepstone (1883), p. 68.
[2] Kuper (1947), p. 71.

on the whole readily obey him and carry out his commands.

IV

The members of the chief's descent group also enjoy certain privileges. We have already seen that they are generally recognized as constituting a separate class within the tribe, that there are always some of them among the chief's confidential advisers, and that many if not most of the major local rulerships, as well as many minor ones, are usually in their hands. But the extent to which the class as a whole is privileged varies a good deal. Among Venda, 'the chief and his clan are something apart from the rest of the tribe'; unlike commoners, they have their own burial groves where they perform sacrificial rites that are unique to them; and their children receive a special training at the chief's village, where 'they learn many things that the *vhalanda*, the ordinary folk, never get to know about, and imbibe that feeling of aloofness from the common people, and of solidarity as a sib against the latter, that is so characteristic of the ruling families among the Venda.' Their detachment from the rest of the population is shown at the first-fruits sacrifice, where they pray: ' "May the country resound with lamentation, may there be sorrow (misfortunes) among the commoners, that we may grow rich thereby" ' (because 'if the commoners have disputes and troubles, they bring them to the chief, who profits thereby in one way or another').[1]

In no other division do the nobles as a class have so exalted a status. But, almost everywhere, they are all normally treated with respect by other people and take precedence at social gatherings; commoners consider it an honour to be allied to them by marriage, and among Tswana no man may marry before the royal leader of his age-regiment; and although in theory all men are equal before the law ('We look not at the person, but at his fault', says a Tswana proverb), in practice it is often more difficult to get justice against a noble than a commoner.

[1] van Warmelo (1932), pp. 109, 151, 160 f.

In all divisions, the more closely a man is related to the chief the more highly privileged he is. The chief himself is expected to find or create personal followings for his senior brothers and sons, thus making them heads of local segments; he should regularly consult them and his uncles and cousins on matters of public concern; and he should give them cattle and provide for them in other ways. As Venda say, 'A man's children share even the head of a locust', i.e. the perquisites of chieftainship belong to the royal line collectively, and not to the incumbent alone. Through the cattle that they inherit or are given by him, these men tend also to be wealthier than most other people. But unless they are sub-chiefs, headmen, or leaders of age-regiments, they have no separate judicial powers and do not receive tribute of their own. The chief's more remote relatives, and sometimes even his brothers and sons by lesser wives, are seldom as important. Their rank entitles them to take charge on occasions when all others present are junior to them; otherwise, unless they happen to be local rulers or commend themselves to their superiors by personal ability, they have no special influence or authority.

All local rulers, even if not nobles, possess distinctive powers and privileges, There is considerable difference in this respect between say a sub-chief with several thousand followers and a headman with less than fifty. But within his own group each of them predominates. We have already seen that in his judicial capacity he can settle disputes and punish offenders. He is also entitled to obedience in all official matters. He relies upon his subjects generally to enforce his verdicts and commands, and if necessary will be supported by the next higher authority. But he always has less power than the chief, who on appeal can override any of his decisions; with very rare exceptions he cannot sentence people to death or 'eat them up', though he can expel them from his group; and if merely a headman even the fines that he imposes tend to be fairly small, since cases involving more serious punishment usually find their way to a higher court.

Every local ruler takes precedence among his own people on social and ritual occasions; they often treat him with ceremonial respect, and mourn for him publicly when he dies. He has the pick of the land for his home and fields, if popular he may be given help in domestic work and presents of meat, beer, and other commodities, and he is entitled to the fines imposed in his court. Subchiefs, in addition, usually have tribute fields specially cultivated for them, can often claim payment from people wishing to settle in their area or move away, and may receive special fees if initiation ceremonies are held locally under their auspices. The chief gives them some of the cattle taken in war by their men, and part of the death dues and other tribute that they collect for him. Because of their official position they are normally members of the tribal council, and those living outside receive special hospitality from him whenever they visit the capital. If they have many adherents they may also play an important part in tribal politics generally, being much more influential, for example, than colleagues in charge of small groups.

Throughout the tribe, heads of administrative divisions thus benefit both materially and in other ways. Bantu themselves are well aware of this. As a widespread proverb says, 'Hunger does not enter a chief's home'; one praise-name for chiefs among Venda is *tsetsema*, 'shuffler', because he 'is supposed to be so fat that he can only shuffle along';[1] and the Zulu verb *-busa* means not only 'to rule over, govern, reign', but also 'to enjoy life, to live in freedom and comfort, as one with plenty to eat and drink and nothing to do'.[2] Consequently it is not surprising that both the chief and other rulers are often envied, and that attempts may be made to usurp their position; the fruits of office are after all well worth having, even if office itself is by no means always the sinecure implied in the Zulu verb. Nor, on the other hand, need we wonder that subjects lay so much stress on generosity when describing how a ruler should behave; they contribute directly to his prosperity, and regard it as only right that he in turn should share his wealth with them. It may be added, in this context, that everywhere among Bantu people habitually make gifts of food and other

[1] van Warmelo (1937), p. 263.
[2] Doke and Vilakazi (1953), p. 53; Bryant (1905), p. 59.

commodities to their own relatives, and help them and neighbours in tasks requiring many hands. Such gifts and services are
reciprocal, and constitute one of the principal ways in which a
household can make good momentary deficits. The tribute given
to the chief and other rulers is often viewed in the same light: it
enriches them, but also obliges them to respond to the needs of
their subjects. 'The chief has nothing of his own', say the Tswana;
'whatever he possesses belongs to the tribe.'

v

In contrast with his Bantu counterpart, a Hottentot chief has
relatively few privileges. Because of his position his subjects
usually respect him, but they show him nothing like the obsequi-
ous deference found in many Bantu tribes, nor do they observe
any formal etiquette in relation to him. He has no special dress or
insignia except a metal-headed wooden staff (originally introduced by the Dutch), his household and home are similar to those
of other people, and he is not conspicuous for the number of his
wives. His installation is a festive occasion, but his death, though
it may be widely mourned, is apparently not marked by distinctive ceremonies. Perhaps the main index of his status is that offences against him are treated more severely than usual; for example,
attempts to kill him are punished by death, and whoever speaks
disparagingly of him is violently beaten.

His office also secures for him certain material benefits. He receives the main share of the fines imposed in his court and occasional presents from successful litigants, takes as fee one or more
animals from every estate that he distributes, is entitled to part of
every ox or big game animal killed by any of his subjects, divides
with his warriors the booty that they seize on raids, and claims
tribute in cattle or other goods from people allowed to settle in
his country. In consequence he too, like the Bantu chief, is usually the richest man in his tribe. But not always: it is recorded of
the chief ruling the Tsaib in 1883 that through losses in war and

bad management he had been reduced to the ownership of a single cow, whereupon he went on a 'begging expedition' among his well-to-do subjects, staying with each in turn until speeded on his way with a fat sheep or goat.[1] Nor is he entitled to service from his people for any but official purposes, though if generous and popular he may be given help willingly if required for himself.

As among Bantu, he has power to enforce the law and compel obedience of his commands. Through his courts he can punish offenders by fines, flogging, confiscation of property, banishment, and (subject to his personal confirmation) even death. In more recent times punishments have usually been administered by the 'messengers' or other court officers; formerly any of the men at the chief's village were used for the purpose, and he himself often struck the first blow if the penalty was death. If additional force is required, as in cases of resistance, warriors are specially mobilized; for example, according to an account written in 1882, 'In one or two instances the chief's judgment was disregarded, and he sent a command of forty men against the rebels, confiscated their property, and had them well flogged, and ordered them to live for some considerable time under his eyes, until they repented their conduct and rendered an open apology.'[2]

But legitimate use of force was not originally confined to the chief and his officers. Until well into the nineteenth century, as already mentioned, Hottentots recognized a man's right, and considered it his duty, to take personal vengeance for the killing of a near relative, and this right could be exercised even against a homicide whom the tribal court had acquitted of murder. Sometimes, too, if the courts could not reconcile them, men at loggerheads were allowed to fight a duel, and should it end fatally the victor was not liable to legal punishment. The main tribal court, moreover, dealt only with disputes between members of different clans, and could not hear appeals from a clan-head's decisions in matters confined to his own people.

[1] Schinz (1891), p. 39.
[2] Hahn (1883), p. 251.

Such authority as the chief possesses seems to be derived mainly from his command of force, and even that he cannot employ except judicially or with the prior consent of his council. His people do not depend upon him personally to anything like the same extent as in a Bantu tribe. His office is not specially venerated, he is virtually insignificant in ritual life and devoid of mystical or sacred attributes, and his rôle in the tribal economy gives him little scope for patronage. Although he is expected to entertain generously and to help the destitute, people do not regard him as a source of wealth and reward (nor, as shown by the example quoted above, is he always rich enough to perform such a function); and except for the judges, who share the court fees and fines, his assistants derive little more than prestige from their official positions.

Chieftainship among Bergdama is a more honoured office. The simple economy and very small communities of the people do not permit of much pomp, but whatever privileges are available pertain to the chief. He is treated with universal respect, being specially addressed as 'great man' by adults and 'grandfather' by children; he usually has most wives (sometimes three or more); he has the pick of all wild animal skins for clothing himself and his family, and only his wives wear necklaces or girdles of ostrich egg-shell beads; and he receives special portions of all game killed in the chase, and tribute from men finding honey or growing tobacco. His death and burial are also marked by distinctive ceremonies; and since the birth of twins is held to forecast his death, one of the children is buried alive to avert the omen. Such details are perhaps trivial in comparison with those defining the status of a Bantu chief, but they do at least show that the Bergdama chief receives special homage from his dependants.

The significance of his office is reflected in several proverbs and riddles, the gist of which is that he alone keeps the band together and that without him the people would scatter. But although he has more authority than anyone else, and if present can sometimes prevent quarrels from leading to violence, he cannot be said to have any real power. He has no recognized jurisdiction over wrongdoers, nor any command of physical force. People comply with his wishes only if it suits them, and should they disobey he has no effective means of punishing them; and in contrast with what we have noted for the Bantu, if they themselves are injured they do not look to him for redress.

A Bushman chief has less privilege than chiefs anywhere else in South Africa. Except for Heikum and Kung, where he receives choice portions of game and where his huts are always located in the eastern arc of the camp, there is no mention of his being specially distinguished in any way. If an elderly man he may have two or more wives, but this is not confined to him; his accession, marriage, and death are apparently not occasions of special importance; and we are explicitly told that he has the same dress, decoration, and standard of living as all other men. If patriarch of his group, he will usually be treated with deference and his views may carry greater weight than those of others; among Heikum and Kung the ritual activities that he alone can perform, especially in connection with the sacred fire, tend also to add to his influence. But he has no coercive power over other members of the band; he lacks judicial functions, he has no special assistants to see that his commands are obeyed, and he cannot enforce his wishes in any other way. Both here and among Bergdama it is only if people offend against the band as a whole, for example by repeated and indiscriminate acts of violence, that concerted action will be taken against them; and there is nothing to suggest that in such cases the chief himself necessarily takes the initiative or organizes the punishment.

VI

The powers and privileges of South African chiefs obviously vary greatly from one people to another. Among Bantu the chief can uphold the law and enforce his decisions even to the point of imposing capital punishment, his authority extends over a wide range of tribal activity, and he enjoys many conspicuous privileges. These rights are shared in varying degrees by his local subordinates.

The Hottentot chief also has coercive powers, but little extraneous authority and relatively few privileges. The Bergdama chief has some authority and certain privileges, but cannot use organized physical force to compel obedience to his will or to punish people who wrongfully injure others. The Bushman chief also has no such power, and except among Heikum and Kung virtually no distinctive authority or privileges. Among Bantu themselves there are local variations in the kinds of tribute paid to the chief, in the deference shown to him, in the extent to which his authority depends upon mystical sanctions, and in the composition of the armed forces at his disposal; but these variations nowhere invalidate the definition of his status just given.

If we accept the view of Weber and other writers quoted at the beginning of this chapter, we should thus have to say that 'political organization' occurs only among Bantu and Hottentots, and not among Bergdama or Bushmen. But this view seems to lay undue stress upon the use of physical force as a means of social control. Despite their lack of courts and other judicial institutions, Bergdama and Bushmen do not live in a state of anarchy. Like Bantu and Hottentots, they recognize personal rights (for example over wives and property), and have standard ways of dealing with their breach; they punish by collective attack people who become a public menace; the members of a band all cooperate in such activities as moving camp, hunting, ceremonial, defending their territory against trespass, and taking offensive action against other groups; they retaliate if one of themselves is killed by outsiders, and are collectively responsible should he inflict the same injury upon people of another band. Decisions are made by the men generally, elders having more influence than the rest. But the chief, as acknowledged head, takes the lead in moving camp, hunting, and warfare, and among Bergdama and certain Bushmen he also conducts ceremonies on behalf of his people as a whole. Except that self-help is the only recognized method of settling private disputes or redressing personal wrongs, the band is thus an organized unit with specific arrangements for maintaining its cohesion, order, and independence. One may therefore reasonably contend that it is also a political entity; its public life, though regulated in a manner markedly different from that found among Bantu and Hottentots, is, after all, subject to a definite system of control, and is neither chaotic nor casual in operation.

Bantu and Hottentots also differ in certain respects. The Bantu chief has unique supremacy and jurisdiction over the whole of his tribe, and the heads of all its segments are subordinate to him either directly or through intervening officers; with relatively unimportant exceptions only he and his administrative assistants have the right to use force, and (except among Cape Nguni and Southern Sotho) he controls a military and labour organization based on a formal system of age-regiments. Among Hottentots the traditional pattern of government was a federal council of clan-heads, of whom the senior in rank was acknowledged as chief; he had no jurisdiction over internal disputes between members of any clan but his own, his judicial power was also restricted by the practice of blood-vengeance (not found among the Bantu), and he had no special corps of men always at his command. It is only since the creation of permanent tribal centres that some of these limits to his power have tended to disappear.

The Bantu chief, moreover, does not depend solely upon force for his control of the tribe. His authority is greatly strengthened by such other factors as the conviction that his office is indispensable, the respect traditionally attached to it, his claim to legitimacy, his position as symbol of the tribe's unity and exclusiveness, his rôle of tribal priest, and the belief in the potency of his personal magic. He can reinforce it still further by using his wealth to reward those who are loyal to him, and by placing his relatives and favourites in charge of local segments. The Hottentot chief lacks ritual and symbolic importance, and does not use his wealth to attract personal adherents; unlike all other South African chiefs, he has hardly any sanction but force to sustain his authority.

The distinctions just noted can be related partly to economic factors. Among all our peoples every family is largely self-sufficient; for example, it normally produces its own food, builds its own home, and makes most if not all of its own clothing and household utensils. But sometimes it may also depend upon others, especially for means of subsistence. Among Bergdama and Bushmen, who live solely upon the natural resources of their environment, conspicuous differences between rich and poor do not and cannot exist. Edible wild plants are available freely to all, and game, no matter who kills it, is habitually shared by everybody present. Consequently if food is scarce the whole band is affected, and not merely certain families; all have the same opportunities, and if times are bad all suffer alike. Among Hottentots, where the community is much larger and was formerly always dispersed, comprehensive sharing of food is unknown. Private ownership of live-stock, moreover, makes for inequality of resources: even if people start on the same level, one man's herds may flourish and multiply, whereas another suffers loss through disease, theft, or destruction by beasts of prey. Similar inequalities occur among the Bantu, where still others may result from the hazards of cultivation: some people may reap ample harvests, and some be adversely affected by local drought, blight, locusts, etc.

Families may thus become relatively more destitute among the food-producing peoples than is possible among the food-gatherers. In such cases kinship obligations often help to relieve temporary shortages. But normally the only way in which poor people can obtain regular access to domestic animals as a source of livelihood is by taking service with others. This in turn means that wealthy men acquire dependants, and enables the chief, as owner of the largest herds, to become the personal lord of many of his subjects. Among Bantu, moreover, he or his local subordinates acting for him control the distribution of residential and arable land; this gives him more authority over his subjects, since they depend upon him for the right to live in his country and grow their crops. In addition, he receives agricultural and other tribute for the specific purpose, *inter alia*, of allowing him to entertain generously and to feed needy people. Hence, owing to their economic systems, Bantu and to a lesser degree Hottentots may depend much more upon their rulers for means of subsistence than do Bergdama or Bushmen.

The chief's status and powers are further affected by the size and settlement patterns of his community. Among Bergdama and Bushmen he has relatively little to do, and his recognized duties are generally so simple that he can attend to them all personally without special assistance. Owing to the smallness and residential unity of his group, he is normally also in direct and continuous contact with all his dependants. Decisions on matters of common concern are made not by himself alone, but by the men generally, and since they usually reflect the consensus of public opinion they are seldom of a kind that people might want to disobey. To this extent, therefore, he has little need of special coercive power.

The members of a Hottentot tribe were formerly scattered over their territory in small widely separated local groups. This meant that the chief had to rely upon others to control people not in his own settlement. Since each local group consisted basically of a single clan, whose men-folk were expected to live together, he could not appoint his brothers or other near kin as his deputies, but ruled with the cooperation of the clan-heads themselves. The nomadic life due to pastoralism, and the absence of territorial exclusiveness, further encouraged local autonomy, by making secession both possible and fairly easy. The chief had no special means of checking this. His status was due primarily to his being hereditary head of the senior clan, and his junior colleagues cooperated with him and with one another mainly to prevent internal hostilities and to protect themselves and their herds. The system of government tended therefore to be of a federal type, with each clan-head managing the affairs of his own group and the clan-heads together attending to matters of common concern. The tradition thus created persisted after the establishment of a central village, where each clan is still a separate local segment; the tribal council remains the dominant organ of government, and the chief is often little more than *primus inter pares*.

Among Bantu the tribe is usually much larger and more dispersed than among Hottentots, but the population is both sedentary and more closely settled. Its local divisions, moreover, are essentially territorial; sub-chiefs and headmen are in charge of defined areas instead of nomadic groups, and their followers are linked together not so much by kinship ties as by allegiance to a common head. The chief is consequently able to extend his authority by appointing his own relatives and retainers to administer such divisions on his behalf, and his control of the appointments, together with his use of wealth to reward his officers, give him a more pervasive command of the tribe than was formerly possible to his Hottentot counterpart. The trend towards centralization is reinforced by other factors, notably the widespread grouping of the people into age-sets whose creation is regulated by the chief. The initiation ceremonies undergone simultaneously by the members of each set, their organization into a single named body always headed by a member of the royal family, the mutual obligations imposed upon them and distinguishing their age-mates from all other adults, and the many activities that they are called upon to carry out collectively, give them a strong feeling of solidarity cutting across parochial attachments to kin or local group. The age organization serves therefore as an effective means of binding people together, and except for the chieftainship and the hierarchy of regional authorities it is perhaps the most conspicuous factor in the promotion of tribal unity.

The chief's rôle in public life is governed also by the social composition of his community. Among Bergdama and Bushmen he is normally the head of a single extended family; except very occasionally among Bergdama, the members of his band are all closely related to him, and are therefore his dependants rather than his subjects. Among Bantu and Hottentots the kinship system also stresses the importance of seniority in line of descent, and the hereditary head of every group has recognized authority over all its other members. It is upon this basic pattern that the system of centralized government has been developed. Our problem is to decide, not why the chief has individual authority (which, after all, he shares with the head of every other group in his tribe, and which the Bergdama chief also has to some extent), but why his authority extends over so many different groups and why the ways in which it is exercised are not the same everywhere. The answer seems to be that in a Bantu or Hottentot tribe many and often most of the chief's subjects are of alien origin; and since those particular people (or their ancestors) had joined the group through conquest or immigration, they were from the beginning in a condition of special dependence upon him. We thus get the basis of a system in which his descent group may be not only politically dominant but may also constitute a separate class in the community.[1] Among Bantu his personal status is further emphasized by the widespread grading of classes, and of people inside each class; the result is that he himself heads a hierarchy in which, as among certain Tswana, every person may have a unique social position.

The features just noted may have further implications. Among Bantu and Hottentots the maintenance of law and order does not and cannot depend upon kinship ties alone, or upon the public opinion that is so very important an element in the tiny compact communities of Bergdama and Bushmen. Among Bantu, for example, the members of an extended family or other localized kinship group deal with all internal disputes. Their hereditary head presides and gives the verdict. But his authority is persuasive and moral rather than coercive and legal; his primary function is not so much to administer justice as to reconcile those who are at variance, and in trying to achieve this he appeals mainly to their family sentiments. When disputes occur between members of different kinship groups (and this obviously cannot happen within a Bergdama or Bushman band), reconciliation along such lines is seldom feasible; and, owing to the obligations of mutual aid that form part of the kinship system, there is always the danger that other people may come to be involved. Some neutral authority is therefore required, some kind of overlord who can intervene before matters get out of hand. By settling such disputes, and so preventing general disturbance of the peace, the Bantu chief (either directly or through his local subordinates) performs a service whose value, as we have seen, is fully appreciated and explicitly recognized by his people. Among Hottentots a similar though less effective rôle was

[1] This point is further developed below, see p. 127 ff.

formerly played by the council of clan-heads, and now that blood-vengeance is no longer practised the tribal court has greater authority. The data thus suggest that in South Africa the government tends to have judicial powers only where the community consists of more than one local group and has a population of mixed origins.

The data indicate also that the chief's authority depends in part upon the nature of his religious functions. Among Bantu the dominant form of religion is ancestor worship, and just as the head of every social group from the family upwards prays and sacrifices to his own ancestors on behalf of all his dependants, so the chief acts as priest for the tribe as a whole. This he does not so much *ex officio* as because he personally is the senior living descendant of the tribal gods, and therefore the proper person to intercede with them. So much importance is attached to this personal aspect that among Sotho the hereditary head of the royal descent group always retains ritual precedence, say at initiation and first-fruits ceremonies, even though the chieftainship itself may have passed to a junior line.

Bushmen, Bergdama, and Hottentots occasionally also invoke the spirits of the dead, but they have no organized ancestor cult. Among all three, worship is directed mainly to certain deities associated partly with animistic beliefs and partly with rain and other natural phenomena; one of these deities is common to them all, and another occurs among both Bushmen and Hottentots. Except among Bergdama and those Bushmen (Heikum and Kung) where he maintains a sacred fire, the chief has little official connection with religious practices; and it is precisely in the groups just named that he is said to have special influence, though even here his ritual duties are a function of his office and not necessarily of his status by descent. We may therefore conclude that religion contributes more to the chief's authority among Bantu, because of the essentially personal tie between gods and priest, than it does among any of the other peoples.

I have tried to show here that the differences in the chief's powers and privileges may be related to such factors as mode of subsistence, social composition of the community, and religion. These are not interdependent. Although mode of subsistence affects the size and territorial distribution of the community, it does not determine the basis of membership; and although many forms of ritual are also directly connected with it (agricultural ceremonies, for example, are necessarily confined to the Bantu), it does not determine the whole religious system, since Hottentots share many beliefs and practices with Bergdama and Bushmen.

The first broad generalization to emerge is that the chief's powers seem to vary primarily with mode of subsistence: he has command of organized physical force only among the food-producers (Bantu and Hottentots), and not among the food-gatherers (Bergdama and Bushmen). The difference may perhaps be linked to certain features that are partly determined, or at least rendered possible, by mode of subsistence itself. Among Bantu and Hottentots the community is relatively large (and among Bantu sometimes very large), its members are dispersed over their territory in discrete settlements, and the population is of mixed origins. All these necessitate mechanisms of organization and control that are not required in the very small, localized, and homogeneous bands of Bergdama and Bushmen. One might thus say, from the South African data, that 'centralized authority, administrative machinery, and judicial institutions' do not occur among the food gatherers, simply because the conditions for their existence are lacking. On the other hand, since ethnographical data show that 'government' as just defined is not characteristic of all food-producing societies, notably the kind that Fortes and Evans-Pritchard term 'stateless', we cannot assume that improved mode of subsistence is alone sufficient to account for its occurrence.

VII

The comments just made bear upon what is commonly termed the 'conquest theory' of the origin of the state. This theory maintains, in brief, that the state is characterized by the domination of one class by another for purposes of economic exploitation, and that the class system itself results from the conquest and subjugation of one group by another. Barnes speaks of it as 'the distinctive sociological theory of the origin of the state'. Elsewhere he says: 'The majority of sociologists have accepted the point of view . . . that the political state was welded together as the result of warfare among primitive groups. The successive conquests of group by group brought about an ever greater amount of authoritative and coercive control by the conquerors over the conquered. In the process there were wrought out the various institutions and organizations within the state which are devoted to the exercise of this political control.'[1]

Although it has been adversely criticized, for example by Lowie and MacLeod, the conquest theory has also found favour among anthropologists. For example, Linton writes that 'States may come into being either through the voluntary federation of two or more tribes or through the subjugation of weak groups by stronger ones, with the loss of their political autonomy', adding that 'Conquest states are much more numerous than confederacies'; and Beals and Hoijer claim that 'The investment of leaders with the exclusive right to employ force or coercion in government occurs only with the formation of the conquest state.'[2]

The South African data, especially for Bantu, provide several instances to support the view that conquest may result in the creation of social classes, one of which clearly dominates the rest. I have already referred to the special position of the Venda nobility. Their ancestors invaded the Transvaal from the north about three centuries ago, and subjugated the various more primitive peoples, mostly Sotho, whom they found already living there. 'The conquerors made themselves masters of the country and became an aristocracy, unassimilated to this day. Here lies the explanation of a notable feature of Venda social organization,

[1] H. E. Barnes, 'Some Contributions of Sociology to Modern Political Theory' (1924), p. 368; 'Sociological Contributions to Political Thought' (1940), p. 653.
[2] R. Linton, *The Study of Man* (1936), pp. 240 f.; R. L. Beals and H. Hoijer, *An Introduction to Anthropology* (1953), p. 466.

namely the unique position of the ruling families and the exalted status of their chiefs.'[1]

Two even more striking examples are the Western Tswana and the Rhodesian Ndebele. The Western Tswana tribes entered Bechuanaland from the Transvaal in the first half of the eighteenth century. They found the country occupied by many small and scattered groups of Bushmen, Kgalagadi, Tswapong, Yeei, and other peoples, whom in some instances they fought and conquered, but who as a rule submitted to them without resistance. The territory thus annexed was then divided into districts, each being placed under the control of an 'overseer' (*modisa*), who was either a senior noble or one of the chief's trusted retainers (*batlhanka*). The inhabitants of each district became the serfs (*malata*) of the local overseer. He made them herd his cattle and cultivate his fields, and usually also brought some of them into the capital to do the menial work in his home. In addition, he could appropriate whatever property they acquired. This referred especially to such hunting spoils as ivory, ostrich feathers, and the skins of wild animals, all of which he claimed for himself, leaving them only the meat. Noble overseers kept these goods for themselves, but retainers had to deliver everything to the chief, who gave them a share as reward for their trouble. Serfs remained permanently attached to the family of their master, and after his death were inherited by his children. They were apparently seldom, if ever, bought or sold, though their master could give or lend them to other men, and they often formed part of a daughter's dowry; but they themselves were not free to seek work with anybody else or to move away from their district. If oppressed, as they often were, they had no access to the tribal courts, and should they run away they might be followed up and brought back by force. They lacked many other civic rights, including participation in political assemblies, and were not admitted into membership of age-regiments, nor were they allowed to possess live-stock of their own. Under colonial rule most of their obligations and social inequalities have now been abolished and they are usually classed as

[1] van Warmelo and Phophi (1948), i, p. 7.

commoners; but some, especially the Bushmen, are still considered inferior to other members of the tribe, who deem it degrading, for instance, to intermarry with them.

If 'the lot of these vassals is just bearable in time of peace', John Mackenzie wrote in 1871,[1]

'it is beyond conception wretched in time of war. I do not mean war among themselves in the country; they are too poor to quarrel seriously, or for a long time: but they are deeply interested in all the political questions of the town, being part of the property of the head men—a quarrel among whom is often followed up in the country in a way which astonishes as it shocks the Christian man. The contest for the possession of certain villages of Bakalahari [Kgalagadi] or Bushmen, is a fruitful source of strife in Bechuana towns. The vassals with all their belongings are the subject of litigation and endless jealousies; and it needs all the skill of a chief to settle these matters between greedy and plausible rivals. When a decision is come to, the poor people in the country are hastily "lifted" by the successful litigant, to be brought back again should he afterwards lose his case. When rival chiefs fight for supremacy in the same tribe, the condition of the harmless vassals is wretched in the extreme. They are then scattered and peeled, driven hither and thither, and mercilessly killed, as the jealousy, caprice, or revenge of their masters may dictate. It is quite fair in such a struggle to kill all the vassals, as it would be to lift the cattle, of him who cannot be displaced from his chieftainship. And so with the varying fortunes of a "civil war", the vassals might be attacked by both parties in turn. Again, when one Bechuana tribe attacks another, the Bushmen and Bakalahari belonging to both are placed in the same category with cattle and sheep—they are to be "lifted" or killed as opportunity offers. In such cases, therefore, all Bakalahari and Bushmen flee into wastes and inaccessible forests, and hide themselves until the commotion is past.

The Rhodesian Ndebele owe their origin as a separate tribe to Mzilikazi, a Khumalo chief who became subject to Shaka and

[1] Mackenzie (1871), p. 132 f.

subsequently one of his generals. In 1821 or thereabouts he fled with his people and settled for a while in the Central and Western Transvaal, harrying the local Sotho tribes; in 1837 he was driven out by the immigrant Boer Voortrekkers and led his people over the Limpopo into the present Matebeleland (named after his tribe). There he established a kingdom that lasted until it was destroyed by the English in 1896. At the height of its power, its population consisted of three distinct social classes: *abezansi*, descendants of Mzilikazi's original Nguni following; *abenhla*, descendants of Sotho and other peoples absorbed into the tribe during its stay in the Transvaal; and *amahole*, the Shona and other indigenous peoples of Matebeleland who were conquered or captured on raids after Mzilikazi had settled in the country. The *amahole* were a distinctly servile class, with whom neither of the others might intermarry; they did all the menial work, their boys were forcibly drafted into the army to serve as common soldiers, and they paid special tribute to their rulers.

These two examples, and there were others, conform in all essential respects to the standard theory about the origin of the class state. But there were many other instances in Bantu history where conquest did not lead to the systematic exploitation and degradation of the subject peoples by their new rulers. Shaka himself, who during his relatively short career (1816-28) conquered well over a hundred separate tribes, treated as integral parts of his own tribe all who became subject to him; there were no social or economic discriminations placing them in a position markedly inferior to the rest of the community, and, as shown by the example of Mzilikazi, their chiefs sometimes became his generals or civil indunas. Even among the Tswana, conquered peoples of Sotho and especially Tswana stock were in time allowed the same political and other rights as all other citizens, though they always ranked below members of long standing. The victorious chief often enough allied himself by marriage to their royal family, and so attempted to make more sure of their future allegiance.

Admittedly, in the instances just given, the lineage or clan of the conquering chief constituted a ruling aristocracy with special powers and privileges. But, as already shown, the hereditary leader of a subject group was often allowed to retain immediate control over his followers and the land that they occupied, and usually too there was no interference with their traditional laws and customs. Moreover, the ruling houses of Venda, Tswana, Ndebele, and Zulu, all existed even before the conquest and were not created by it, and, as will be gathered from what has just been said, conquered peoples usually also had rulers of their own before being subdued. Indeed, the institution of chieftainship and the privileged position of the royal family are said by the Bantu themselves to have 'always' been a feature of their political system. Every tribe of which we know, whether or not still independent, has traditions of a ruling dynasty of its own and can usually name the present head of that dynasty, and no myths or legends have been recorded of a state of society in which chiefs did not exist. It seems probable, therefore, that the distinctive position of the royal family is due not to conquest, but to some other factor, though undoubtedly the chief and his kin gained in power and prestige as their tribe expanded by force of arms.

There are also many instances among Bantu where inter-tribal wars did not lead to the subjugation of the defeated group; in other words, absorption of the defeated as a subject class was not the inevitable outcome of victory. On the other hand, too, almost all tribes have gained members by the accession of refugees, seceding groups, and other immigrants. Although such people are always inferior in status to the local ruling aristocracy, the only known instances in which there is marked discrimination between them and ordinary members of the tribe are when they differ from the others in language or culture. For example, the 'Fingoes' (Natal Nguni) who fled from Southern Natal to escape Shaka's conquests were at first 'looked down upon' by the various Cape Nguni tribes to whom they attached themselves; in Basutoland there are immigrant groups of Nguni with whom 'the true Basuto' have little to do socially and who are treated with contempt, so that they usually try to conceal their origin; and the Kalanga who fled to the Ngwato from Mzilikazi were at one time regarded with such scorn that marriage with them was considered degrading and it was even an offence to call a true Ngwato a 'Kalanga'.[1]

On the available evidence, indeed, it seems that a class system like that found among Western Tswana, Ndebele, and Venda is the outcome not so much of conquest itself as of ethnic or cultural differences between conquerors and conquered. As shown especially by the Tswana, there is seldom marked discrimination against conquered or immigrant peoples of the same stock as their overlords, and it may be noted that Eastern Tswana tribes, who expanded very largely at the expense of others of their own division, never developed a servile class at all. It is only if subject groups differ obviously in language, culture, or race from their new rulers that they tend to be exploited, and this applies even if they were not conquered but came as immigrants. Certainly among both Western Tswana and Ndebele the serfs were all peoples of alien stock, with distinctive languages and cultures, whereas the absence of a similar system among the Zulu may be due to the fact that Shaka's conquests were all made among peoples of the Natal Nguni division to which the Zulu themselves also belonged.[2]

What I have just said applies also to the Hottentots. When one tribe defeated another in war, the conquered tribe as a whole was seldom absorbed into the ranks of the victors, but captives, like refugees and other immigrants of Hottentot stock, were granted the same political and economic rights as members by birth. It was only Bergdama and Bushmen, peoples differing from the ruling section in race, culture, and sometimes also language, who were treated as 'servants'; indeed, as already noted, Bergdama have constituted a distinct servile class among Hottentots from the earliest recorded times.

[1] Hunter (1936,) p. 189; Ashton (1952), p. 11; Schapera, unpublished field notes.
[2] The same point is made by Gluckman, who writes (1940. b, p. 151): 'The Zulu had subjugated people of more or less the same culture as themselves, and probably therefore their state was "caste-less", while on the other hand Nguni tribes who fled from the Zulu and conquered peoples of alien culture established "caste" states in which the core of Nguni aristocrats strove to maintain their identity.'

Warfare among Bergdama and Bushmen themselves does not as a rule lead to the subjugation of one group by another. Disputes for the ownership of land sometimes occur between neighbouring bands, but the evidence suggests that in such cases the local group, if defeated, usually moves somewhere else. However, it does appear that among Bushmen a man of forceful personality may occasionally succeed in dominating the members not only of his own but also of other bands. Of one such man, an Auen who lived towards the end of the nineteenth century, we are told that through military prowess he had gained control of several bands of Auen and Naron round Sandfontein; he always had 'many' people about him, claimed annual tribute from all his subjects in skins, ivory, and chains of ostrich egg-shell beads, settled local disputes arising out of murder, theft, and adultery, and if any band refused to obey him led the others against it in a war of extermination. Some of the details are suspect, being based solely on hearsay; the same man, however, is mentioned in a later source, which adds that after his death his son tried to emulate his rôle but on being defeated in a fight against Bergdama lost all authority outside his own family.[1] Since several other 'great chiefs' of the same kind are named by writers on the Kung,[2] there is little reason to doubt that such men may have acquired personal authority beyond the limits of their own band. But how this was done, and what powers they were able to exercise, cannot be satisfactorily determined from the data; the only important hint is that they were sometimes leaders in resisting the encroachment of Europeans and other alien peoples. In any event, the occurrence of rulers with recognized and permanent authority over several different bands is certainly not a common feature of Bushman public life, and indeed it is difficult to see how they could continue for any length of time to control such scattered groups.

Nowadays there are also in South West Africa large Bergdama communities with chiefs who in powers and functions correspond

[1] Passarge (1907), p. 114 f.; Bleek (1928.a), p. 36.
[2] Lebzelter (1934), pp. 42, 66; Brownlee (1943), p. 124 f.; Metzger (1950), p. 8; Wilhelm (1953), p. 154.

more to a Hottentot chief than to the usual Bergdama patriarch. But such communities have all been artificially created under European influence on Mission stations, and nothing like them has emerged among the groups that still retain their traditional mode of life.

The South African data thus show that, with the very dubious exception of one Bushman instance, 'government' (as defined by Fortes and Evans-Pritchard) has nowhere been the outcome of conquest; chieftainship seems to have been a traditional feature among all our peoples, whether or not they expanded by subjugating other groups. The main effect of conquest usually was to enhance the chief's power, not to create it; and it was only if conquerors and conquered differed markedly in such traits as language and culture that the conventional social distinctions found among Bantu and Hottentots sometimes developed so far as to lead to the systematic exploitation of one particular section of the population.

V

Rulers and Subjects

I

IN the preceding chapters I described the persons who manage the affairs of a South African community, the functions that they perform, and the powers and privileges that they possess. We saw that among all our peoples accession to office, and the duties and prerogatives of office-holders, are in no way capricious but are governed by special rules. The existence of such rules suggests that there must also be some provision for their enforcement. In discussing the powers and privileges of office I indicated by what methods and to what degree chiefs and other authorities can normally hope to secure the obedience of the people under them. I shall assume, as a corollary, that everywhere in South Africa there are also means of trying to ensure that they in turn fulfil the obligations traditionally assigned to them. The assumption raises several questions that we shall have to consider if the data permit: what are the inducements that might tend to make office-holders do as expected instead of as they please, what degree of latitude is allowed to them, to whom must they answer for their conduct and what are the checks to prevent them from going astray, and what happens if they nevertheless neglect their duties, prove to be incompetent, or abuse the powers vested in them?

Since office-holders everywhere in South Africa have obligations, such questions would apply to all the peoples with whom we are here concerned. But the management of public affairs may also present problems of other kinds. We do not necessarily have to accept the Marxist conception of the class struggle to postulate that in the composite communities of Bantu and Hottentots there may be groups or persons resenting inferiority of social status or, if originally conquered, wishing to regain their independence;

and what we already know of a chief's powers and privileges suggests also that among those peoples, and especially Bantu, there are likely to be serious rivalries for his office, or factions contending for his favour. We can further postulate that among them, but not among Bergdama or Bushmen, a chief will tend to have dual responsibility: on the one hand towards his own class, perhaps intent on maintaining its privileged position, and on the other towards the rest of the population. This in turn suggests that we should ascertain how far he identifies his own interests with one class rather than another, and what effect such a policy may have upon the extent of his personal power.

In this connection another series of problems arises. It is characteristic of Western societies that there is, and has been for many centuries, a good deal of discussion about such topics as the powers and functions of governments, the limits of state action, the obligations of rulers, and the rights of the private citizen; political science, political philosophy, and the history of political ideas are systematically studied and taught at universities and other institutions of learning; attempts are continually being made to improve the efficiency of the government; political philosophers and others plan ideal systems of government to suit either existing conditions or utopian societies; and there is usually widespread and keen public interest in political events of all kinds. Sometimes there have also been armed revolts resulting in, or aimimg at, the overthrow of one system of government and the substitution of another, such as a republic in place of a monarchy or a totalitarian dictatorship in place of a parliamentary democracy.

Relatively little attention seems to have been given to the investigation of analogous phenomena in primitive societies. The lack of written records in such societies does of course mean that adequate data for study are seldom available, and it is in any case unlikely that we should find among them as highly developed and systematized a theoretical interest in the forms and functions of government generally. But it is certainly possible for field-workers to ascertain what people say or think about an existing system of government, and to what extent there is speculation about amending it or replacing it by some other system. Oral tradition may preserve accounts of earlier reforms or revolts and the underlying reasons, the ideals to which rulers should conform are often reflected in proverbs and maxims, and the way in which a chief or other authority behaves may arouse adverse comment or meet with public approval. We shall have to consider all available information of this kind, and determine what bearing local conceptions of 'good government' may in fact have upon the relations between rulers and subjects.

II

Among Bantu, so far as one can judge from the data, people are not particularly interested in abstract problems or theories of government. They take the existing system for granted, and do not question its suitability or strive for something better. As Kgatla say when installing a new chief, 'It always was so, and so it will still be to-morrow'; and we saw in the previous chapter how great is the reverence normally shown towards the chieftainship. But uncritical acceptance of the system does not imply uncritical tolerance of every chief or subordinate authority. There are definite ideas of how rulers should behave, and in concrete situations those ideas do much to determine the popular reaction.

What people expect of their chief may be seen, first, from the kind of advice given to him at his installation ceremony. The Xhosa chief Ngqika, for example, is said to have been exhorted as follows by the senior officiant (c. 1797): 'Son of Mlawu, grandson of Rarabe, this day you are invested with the chieftainship of your contrymen. May your conduct be reputable. Let worthiness become you, and may you be just. These are your people, be a father to them, and rule them with wisdom. May your hand be beautiful (literally, be generous) and not seek out a person's body (literally, lift up the hand against another), for as your country's proverb has it, "The stick has no kraal" (i.e. misuse of power destroys the home).'[1]

[1] Soga (1932), p. 31 f.

Among Tswana, similarly, the new chief is told to look after his tribe properly and keep it at peace; to rule firmly but justly and impartially, and not favour his own kin ('We look not at the person, but at his fault', says the proverb); to attend constantly at his council-place, 'so that you may get to know your people, and they may get to know you'; to abandon his boyhood practices and youthful associates, and listen to his advisers; to respect the persons and property of his subjects, and not abduct their wives, seduce their daughters, or take their cattle to enrich himself; to support orphans, old people, and cripples, and feed his people generally ('the chief is the wife of the tribe'); to be long-suffering and patient, though he will have much to annoy and tire him ('the chief is a dirt-heap on which the tribe's rubbish is piled'); and to remember always that he will be ruling not dumb cattle but human beings, who if he ill-treats or troubles them will abandon him ('a chief is chief by grace of his people').[1] And it is recorded of the famous Southern Sotho chief Moshesh that when in early manhood he asked his wise old kinsman Mohlomi for the secret of successful government, he received the following advice, which for the rest of his long life he tried to put into practice: 'One day thou wilt rule men: learn, then, to know them; and when thou judgest, let thy judgments be just.'[2]

Expressed in more general and comprehensive terms, the conduct of the ideal chief as visualized by the Bantu may be summarized as follows. He should attend faithfully to his official duties and not give priority to his private affairs; above all, he should deal promptly with cases that come to his court and with any other matters requiring his personal attention. He should always consult his councils, and seek confidential advice from men of recognized standing, not from toadies or upstarts. He should preserve law and order, and administer justice fairly and impartially; his sentences should not be unduly harsh, and he should not inflict punishments wantonly. He should consider the welfare and security of his people, and to this end perform the appropriate

[1] Schapera (ed.) (1938), pp. 111, 119 f.
[2] Ellenberger (1912), p. 96.

rituals for rain, good harvests, etc., and try to preserve peaceful relations with his neighbours. He should safeguard the land and other rights of his subjects, and protect them from misrule by his subordinates, but he should not interfere arbitrarily with the internal affairs of any local group. He should also be generous and hospitable, and reward his assistants: 'he may be forgiven much, but never for meanness and want of open-handedness'; his retainers 'serve him for cattle; nor is it expected that he could maintain his influence, or indeed secure any number of followers, if unable to provide them with what at once constitutes their money, food, and clothing.'[1]

In addition, he should have certain desirable personal qualities. What these are may best be illustrated by reference to some notable chiefs of the past whose memory is still cherished by their people. The 'most famous' of all Southern Sotho, Mohlomi (died 1814), was 'kind, affable, and easy of access', and conspicuous among his contemporaries 'for his love of peace, for his charity to all, for his wisdom, and for the love he bore to all men'; Kgari (Ngwato, 1817-28) was 'all that Bechuanas desire their chief to be: brave in the field, wise in the council, kind to his vassals'; Sarili (Xhosa, 1837-92) was 'a ruler of great wisdom, moderation and kindness; a chief "with a wing", wherewith he protected his people'; and Mbandzeni (Swazi, 1874-89) 'was a man of singularly kind and gentle disposition, . . . remarkable shrewdness and tact.'[2] Such great warriors and statesmen as Shaka (Zulu), Mzilikazi (Ndebele), Moshesh (Southern Sotho), Thulare and Sekwati (Pedi), Makaba II (Ngwaketse), and Kgama III (Ngwato), are also remembered with admiration and pride, but not always with affection. That, on the whole, is reserved for chiefs who were open-handed and friendly, patient and tactful, and above all compassionate and gentle. *O ne a busitse batho ba gagwê ka pelo e ntlê*, 'he ruled his people with a kind heart', is the final verdict of the Ngwaketse about their beloved chief Gaseitsiwe

[1] Soga (1930), p. 98; MacLean (1858), p. 27 f. (Dugmore).
[2] Ellenberger (1912), pp. 91, 97; Mackenzie (1871), p. 358; Bennie (1939), p. 22; Kuper (1947), p. 22.

(1845-89), a man not otherwise noted for his achievements.[1]

Such personal qualities, it is recognized, cannot usually be acquired or instilled; but, as already noted, their obvious lack may sometimes lead to an heir's being rejected in favour of a more promising brother.[2] The normal work of government, on the other hand, can be learned, and the heir apparent is often specially trained for his future post. Among Tswana, for example, he is made to attend regularly at the council-place, where he sees how cases and meetings are conducted and is taught tribal laws and customs; he may in time be given jurisdiction in minor cases and other matters during his father's illness or absence, and he may even take full charge of tribal affairs should his father become very old and feeble. Elsewhere, as among Southern Sotho, he may acquire administrative experience not at the capital but by being placed at the head of a district; or, as among Swazi, during his minority selected men instruct him in the ritual and other duties that he will in due course have to perform. Occasionally, as among some Northern Sotho, he may even be sent for training (and protection) to the court of a neighbouring chief. But deliberate preparation of such kinds is not always possible; among Venda, for example, the future chief is not known until after his father's death, or, in other divisions, a man may unexpectedly become chief or regent owing to the early death of a senior brother. However, since all the main sons of a chief are normally brought up aware of their position, and when old enough are given followers of their own, it seldom happens that one of them succeeds to the office without having had some grounding in the art of administration.

In any event, however immature a new chief may be, his predecessor's confidential advisers and council are always at hand to guide and assist him. Since the former, especially, include some of his uncles and other near kin, he starts his reign under the aegis of men not only versed in the conduct of public affairs but also very well known to him through long and intimate personal association.

[1] Schapera (ed.) (1940), p. 141.
[2] See above, p. 52.

Provided that he consults them frequently and is ready to listen to their advice, and provided also that they are loyal to him, he need seldom find his task either burdensome or difficult. The council, too, consists mainly of influential men, most of whom as heads of local segments are in closer touch than he with the bulk of the people; and so long as he has their agreement and support he can normally be sure that his wishes will be respected. It is extremely unlikely that the council's decisions will be resisted by the tribe generally. For example, the Mpondo chief Faku (died 1867) succeeded with the help of his subordinates in ending circumcision, though 'there seems to have been no general feeling among the people in favour of its abolition' and despite sporadic instances of local opposition; and in more recent times the same and many other radical departures from traditional usage have been similarly imposed in Tswana tribes.[1]

To illustrate procedure at council meetings, I give here an account of one stage in the process of legislation among the Kgatla. Isang, while regent (1921-9), wished to introduce some form of control over beer-drinking, excessive indulgence in which had recently caused some local trouble. After discussing the matter privately with his confidential advisers, he referred it to the full tribal council (May 1924). He considered the occasion important enough for his secretary to take minutes, from which I quote the relevant passages (in translation):

'*Chief Isang:* I do not say that beer should be prohibited, but that a law should be made about it.

Segale Pilane (chief's uncle and principal adviser):We seek a plan for dealing with beer-drinking. Beer has ruined us; we have no children; we tried to educate them, but beer has spoiled them.

Komane Pilane (another senior uncle): Let there be a law about beer-drinking, and let whoever violates it be punished.

Abel Madisa: Let the sale of beer be prohibited. (Supported by *Nasone Pilane, Montswe Rapalai, Mokalane Makgale, Ramodisa, Klaas Segogwane, Antipas Sello, Masilo Ntshole.*)

1 Hunter (1936), pp. 165, 396; Schapera (1943.c), p. 19.

Chief Isang: I endorse the suggestion that beer should no longer be sold. But now I ask, is there not some one who can suggest a law whereby beer may continue to be sold, but in such a way as not to cause trouble among the people?

Maretele Mangole: Let beer be sold, but the purchaser should go home to drink it.

Pule Mogomotsi: Let it be sold, but on condition that it is no longer drunk at night.

Motshwane Pilane: Let beer-drinking at night be prohibited, and also let beer be sold only for consumption at home.

Kgari Pilane: Beer-drinking goes together with sexual immorality. You should not find fault with the boys alone, and ignore the girls. As long as beer continues to be brewed, immorality will be associated with it.

Mabuse Letsebe: I say, let beer continue to be sold.

Segale Pilane: Headmen, you have helped us; it is you who are the chief's policemen, and whoever breaks the law must be dealt with by you.

Chief Isang: Let those who say that beer should not be sold raise their hands.

(85 men raised their hands; only two said that beer should still be sold.)

Chief Isang: You are not of two opinions, you are unanimous. And what I say to you is that when you go astray and are turned back you should listen. To err is human, but to find fault with oneself is often lacking. Therefore I say: Beer must no longer be drunk at night. See to it that beer is brewed not by the girls but by their mothers. I shall allow the brewing and sale of beer from the beginning of June until December, and if there is no improvement I shall call you together again to kill the sale of beer. Women of the Maatlametlo age-regiment and downwards must not any one of them drink beer. Headmen, help to support the law.'

The report, though obviously a very brief summary of what was said, is detailed enough for our present purpose. The chief and his main adviser put their problem to the headmen. Some of the latter advance a suggestion that does not immediately satisfy the chief, and he asks them to consider a more specific issue. After further discussion, during which several different views are expressed, a vote (not a feature of the traditional procedure!) is taken on the original and more drastic proposal. Despite almost unanimous agreement, the chief finally decides not to prohibit the sale of beer, but to try out a compromise for an experimental period. The two relevant points in the proceedings are the method of consultation, which allows for the free exchange of opinions, and the fact that the chief is guided but not bound by the views of his council: in the end, he follows the course that seems best to himself, which here happens to be milder than was generally agreed upon. Immediately after the meeting, Isang had a list of regulations governing the sale and consumption of beer drawn up in writing and read out to the tribe. The preamble states: 'Let it be known by every member of the Kgatla tribe that the chief has found it necessary, on the advice of the ward-heads and chieftains of the tribe, to frame a law about beer for the whole territory of the Kgatla.' From this it would seem that the law was not submitted as usual to the tribal assembly for approval, the overwhelming support of the council being apparently considered sufficient.[1]

His advisers and councils not only help the chief to determine policy, but also limit the power that he personally can exercise. As indicated by the example just given, he is not bound to follow their advice and may even ignore it if he wishes. But he depends upon them, and especially upon the local rulers, to carry out his policy. As Segale Pilane said, they are his 'policemen', and whoever breaks the law must be dealt with by them; and in the regulations about beer-drinking promulgated by Isang one section reads: 'Every headman is responsible to the chief for the enforcement of the law in his village or district.'[2] Hence, if he tries to impose a measure of which all or most of them disapprove, he can seldom get his way, for should he persist he will encounter

[1] Schapera (1943.c), p. 14 ff.; for the regulations, *ibid.*, p. 91 f.
[2] *Ibid.* p. 92.

obstruction, delay, or passive resistance, if nothing worse. As the proverb says, 'A chief is chief by grace of his people', and without their co-operation he cannot do much; or, in a Tsonga variant, 'The elephant is the trunk', i.e. just as the elephant cannot seize anything without its trunk, so the chief cannot do his work without his subjects.[1]

Cases have in fact occurred where a chief's policy proved so unpopular, and the opposition to it so successful, that it became unworkable and had to be modified or abandoned. Among both Ngwaketse and Kwena, for example, chiefs had to repeal legislation altering the traditional penalties for seduction, since the innovations were so unwelcome that people stopped taking offenders to court; and in the same and several other Tswana tribes early attempts to control the use of alcohol, and the sale of crops to European traders, could also not be enforced effectively.[2] One major reason was that local rulers failed to take action against their followers. As Seêpapitsô, the very progressive chief of the Ngwaketse, bitterly complained at a tribal assembly in 1913 when denouncing disobedience of his liquor laws: 'Why do you still persist in drinking honey-beer, though you know that it has been forbidden here? It is you headmen who are spoiling things, because you have made the town a burden for me to manage, and I am alone.'[3] The words, 'I am alone', are significant; they show how helpless the chief may be when faced by collective resistance to his commands.

It is not only among Tswana that the chief's power thus depends upon the co-operation of his councillors. Their importance in public life is a feature reported also of all other Bantu. Among Xhosa, for example, 'The principal safeguard against an abuse of power by the chief is the existence of the Court of Councillors . . . The chief is head of the council, but he dare not veto a decision of this court except at the peril of his reputation and authority in the tribe.' Among Southern Sotho, 'A chief should be

1 Junod and Jacques (1936), p. 11.
2 Schapera (1943c.), p. 58 ff.
3 Schapera (1947), p. 65.

assisted by and pay heed to the advice and counsel of his people', especially his near relatives and the heads of local segments; in the old days 'consultation with them was essential, for [he] relied almost entirely on their support in carrying out his policy; . . . in agreement with them he was strong, in opposition powerless.' 'The king is ruled by his councillors', say the Swazi. A Venda chief, similarly, 'in order to get anything done, must first assure himself of the cooperation' of his headmen and indunas, of his council, 'and in fact of every one of any real importance in the tribe. He cannot drive his will through without such co-operation, and if he attempts to do so he will fail, and in olden days would run severe risk of dying by poisoning.'[1]

In practice, the extent to which the chief is restrained by his councillors varies considerably. As hereditary head of the tribe, he has marked personal powers and privileges, much patronage at his command, and, unless he behaves very badly, the goodwill and respect of the people generally. His ritual status, as we have seen, also gives him unrivalled authority; among Venda, especially, where 'greater stress is laid on the sacred as opposed to the secular character of [his] person', his word 'is law to an extent not met with among other South African tribes', and he 'may be truly said to be an almost absolute lord and master over his people'.[2] He is thus normally in a much stronger position than any of his subjects; and if, as often happens, his councillors are jealous of one another and compete for his favours ('habitués of the capital do not love one another', says a Pedi proverb), he may be able to consolidate himself still further by manipulating the rival factions to his own advantage.

However, much also depends upon casual factors. If still fairly young when he starts to rule, the chief may be overawed by his father's advisers, secure in the authority that they have so long exercised; but gradually, as one by one they die or retire, he

[1] Soga (1932), p. 28; Ashton (1952), p. 215; Kuper (1952), p. 36; Lestrade (1930), p. 313. For similar statements about other divisions, cf. Gluckman (1940. a), p. 33 (Zulu); Junod (1927), i, p. 413 (Tsonga).

[2] Lestrade (1930), pp. 311, 312.

replaces them by men of his own choice and closer to him in age, whom he can handle with more confidence and with the ease gained from experience. Hence the older he gets and the longer he rules—and I have already indicated that age in itself normally adds to a person's influence in social life—the more likely it will be that he can lead his advisers instead of being dominated by them. Again, if the tribe is at war or threatened by invasion, common danger rallies the people around him and his power is increased by the belief that his magic is essential to the army's success; but if times are peaceful there is more opportunity for domestic intrigues and the expression of discontent, so that he cannot so readily afford to antagonize men of standing.

His personal conception of his duties is obviously another important element in the situation. Undoubtedly he is sometimes genuinely concerned with the welfare of his people, and to this end may even insist upon pursuing policies that are not always popular. I have already referred to the difficulties that the Ngwaketse chief Seêpapitsô had about this with his headmen. The matter came up again shortly afterwards in the same connection. Seêpapitsô had himself entered and searched the hut of a man whom he suspected of breaking the liquor laws. At the man's trial, several headmen said that the chief had acted wrongly; as one of them put it, 'It is our work, not yours, to catch those who break the law'. To this Seêpapitsô replied: 'I hear some of you say that I have no right to catch people; but the fault is yours, because you don't do your duty. I shall continue entering your huts, because you headmen don't help me to carry out the law.'[1]

Another good example is provided by the great Christian chief of the Ngwato, Kgama III (1875-1923). He was so notorious an autocrat that a fellow-chief once remarked to him in a letter:[2]

'Chief, the proverb says: "The lion said, I am strong when alone; the man said, I am strong through the help of others." If you have

[1] *Chief v. Mohubidu*, Chief's Court, Kanye, Case No. 20 of 1913.
[2] Isang (Kgatla) to Kgama, 17 June 1921, quoted in Schapera, 'The Native as Letter-Writer', *The Critic* (Cape Town), vol. 2 (1933), p. 28. In the original, the words italicized are in English, not Tswana.

governed by *Absolute Monarchy*, that is through the luck that God has given you, but I deny to you that Sekgoma [Kgama's heir] will ever be able to maintain a government like yours unless he relies on consulting his people and on ruling *constitutionally*.'

Kgama's own view of his official responsibilities is best illustrated by the following extract from a letter written on his behalf by a local missionary to a visiting educational expert in 1905:[1]

'He wished me to tell you that he was personally anxious for his tribe to advance in Education; but that under tribal government it was necessary that the people themselves should endorse any suggestion emanating from the Chief, and his refusal to bring up the matter before them was simply because he did not believe that the tribe as such would endorse such a proposition. He then gave me a résumé of various propositions that he had brought before the tribe in days gone by, which in his own opinion were for the advancement of the tribe. In the early days of his reign he had brought up the subject of the *Bogwera* and *Boyali* ceremonies (the native circumcision rites), as he knew that the tendency of these ceremonies was against the advancement of the tribe and of Education. About the same time he also stopped secular work on the Sabbath for the same reason. He carried out these reforms solely in virtue of his powers as Chief, against the wishes of the majority of his people, but believing them to be for their advantage. Later on he forbade the use of Kaffir beer, beginning with the younger Tribal Regiments. Upon this the elder members of the tribe objected, saying that it was very difficult for them to forbid their children drinking Kaffir beer when they habitually saw their parents drinking it; thus hoping Khama would rescind the law; whereupon Khama entirely forbade its use to the whole tribe, both young and old; and for years there was no Kaffir beer-drinking in Khama's town.'

Evidently Kgama, despite his professed regard for public opinion, did not always feel bound to seek or obtain the tribe's

[1] E. B. Sargant, *Report on Native Education in South Africa*, Part III (1908), p. 46.

'endorsement' of his 'suggestions'. He was a forceful and energetic man, intolerant of opposition, and in the later years of his very long life (he died at the age of about ninety-three) he ruled in effect as a dictator—though not before he had been involved in some painful disputes with his nearest kin. But he was also an able administrator, scrupulously honest, generous and even liberal with his wealth, and considerate of the serfs, whom he freed from many of their disabilities; his verdicts in court cases are still remembered for their justice and equity, and some of his reforms were very welcome; and he tried to do what he sincerely thought was best for the tribe. Undoubtedly his conversion to Christianity greatly influenced the way in which he ruled. But pagan chiefs too sometimes cared equally for their people, for example Mohlomi and Sarili; and the great Mthethwa chief Dingiswayo (1808-18), protector and patron of Shaka, has been described as 'a man of progressive and praiseworthy ambitions; enlightened and constructive in his policy of social improvement and political reform; an able military organizer and a clean fighter; magnanimous in his wars of conquest, benevolent in his rule at home, [his] name . . . unsullied by deeds of barbarism and tyranny.'[1]

By no means all Bantu chiefs have as noble a conception of their duties. We are told of Southern Sotho chiefs, for example, that 'Some were just, public-spirited and accessible; others became preoccupied with the maintenance and increase of their wealth and were thus tempted to indulge in dishonest and unjust action'; and the Venda proverb, 'At the capital they love the big drum only' (i.e. the drum beaten during certain ceremonies 'for participation in which considerable fees are collected'), is said to refer primarily to the fact that 'the chief and his entourage don't care for the welfare of their people, but only for the profit they can make out of them.'[2]

As Kgama's history indicates, the chief's character and personality also help to determine what use he actually makes or tries to make of the power at his command. It is a truism to say that

[1] Bryant (1929), p. 171.
[2] Ashton (1952), p. 220; van Warmelo (1937), p. 176.

much individual variation is to be found among the many thousands of chiefs who have ruled over Bantu tribes. Examples are readily available of chiefs who were forceful or timid, intelligent or stupid, temperate or dissolute, open-handed or mean, kind-hearted or cruel, phlegmatic or hot-tempered, ambitious or unaspiring; and one does not necessarily have to subscribe to the 'great man' theory of history in order to believe that such characteristics undoubtedly influenced their relations with their subjects.

Kwena tradition, for example, relates that an ancestor of Ntloedibê ward was originally chief of the tribe, but through sheer indolence allowed all public business to be conducted by his younger brother, who ultimately ousted him completely; Kgama's own son Sekgoma II (1923-6), a weak and ineffective man, became the virtual puppet of certain senior nobles, whose influence over him created a rival faction that subsequently caused much trouble; and Sandile (Ngqika, 1840-78) was not only a drunkard but had so little 'resolution and strength of mind' that 'the councillors took matters very much into their own hands.'[1] In contrast, instances are known of great warrior chiefs who dominated their people to such an extent that they were able to rule with almost absolute tyranny. Among them were Sebego (Ngwaketse, 1825-44), Mzilikazi (Ndebele), and above all Shaka (Zulu), of whom contemporary and reliable European observers record that he had literally thousands of his own subjects put to death for no apparent reason except sheer personal whim. Such less famous men as Ncobo (Hlubi), Mahakane (Venda), and Motlotle (Kgatla), are also remembered locally for their bloodthirsty nature and for the many cruelties that they practised.

III

However, as shown by the fate of Shaka himself and several others, whose conduct led to their assassination, there are limits to the chief's autocracy. So great is the reverence for his office that

[1] C. G. H. Commission 1883, p. 151 (Chalmers).

people will normally put up with much from him that would never be tolerated in one of lesser rank. In theory, nevertheless, he is not above the law. It is virtually unknown and almost unthinkable for him to be publicly sued in his own court. But should he wrong one of his subjects—for example, by damage to property (as when his cattle injure growing crops), or by seducing a daughter or wife—the victim may approach him either directly or, more commonly, through a senior noble or induna. He is then expected to make reparation. But should he refuse he cannot be compelled, and in such cases the victim has no remedy save to leave the tribe if he can.

Nevertheless, as we have already seen in regard to Seêpapitsô, a chief who misbehaves in such and other ways is always adversely criticized. Commoners do not usually venture to be outspoken; 'The man who complains about the chief does so only after leaving his country', says the proverb, i.e. it is dangerous when close by to attract his attention by unfavourable comment. But his senior relatives and other councillors are everywhere expected to rebuke him privately and warn him to mend his ways; as Xhosa say, 'They have the privilege of confronting him when he does wrong'. 'Treat the people well', he is told, 'they are not yours (to do with as you please), but your father's'; and they remind him of the well-known proverb, 'When the chief limps, his subjects also limp', i.e. if he himself sets a bad example others too will tend to disregard the law. Occasionally, as among Swazi, Tswana, and Venda, his councillors have even been known to fine him secretly for his misconduct. They are what Tswana call 'upholders of the law' and 'guardians of the tribe', not merely the chief's assistants and agents but also the representatives and defenders of the people; and should he go astray they may themselves be publicly blamed for not keeping him in check.

Among Sotho, and especially Tswana, this is where the national assemblies are so important. Their proceedings are characterized by great freedom of speech; as the proverb says, 'He who trips in an assembly is not to be blamed', i.e. no exception should be taken to his words. In practice, well-founded fear of subsequent reprisal often restrains all but brave or reckless men from openly attacking the chief and so exposing themselves to a charge of disloyalty. But if the occasion calls for it—if the chief has behaved very badly, or wishes to impose a policy that is highly unpopular—then he and his intimates will be contradicted, reprimanded, or even violently blamed, with little hesitation. At such a meeting among the Kgatla early in the nineteenth century the former regent Senwêlô, who had recently caused the murder of his nephew Chief Letsêbê, was told that by his deed he had set a precedent from which he himself would soon suffer (as in fact he did); at another, in 1926, the Kwena chief Sebele II heard several speakers say that they were ashamed of his conduct, which had brought disgrace upon the tribe; and again among the Kgatla, in 1934, the chief was publicly criticized in his own presence because he had been neglecting tribal business, was often absent from home, relied upon bad councillors, tried cases away from the council-place, and was drunk far too often.

As Willoughby suggests, the assembly may be 'a great safety-valve, which allows sections of the community that have generated much wrath against the chief or some other high-born person to blow off in violent language, and thus avert an explosion that might wreck the tribe.'[1] But it also enables the chief and others to assess how much opposition there is to him, and unless sure of enough support he will seldom persist in ignoring public opinion as here revealed, especially if his critics include men of great standing and influence. For example, the Hurutshe chief Dibetswe was so disliked by his people, 'because he took away their cattle and seduced their wives', that the tribe ultimately 'held a meeting with a view to banishing him', whereupon he fled with a few followers to Basutoland (c. 1814); and the Kwena chief Motswasele II was in fact assassinated in full view of his tribe on such an occasion.[2]

The relative frequency of the assemblies, and the fact that all tribesmen may attend and are sometimes compelled to, helps to

[1] W. C. Willoughby, *Race Problems in the New Africa* (1923), p. 97.
[2] Breutz (1953.b), p. 95; Schapera (ed.) (1940), p. 43 f.

explain why on the whole Tswana chiefs are seldom autocratic; they are directly and often in contact with the mass of their people, and it is therefore difficult for them to remain indifferent to a publicly-expressed threat of opposition. Elsewhere the chief never has to face his people collectively, except perhaps on great ceremonial occasions, nor do his opponents have the same excellent opportunity of being able to influence the tribe as a whole. Hence it may happen, as among the Lobedu, that 'No one in the tribe ever knows what is happening even in important matters affecting them all, and the tribe accepts with equanimity the most outrageous favouritism of the royal family.'[1] In such cases the chief is subject primarily to whatever restraining influence his confidential advisers, and especially his senior kin, are able to exercise; and we may recall in this connection that among Swazi the queen-mother, and among Venda the *makhadzi* (senior paternal aunt), are both said to have the specific duty of rebuking him should he do wrong.[2]

If the chief heeds his advisers and mends his ways, he need have nothing to fear; but if he persists in his misconduct there will almost certainly be trouble. Given sufficient provocation, his opponents may resort to violent action. This occasionally takes the form of a plot against his life. Since attempts to kill him may also be made by ambitious rivals or embittered relatives, his murder does not necessarily mean that he was widely detested. But among those assassinated primarily because their rule had become intolerable were Shaka (1828) and Motswasele II (Kwena, c. 1821).[3] To this day Motswasele's fate is often cited to Tswana chiefs as a warning of what to expect if they try to behave as he did: he took cattle and corn from his subjects, abducted their wives, and ruthlessly enforced the death penalty. In some divisions, such as Cape Nguni and Venda, it is reportedly taboo to shed the chief's blood except in battle, owing to the sanctity of his person; but he may be strangled or poisoned instead, or, as happened to the ancient Hlubi

[1] E. J. Krige (1938), p. 273.
[2] See above, p. 55 f.
[3] For other examples of chiefs who were murdered, see below, p. 174.

chief Ncobo (who killed each of his wives as she became pregnant), he may be abandoned to his fate in a spot infested by wild
beasts. Venda chiefs, incidentally, are said to be so afraid of poison
that they will not eat or drink anything until it has been tasted beforehand by someone else.

As an alternative to murder, which necessarily involves direct
access to his person, the chief's enemies may try to bring about a
revolt. Here again their basic motive often is ambition or personal
grievance, but if he is at all unpopular they can usually rely upon
the help of others, and if he has been despotic they may be supported by most of the people. The outcome in many instances has
been the expulsion of the chief and his replacement by someone
else. Among those driven from home by civil wars due mainly to
their own tyranny were such well-known rulers as Dingane (Zulu,
1840), Macheng (Ngwato, 1858), and Mawewe (Shangana, 1861).

Since ordinary tribesmen can hardly hope to command enough
support, plots against a chief are almost invariably organized by or
under the leadership of one or more of his near agnates, and sometimes, as seems to have happened in regard to both Shaka and Motswasele II, they are confined to a small group of men very close to
him. There is no instance on record of extensive popular risings
among Bantu similar to the French or Russian revolutions. Nor
is there any known instance of an attempt to change the existing
type of government. A chief might be killed or expelled, but he
was always succeeded by a near relative, never by an outsider,
and the chieftainship itself was always retained. It was not
the institution as such that was condemned, but merely the
conduct of the person who at the moment happened to be in
office.

Normally the only ways in which commoners can show
marked disapproval of a chief's rule are to support one of his
rivals, or else to withdraw from his tribe and go somewhere else.
Secession is in the long run perhaps the most important sanction
that people in general can bring to bear against him; and, as already noted, among Tswana he is explicitly warned at his installation that if he does not treat his subjects well they will abandon

him. What Stayt says in this connection about the Venda[1] is equally applicable to all other Bantu:

'The power of rulers depends upon their wealth and the numerical strength of their following. This is an incentive to all rulers, of whatever rank, to endeavour to attract new people and to maintain their hold over their present subjects by ruling with equity and justice, acting in all things with consideration and giving wise council. A great deal depends upon the ruler's personality, and often an unwise heir will find a strong heritage quickly weakened, resulting in the lowering of his prestige . . . If a leader is unpopular with any of his following, and an individual feels that he has not been treated fairly, or that his overlord is unworthy of the services he is bound to offer him, he has one method of revenge: he can desert his unjust lord and offer his services to another man. This power of achieving retribution by desertion, possibly to join the ranks of a rival, forms a natural check on the absolute power of the rulers and prevents them from indulging too often in arbitrary acts of cruelty and injustice.'

Since few chiefs will submit readily to loss of their subjects, secession is not always easy, especially for people living in or fairly close to the capital. Among Tswana, for example, a man is rarely allowed to depart peacefully with all his movable property. The alternative is surreptitious flight, and if his intention becomes known to the chief his cattle may be confiscated before he can get them away. In many instances attempts have also been made to bring fugitives back by force, and often it was only after fighting and bloodshed that they either made good their escape or were compelled to return and suffer the penalty. Thus, when the Ngwaketse broke away from the Kwena (c. 1750), and the Tawana from the Ngwato (c. 1795), punitive expeditions were sent after them, which however they defeated; but when Phethu and Bathoen, half-brothers of the Ngwato chief Sekgoma I, seceded with the intention of forming their own tribe (c. 1840), he pursued and killed them and brought their followers back under his rule.

[1] Stayt (1931), p. 217.

In spite of such difficulties, history shows that many a chief has been abandoned by portions of his tribe. His own conduct was by no means always responsible, but it has certainly often been a major factor. A few Tswana examples may be cited. The whole of Maoto ward seceded from the Kwena to the Ngwaketse (c. 1790) because the chief attacked them, and killed one of their men, for their failure to attend a tribal assembly of which in fact they had not been notified; the Tlôkwa chief Kgosi became so unpopular, 'because he feeds only his dogs, and neglects us', that his followers deserted him in battle and he was killed (c. 1820); and the quick temper and autocratic tendencies of the Kgatla chief Kgamanyane alienated his brother Letsêbê, who with many other people left the tribe (1863). Tradition describes the Mogôpa chief Tsoku (c. 1750-60) as an avaricious and cruel man who, apart from slaughtering people's cattle and committing other misdeeds, once had a pregnant woman cut open 'so that he might see what direction an unborn child faces in its mother's womb'; his subjects thereupon broke away from him in large numbers, and he himself was afterwards strangled to death by a half-brother with whom he had sought refuge from invading enemies.[1]

Two Northern Sotho examples may be added. Among the Birwa, Motshabi succeeded to the chieftainship after his father's death (c. 1830); but owing to cowardice he refused to go through part of the installation ceremonies that involved 'meeting the spirits of his ancestors'. Because of this, 'his vassals began to despise him and refused to acknowledge his authority'. In the end they left him, either joining stronger chiefs near by or making themselves independent. 'In this way the strength of the tribe declined very much, and only a fragment remained.'[2] Among the Phalaborwa, Chief Matume (who ruled early in the present century)

1 Schapera (ed.) (1940), pp. 37 f., 174, 224; Breutz (1953. a), p. 86 f. For some other examples, see below, p. 158 ff. According to Bryant (1929, p. 649), Shaka too 'had the habit of having pregnant females opened alive, that he might learn "how the foetus lay"!'

2 van Warmelo (1953), p. 29.

greatly angered the people by his licentious conduct: he used to seduce their wives, and any husband who complained was put to death. Consequently they urged his popular half-brother Selwana to kill him and take his place. Selwana agreed, but fearing Government intervention suggested that the people should all move away from Matume, and kill him only if he pursued. This was duly done, and Matume, deserted by almost the whole of the tribe, attached himself to a neighbouring chief and left Selwana undisturbed as his successor.[1]

In contrast with such chiefs, there have been some whose character and conduct brought them many adherents from other tribes. Perhaps the best known was Moshesh, founder of the present 'Basuto nation'. Born heir to the chieftainship of a small and unimportant tribe (c. 1785), he soon became a noted raider, and although his father survived until 1855 he was from about 1820 onwards the acknowledged ruler of his people. During the troubled times initiated by Shaka's wars, his diplomatic skill and ready hospitality attracted the scattered remnants of many broken tribes. He conquered several neighbouring chiefs and successfully resisted invasion by others, and with the growth of his prestige more people flocked to his rule. When he died, in 1870, he was one of the most powerful chiefs in the whole of South Africa, and widely famed as an intelligent and humane statesman. Mswati II (Swazi, 1841-68) 'was a kind and just ruler, and to his "armpit" fled fugitives from other areas and also relatives of earlier inhabitants'[2]; the Kgatla chief Lentswe (1875-1924) had a high reputation for justice, tolerance, and generosity, which brought to his tribe several groups of seceders from his neighbours; and such other chiefs as Gambushe (Bomvana) and Rarabe (Xhosa) are also among those said to have gained many new subjects because of their personal esteem.

[1] Hoffmann (1934), p. 211. Another version says that the brothers quarrelled about the succession, and that, 'after considerable fighting', Matume (the rightful heir) was driven out (E. J. Krige (1937), p. 358 f.).

[2] Kuper (1952), p. 4.

IV

So far I have been discussing the types of situation due to the chief's own behaviour. But even if he himself rules in a manner acceptable to most of his people, he may still meet with trouble. The powers and privileges of his office are so enviable that he almost always has rivals among his close relatives, who may try to supplant him either before his accession or afterwards. Tribal politics in fact consists very largely of such dynastic disputes. Examples can be found almost everywhere, and rather than cite isolated instances I give here a few representative series (with genealogies) for tribes whose history has been recorded in sufficient detail.

(a) XHOSA

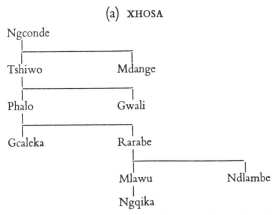

The heir when Chief Tshiwo died (c. 1700) was his infant son Phalo. Mdange, Tshiwo's half-brother, acted as regent. Gwali, Phalo's eldest half-brother, tried to usurp the chieftainship, but was defeated by Mdange and driven away; his people have ever since formed a separate tribe. Phalo in due course became chief. He ruled so long that his heir Gcaleka grew impatient and sought to oust him, but was frustrated by Rarabe, son of another wife. Then, realizing that there was little likelihood of future peace, Rarabe moved away with Phalo and many others, leaving Gcaleka in charge of the main body (c. 1760). The two sections have ever since been independent. Among the reasons why Gcaleka failed to retain the allegiance of all his people were the extreme cruelty of his mother and his own adoption of the dreaded profession of diviner. Rarabe, on the other hand, was very popular. His generosity and outstanding feats of war attracted many additional followers, and when he died in 1787, of wounds received in battle, his tribe was large and powerful. His heir, Mlawu, had previously also been killed in war, leaving as future successor a youthful son named Ngqika. Ndlambe, Mlawu's younger brother, acted as regent. He became so popular that Ngqika, on reaching maturity, had to fight him for the chieftainship (1797). Ndlambe was captured, but escaped shortly afterwards, and was joined by many people. His following was still further increased when Ngqika later abducted one of his wives, an act that was widely condemned as incestuous and that caused thousands to abandon the young chief in favour of his uncle. The hostility between the two steadily grew more bitter, and finally culminated in a great and destructive battle (1818). Ngqika was defeated, and since then the two sections have remained separate tribes.[1]

(b) ZULU

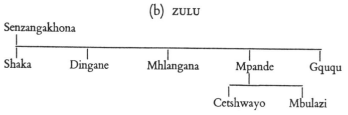

Shaka was stabbed to death in 1828 by his half-brothers Dingane and Mhlangana. Soon afterwards Dingane also had Mhlangana killed, and became undisputed chief. His rule was in some respects even more tyrannical than Shaka's. To strengthen his position, 'he set about a systematic extermination of all that remained of his family and relatives, all his friends and former comrades, the great ones of the nation.' Among the few whom he

---

[1] MacLean (1858), pp. 14 f., 18; Soga (1930), pp. 113, 120 ff., 128 f., 141 f., 148 ff., 153 ff.; Bennie (1939), p. 20 f.

spared was his half-brother Mpande, a quiet and inoffensive youth. In due course Mpande's growing popularity turned Dingane against him. Fearing death, Mpande escaped into Natal with several thousand adherents. He soon returned, reinforced by a party of Boers. In the ensuing battle (1840) Dingane was defeated; he fled into Swaziland, where he was murdered by the local inhabitants. Mpande then became chief. Three years later he caused the murder of his only surviving brother, Gququ, 'a great number' of whose partisans thereupon fled into Natal. Friction afterwards developed between Cetshwayo, his eldest son, and Mbulazi, son of his favourite wife, each of whom had a separate district and many followers. The rivalry between them culminated in battle (1856), Mbulazi and five brothers being among the many killed. The remnants of his following excaped into Natal. Cetshwayo thus became unchallenged heir to the chieftainship, to which he succeeded on Mpande's death (1872).[1]

(c) SWAZI

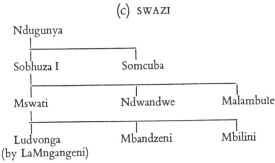

When Sobhuza I died in 1839, his heir Mswati was still a minor. An elder half-brother, Malambule, tried to usurp the chieftainship, but was defeated in battle and killed together with many of his men. Mswati, installed soon afterwards, subsequently had trouble with his paternal uncle and former regent, Somcuba, who was also defeated and killed (1852). He himself died in 1868 after a long and victorious reign, during which the Swazi expanded greatly by conquest and immigration. The heir, Ludvonga, was

[1] Bryant (1905), p. 63* ff.; (1929), *passim.*

too young to rule, and Mswati's mother and half-brother Ndwandwe acted as joint regents. Ludvonga died unexpectedly in 1874, and Ndwandwe, convicted of poisoning him, was clubbed to death. A period of turmoil and fighting followed; Mbilini, one of Mswati's sons, was forced to flee with his adherents into Zululand, where some of their descendants still are, and two other groups, also led by senior princes, joined and have ever since formed part of the Pedi tribe in the Northern Transvaal. Mbandzeni, another son, was ultimately chosen to rule together with Ludvonga's mother LaMngangeni (his own mother being dead). Before Ludvonga's death his future great wife had already been selected. Mbandzeni now begot a son by this woman, but subsequently had him killed because LaMngangeni favoured the child as future heir. This led to fighting between his partisans and hers; the queen-mother fled, but was captured and strangled, and another of Mswati's widows was chosen to take her place.[1]

(d) TAWANA

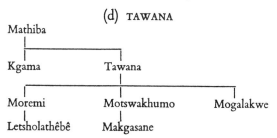

The Tawana are an offshoot of the Ngwato, from whom they broke away during the chieftainship of Mathiba (c. 1780-95). Their secession was due to the rivalry between Kgama, son of Mathiba's great wife, and Tawana, son of the favourite wife. Mathiba wished to recognize Tawana as his heir, but the tribe objected that Kgama was legally entitled to the succession. The outcome was that Tawana moved away with his adherents (c. 1795), thus founding the tribe now known by his name. He was accompanied by Mathiba, Kgama remaining behind as chief of the Ngwato. Tawana afterwards quarrelled with Mathiba, who

[1] Bryant (1929), pp. 322, 326, 332 f.; Kuper (1947), pp. 15, 20, 100 ff.; Kuper (1952), p. 4 f.; Hunt (1931), p. 296.

returned to Kgama but was rebuffed and in despair committed suicide. Tawana ruled a long time, and although his heir Moremi became mature refused to let him share in the government. Moremi at last moved away with some followers; he was pursued, and in the fighting that resulted Tawana was killed. Moremi then returned and took over the chieftainship (c. 1820). He ruled mainly through his personal retainers, and paid little heed to his brothers, who complained that he treated them no better than he did his dogs. One of them, Motswakhumo, consequently seceded with part of the tribe (c. 1825) and went to Angola. But his son Makgasane remained behind, and later became regent for Moremi's heir Letsholathêbê. His conduct showed that he was planning to keep the chieftainship for himself. This antagonized the people, and when they once had to flee hurriedly before an invading enemy, and Makgasane fell ill en route, they abandoned him by the wayside and left him to die alone. Mogalakwe, another of Tawana's sons, then became regent. He ruled well and unselfishly, treated the people with kindness, and in due time installed Letsholathêbê as chief (c. 1840), thereafter remaining his principal and loyal adviser; because of this, he is still remembered with respect and much affection.[1]

(e) KGATLA

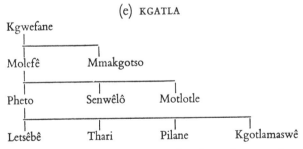

```
Kgwefane
   |
   |_____
   |                    |
Molefê              Mmakgotso
   |
   |_____
   |              |                  |
Pheto         Senwêlô            Motlotle
   |
   |_____
   |              |                  |               |
Letsêbê        Thari              Pilane        Kgotlamaswê
```

When Chief Molefê died (c. 1790), after a long and peaceful reign, his brother Mmakgotso became regent for the young heir Pheto. After Pheto's accession the two quarrelled about the distribution of cattle looted in war. Mmakgotso fled to the Kwena, and with their help returned to attack his nephew. He was

[1] Nettelton (1934), p. 343 ff.; Schapera, unpublished field notes (1940).

defeated and captured, but was soon afterwards released and went to settle among the Kwena, where his descendants still are. Pheto ruled a long time. When he died (c. 1810), his younger brother Senwêlô became regent, Letsêbê the heir being still a minor. Letsêbê later seduced one of Senwêlô's wives. Hearing that his uncle threatened retaliation, he had him driven away and himself began to rule. Soon afterwards he was murdered at Senwêlô's instigation (c. 1820). His younger brother and heir Thari fled for safety, and Senwêlô resumed the chieftainship. Within a short time he too was killed in revenge by Letsêbê's adherents. Motlotle, one of Pheto's minor sons, was then chosen as regent, mainly because he seemed quiet, dull-witted, and unlikely to give trouble. No sooner was he in power than he set about killing his senior relatives. Several escaped to other tribes, but Thari was lured back, ambushed, and murdered. Motlotle's savagery caused most of the people to abandon him, and he was soon left with very few followers. In 1823 they too were scattered by enemy invaders, and he himself fled with only one attendant. He came to a village where he was recognized by other Kgatla refugees; they followed him when he left, and beat him to death with sticks. Pilane, Pheto's senior surviving son, then became chief. His title was later contested by a half-brother named Kgotlamaswê, whom he fought and drove away. Under his long and skilful reign (c. 1825-50) the tribe gradually regained its former cohesion and strength.[1]

(f) PEDI

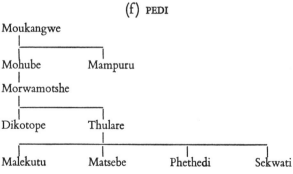

1 Schapera (1942.a), p. 4 ff.

Chief Moukangwe became so old that tribal affairs were managed for him by his son Mohube, after whose death in battle another son, Mampuru, acted as regent. When Moukangwe at last died, Mohube's son Morwamotshe should have succeeded, but Mampuru refused to make way; this led to fighting, whose outcome was that Mampuru and his followers seceded and became a separate tribe. Morwamotshe was succeeded in due course by Dikotope, but Mampuru instigated another son, Thulare, to revolt against the new chief. Dikotope fled and obtained help from other tribes. Thulare attacked and defeated them, killing Dikotope, and then became chief. He ruled long and well, greatly extending the power of the tribe. After his death (1824) his son Malekutu succeeded him, but two years later was poisoned by a brother, Matsebe, who coveted the chieftainship. Matsebe was thereupon driven out by another brother, Phethedi, who pursued and after some fighting killed him, and then himself became chief. Soon afterwards the Pedi were attacked by Mzilikazi's Ndebele, and in a fierce battle Phethedi and all but one of his surviving brothers were killed. Only Sekwati escaped. After living abroad as a refugee for several years he returned, and under him the tribe gradually regained its former strength.[1]

(g) LETSWALO

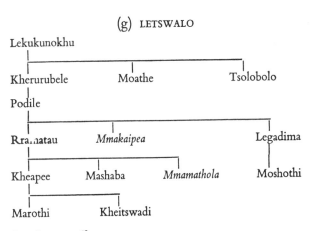

[1] Hunt (1931), p. 278 ff.

The Letswalo are a North-Eastern Sotho tribe. Their chief Kherurubele was murdered (c. 1828) by his younger brother Moathe, who in revenge was strangled by Kherurubele's son Podile; his people thereupon fled under a brother named Tsolobolo and became a separate tribe. Podile ruled for many years and grew very old. His son Rramatau, impatient to succeed, finally tried to starve him to death. The attempt was foiled by a sister, Mmakaipea, to whom Podile in gratitude then taught the secret rainmaking magic. Rramatau duly became chief when Podile died (1859). Three years later he was killed in war by the Swazi. His son Kheapee succeeded. Kheapee by his first wife had a son named Marothi, but afterwards took another woman as great wife and by her begot Kheitswadi. Marothi, who had till then considered himself the heir, waited for a suitable opportunity and then murdered Kheapee; he is said to have been instigated to this by Mmakaipea, who, being ambitious, planned to rule through him. But she was frustrated by Kheapee's half-brother Mashaba, who had the parricide put to death. For the next twenty years or so there was much confusion and strife; Mashaba and Mmakaipea each ruled rival factions, and a third came into being under Moshothi, son of Rramatau's brother Legadima and a noted and successful warrior. Mashaba's faction ultimately became subject to Moshothi, whose people have ever since constituted a separate tribe. Another was created in 1900 by the secession of Kheapee's son Kheitswadi from Mmakaipea's successor Mmamathola (daughter of Rramatau).[1]

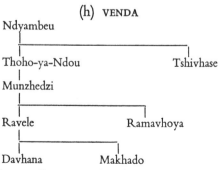

(h) VENDA

Ndyambeu

Thoho-ya-Ndou .... Tshivhase

Munzhedzi

Ravele .... Ramavhoya

Davhana ...... Makhado

Krüger(1936a), p. 180 ff.; J. D. Krige(1937), p. 343; vanWarmelo(1944a), p. 5 ff.

After the death of Thoho-ya-Ndou the chieftainship was usurped by his half-brother Tshivhase. The latter was soon afterwards defeated in battle by Thoho-ya-Ndou's son Munzhedzi, and with his remaining adherents fled to found his own tribe. Munzhedzi then became chief. His oldest son was Ravele, but his favourite was Ramavhoya, to whom he secretly gave many followers. The result was that when their father died Ramavhoya was able to drive Ravele into exile and usurp the chieftainship. He afterwards infuriated the people of an allied tribe by treacherously murdering their chief. In revenge they fetched back Ravele, and with him attacked Ramavhoya, whom they captured; they then forced Ravele personally to strangle him to death (1859). Ravele thus became chief. After his death he was succeeded by his son Davhana, who was however soon driven out by a half-brother named Makhado and with a small following joined another tribe.[1]

As shown by these examples, and very many others like them are known, conflicts within a royal family arise from situations of various kinds. In only a few of our instances was the trouble due primarily to the tyranny or misgovernment of a ruler.[2] More often it was caused by such events as real or attempted usurpation of the chieftainship,[3] personal jealousies or grievances between a chief and his relatives,[4] and attempts to remove real or potential rivals.[5]

Owing to polygamy and the associated practice of ranking wives, disputes about the succession are almost inevitable. The brothers and other connections of each wife watch jealously over the interests of her sons, whose fortunes they usually do all that

[1] van Warmelo (1932), p. 6 ff.; (1940), p. 38 ff., 51 ff.
[2] Cf. Shaka and Dingane (Zulu), Motlotle (Kgatla), Ramavhoya (Venda).
[3] Cf. Gwali and Gcaleka (Xhosa), Malambule (Swazi), Moremi and Makgasane (Tawana), Mampuru, Thulare, and Matsebe (Pedi), Rramatau and Marothi (Letswalo), Tshivhase and Makhado (Venda).
[4] Cf. Ndlambe v. Ngqika (Xhosa), Mswati v. Somcuba (Swazi), Kgama v. Tawana, and Moremi v. Motswakhumo (Tawana), Pheto v. Mmakgotso (Kgatla), Kherurubele v. Moathe (Letswalo).
[5] Cf. Dingane v. Mhlangana and Mpande, Mpande v. Gququ, and Cetshwayo v. Mbulazi (Zulu), Mbandzeni v. LaMngangeni (Swazi), Kgama v. Tawana (Tawana), Motlotle v. Thari etc. (Kgatla); etc.

they can to promote, if only because they themselves expect to benefit in consequence. Hence any irregularity about a chief's marriages, any uncertainty about the relative status of his wives, any undue partiality that he may show for one in particular, will tend to give rise to dispute and intrigue. This is shown, for example, by the rivalries between Cetshwayo and Mbulazi (Zulu) and among the sons of Mswati (Swazi). Indeed, tradition has it that the institution of female chieftainship among the Lobedu was due primarily to such a situation. Chief Mugodo (c. 1800) had two sons who quarrelled and fought for the right of succession while he himself was still alive. In despair because of the unrest that they were causing, he drove them both away, and gave the sacred rainmaking apparatus to his daughter Mojaji, thereby ensuring that she would rule after him.[1]

Even if the heir is definitely known and acknowledged, he is not always assured of the succession. His own conduct may lead to his rejection, as happened long ago to the Pedi prince Thobele, who was banished for cohabiting with his father's wives;[2] his father may favour another son, as with Tawana (Tawana) and Ramavhoya (Venda); he may be murdered, as was the fate of Thari (Kgatla) and Ludvonga (Swazi); or, as illustrated by Gwali (Xhosa), Malambule (Swazi), and Marothi (Letswalo), an ambitious half-brother may try to displace him. And where, as among Venda, North-Eastern Sotho, and some Nguni tribes, the heir is normally not chosen until after his father's death, there may be struggles for supremacy between a chief's sons as soon as he dies (cf. Swazi: Mbilini etc.; Venda: Makhado) or even during his lifetime (cf. Zulu: Cetshwayo v. Mbulazi; Lobedu: Mugodo's sons). So usual is it for the succession to be contested that, in some Tswana and Tsonga tribes, part of the installation ceremony consists in a public challenge to those denying the new chief's title to come forward and fight—and history shows that the challenge was not always a mere gesture; and among Central Sotho a chief's funeral is sometimes marred by a struggle among his sons

[1] Krüger (1936.b), pp. 101, 105; Krige (1943), p. 8 f.
[2] Hunt (1931), p. 277 f.

for the right to turn the first sod of his grave, an act that is both the prerogative and the validation of his successor.[1]

It often also happens that on his father's death the heir is too young to rule. The regent then chosen is expected to make way for him when he comes of age. But many a regent, once in power, becomes unwilling to surrender office, or tries to do away with the heir in order to retain the chieftainship for himself. Examples of the situations that may result are found in the histories of Ndlambe (Xhosa), Ndwandwe (Swazi), Makgasane (Tawana), Senwêlô and Motlotle (Kgatla), and Mampuru (Pedi). And although the regent himself may behave correctly, and of this too our histories contain examples (cf. Xhosa: Mdange; Tawana: Mogalakwe), the period of minority often tempts one of the heir's brothers to try usurping the chieftainship before he is old enough to be installed (cf. Xhosa: Gwali; Swazi: Malambule).

Even if the heir does become chief, he may afterwards have trouble with his brothers or uncles. They are jealous of their rights and actively resent any failure on his part to consult them or to provide adequately for them, or, especially if he rules badly, they may conspire against him in the hope of ousting him and taking his place. On the other hand he himself may fear them sufficiently, especially if they become popular or if his own title is not well founded, to seek their removal before they are a real source of danger. Some of the situations producing conflict between brother and brother, or between uncle and nephew, are illustrated by the histories of Dingane and Mpande (Zulu), Mbandzeni (Swazi), Motswakhumo (Tawana), Mmakgotso and Motlotle (Kgatla), Thulare and Matsebe (Pedi), Moathe, Mmakaipea, and Mashaba (Letswalo), and Ramavhoya (Venda).

Moreover, as shown by what happened to Phalo (Xhosa), Mathiba and Tawana (Tawana), and Podile and Kheapee (Letswalo), the chief's own sons may quarrel with him or become impatient and seek to supplant him if he rules too long for their liking. Among the Mthethwa, to cite another instance, Chief Jobe in old

1 For examples of such conflicts, cf. Hunt (1931), pp. 280, 293; Harries (1929), p. 111.

age designated his son Tana as his heir. Tana soon grew tired of waiting to succeed in the normal way, and with his younger brother Ngodongwana (subsequently and better known as Dingiswayo) plotted against his father's life. This became known to the old chief, who ordered them both to be killed. An armed party one night surrounded and attacked the hut in which the youths were sleeping. Tana was killed, but Dingiswayo managed to escape. After wandering about for several years he returned. He found the tribe being ruled by a junior half-brother named Mawewe, Jobe having meanwhile died. Without attempting resistance Mawewe fled, but he was persuaded to return and on arrival was at once put to death. Dingiswayo then assumed the chieftainship.[1]

Similarly, among the Ngwaketse, Tshosa (son and heir of Makaba II) tried to usurp the chieftainship during his father's lifetime (c. 1817). Defeated, he and his supporters fled to a neighbouring tribe. In 1822 he led a raid against his father's cattleposts, but was beaten off, pursued, and killed.[2] Among the Ngwato, again, a long-standing feud between Chief Sekgoma I and his heir (afterwards Kgama III) resulted in the latter's withdrawal from the capital with many followers, including most of the Christians (1873). He returned early in 1875 and after some fighting drove out his father and made himself chief. Sekgoma was subsequently admitted back into the tribe, but lived in obscurity until his death in 1883. In 1896 Kgama quarrelled with his own heir, also named Sekgoma, who complained of not receiving due recognition but whom he, in turn, accused of insubordination and conspiracy. The quarrel became increasingly bitter and culminated in Sekgoma's banishment (1899). He was accompanied by many people, over whom he ruled as an independent chief until 1920, when he was reconciled to his father and allowed to return. Kgama died three years later, and Sekgoma then became chief of the whole tribe.[3]

[1] Bryant (1905), p, 30* f.; (1929), p. 86 ff.
[2] Schapera (1942.b), p. 5.
[3] Schapera (ed.) (1940), pp. 83 f., 88; Sillery (1952), pp. 121, 125 ff.

V

Bantu are well aware of the dangers threatening the chief from the ambitions and rivalries of his near kin. 'The king should not eat with his brothers, lest they poison him', say the Zulu; 'princes make restless subjects', say the Swazi; 'nobles are the chief's killers', say the Tswana; and the universal and much-quoted proverb, 'There cannot be two bulls in one kraal', usually refers specifically to the struggles for power and elimination that so often occur in the royal family.

To counter such threats, various devices may be employed. One of the most widespread is to balance the power of the nobles by giving power to commoners. Almost everywhere, as we have seen, commoners usually fill some of the central executive posts, often including that of great induna. As Dr. Kuper says of the Swazi, 'In view of the potential rivalry between the king and his brothers, it is not surprising to find that men of specific commoner clans hold key positions. From them are drawn men with whom each king enters a bond of blood brotherhood. They are bound by the ritual to assist him in every way, and at the same time they are too lowly by birth to threaten his powers. Every ruler has a main councillor selected from a commoner family of proven loyalty and intelligence. These men recognize "there is only one king".'[1]

Many commoners are also sub-chiefs or headmen, and thus not only belong to the tribal council but control local segments, whose allegiance may be an important factor in case of civil war. Unlike nobles, moreover, many of them hold the chief's cattle on loan, and are therefore directly indebted to him for their means of subsistence. As already mentioned, the fact that they are not of royal blood prevents them from ever being contenders for the chieftainship, and on the other hand they are attached to the chief not only by economic self-interest but also by traditional conceptions of loyalty and reverence.[2] It does occasionally happen that

[1] Kuper (1941), p. 23
[2] See above, p. 104 ff.

leading commoners may be won over by royal conspirators—one of Shaka's murderers was his household steward Mbopha (the narrator in Rider Haggard's novel *Nada the Lily*), and among Swazi two prominent indunas were executed for treason[1]—but normally the chief can rely upon the support of such men, unless he himself behaves so badly as to alienate them.

Occasionally, as in some Tswana and Cape Nguni tribes, nobles and commoners are even grouped formally into opposite factions. The Kgatla, for example, are divided into five major 'sections'; one, termed *bakgosing* (those of the chief's place'), embraces all wards headed by nobles and some headed by foreigners, and the four others, collectively termed *badintlha* ('outsiders'), embrace all wards headed by commoners and a few headed by foreigners. The sections form separate administrative units, and at tribal assemblies are sometimes called upon individually for their views. The *badintlha*, moreover, pride themselves on being the chief's 'allies and champions' in his disputes with his relatives, and in the past have usually lived up to their claim: it was due primarily to their support that Pilane was able to defeat Kgotlamaswê,[2] and when, after the death of his son and successor Kgamanyane (1874), the *bakgosing* wished to give the chieftainship to the latter's eldest son Tau, the *badintlha* maintained that the true heir was Lentswe, son of the great wife, whom under threat of battle they succeeded in having installed.[3]

A somewhat similar system occurs among the Gcaleka, the senior Xhosa tribe. Here there are two major segments: Ntshinga, embracing all clans of the royal stock, and Qauka, embracing all the others. The segments constitute separate units both in the army and in the administrative system; and it is recorded, though adequate detail is not given, that in 1927 Ntshinga, accused of having often misled chiefs in the past, was after public discussion replaced by Qauka as 'supreme guide in tribal affairs'.[4]

[1] Bryant (1929), p. 658 ff.; Kuper (1947), p. 61.
[2] See above, p. 162.
[3] Schapera (1938), p. 24 ff., and unpublished field notes.
[4] Soga (1932), p. 101 ff.

The Ngwato, again, are divided into four parallel sections each containing wards headed respectively by nobles, commoners, or foreigners. Every section has two leading ward-heads, a noble and a commoner; they normally act together in matters of sectional interest, but the commoner has greater administrative and judicial authority. What mainly concerns us here is that the two headmen are also said 'to watch each other' (*go disana*) on behalf of the chief, i.e. each is responsible for reporting any acts or threats of disloyalty on the part of the other. In most large wards headed by nobles there is likewise a small group of commoners originally placed there by the chief as 'watchmen'; reciprocally, nobles have have sometimes been placed for the same purpose in large wards headed by commoners. The Tawana have an almost identical system, but with three sections instead of four.[1] As will have been gathered, this method of grouping aims at checking disaffection, whether among nobles or commoners; but the significant feature is that it explicitly uses commoners as a counterpoise to the nobles. Nothing similar has been noted in other Tswana tribes, but in many of them (including Ngwato and Tawana) the chief sometimes consults 'common headmen' as a group apart from the nobles, and can thus try to ensure their support in case of trouble with the latter.

Another widespread device is for the chief to send his near relatives to take charge of outlying areas. Since this cannot be done extensively without much disturbance of existing arrangements, he generally selects the nominees from among his senior brothers and sons, who because of their rank would in any case be the most likely to threaten him. The practice not only gives the royal family more direct control of the tribe.[2] It also enables the men concerned to experience individually the powers and privileges of rulership, and may thus tend to reduce the possibility of their becoming restive and insubordinate; according to Kuper, indeed, 'It is a doctrine of Swazi political theory that the appointment of princes to the chieftainship of districts will induce them to guard

[1] Schapera (1938), p. 27 f.; (1952), pp. 90, 92; and unpublished field notes.
[2] See above, p. 123.

the interests of the main heir and to expend their ambition in the exercise of their local authority.'[1] Moreover, by keeping such men away from the capital except on official occasions, it denies them dangerously close access to the chief's person and likewise makes it more difficult for them to combine effectively against him or to gain many adherents outside their own areas. On the other hand it does at the same time allow them to build up strong local support if they are at all capable and popular, and may thus encourage them to seek independence by hiving off to found their own tribes.

Among Tswana, unlike most other divisions, it is only within modern times that the practice was begun of appointing senior nobles as resident governors of outlying districts. Traditionally, the chief's agnates all live in his capital, where they are grouped into several wards each consisting basically of a lineage segment with its own headman. The town generally also contains other wards headed by commoners or foreigners. The disposition of wards, among Western Tswana, once again tends towards protecting the chief. His own ward is in the centre, around it are located the wards of his retainers (mostly commoners), and beyond them, finally, are the wards of people not specially attached to him, mostly nobles and foreigners. The arrangement thus ensures that he always has his personal adherents between him and the potentially hostile elements. A similar function is served elsewhere, as among Zulu and Swazi, by the military garrison always maintained at the chief's village;[2] and it has been pointed out, in this connection, that Shaka's murder was made possible only because he had left himself undefended by sending his whole army away on a foreign campaign.[3]

The Nguni and Tsonga rule that a chief should not marry his great wife until he is already in office, and preferably not until late in life, is often said by the people themselves to be yet another attempted safeguard: it aims at ensuring that his heir is never old

[1] Kuper (1941), p. 23.
[2] See above, p. 48.
[3] Bryant (1929), p. 660 f.

enough to be able to challenge him before he dies. As shown by the histories of Phalo (Xhosa) and Jobe (Mthethwa), it does not always succeed. One consequence, moreover, is that the heir is often a minor at his father's death, and may then himself have difficulty in afterwards becoming chief.

In most Sotho tribes, on the other hand, the system of royal marriages is such that the heir often reaches manhood early in his father's reign, if not sooner. In such cases the chief as he grows older may employ the heir as his deputy and subsequently even entrust him with all the essential duties of government. We have already seen that among the Southern Sotho Moshesh was *de facto* chief for many years before his father died, and that among the Pedi two of Moukangwe's sons successively acted for him in his old age. Among the Kwena, similarly, Chief Motshodi (c. 1740–70) outlived his son and heir Legojane, and in the closing years of his life had as regent Legojane's son Motswasele I. However, as shown by the examples of Moremi (Tawana), Tshosa (Ngwaketse), and Kgama and Sekgoma II (Ngwato), conflicts between father and son do often occur. It seems reasonable to assume that they are facilitated by the relative absence of appropriate safeguards such as those found in other divisions.

Among Venda, again, it is said to have been the rule until the time of Ravele to kill at birth all a chief's sons except the first three, 'lest they be too many and cause strife about the chieftainship'; and among Swazi the queen-mother, once chosen, is expected to remain continent so that her son should not have any full brothers 'who might be tempted to usurp his birthright'.[1]

Apart from being helped by such institutional methods of eliminating or restricting potential rivals, individual rulers may resort to personal measures of security. Among Zulu, for example, both Shaka and Dingane (who although they did not marry took concubines) had all their sons killed at birth, to prevent the possibility of afterwards being ousted by them, and both Dingane and Mpande also killed brothers; the Ncunu (Natal Nguni) chief Macingwane likewise did away with all his sons but two, 'lest,

[1] van Warmelo (1932), pp. 11, 15, 29; Kuper (1947), p. 55.

perchance, they should . . murder him';[1] and, as we saw above, Ncobo (Hlubi) killed each of his wives as she became pregnant, and Mbandzeni (Swazi) killed one of his sons because the child was regarded by some as the future heir. Among Tsonga, similarly, 'a chief, when he ascends the throne, will do his best to get rid of troublesome brothers in order to reign alone and to ensure the chieftainship to his son. This has often happened, especially in the case of Maphunga, chief of Nondwane, who killed as many as four brothers or near relations . . . [One of these] was very courageous, and the cunning Maphunga succeeded in poisoning him treacherously, through the agency of a dissolute woman.'[2] But on the whole such practices are not very common, and although in all divisions many instances are known of chiefs killing brothers or other near kin the victims were usually true rebels or conspirators and not merely potential rivals.

Our examples show that chiefs do sometimes die of old age after a long if not necessarily peaceful reign.[3] They also contain instances of aspiring usurpers being foiled or repulsed,[4] and perhaps meeting with death[5] or expulsion.[6] But there are likewise instances of an acknowledged heir being murdered,[7] and of rulers in office being expelled or forced to move away,[8] being killed in civil war or after capture,[9] or being deliberately assassinated.[10] The

[1] Bryant (1929), p. 264.
[2] Junod (1927), i, 413 f.
[3] Phalo, Rarabe (Xhosa); Mpande (Zulu); Mswati (Swazi); Molefê, Pheto, Pilane (Kgatla); Moukangwe, Thulare (Pedi); Podile (Letswalo); Moshesh (S. Sotho); Motshodi (Kwena).
[4] Gcaleka (Xhosa); Rramatau (Letswalo).
[5] Malambule (Swazi); Makgasane (Tawana); Matsebe (Pedi); Marothi (Letswalo); Tana (Mthethwa).
[6] Gwali (Xhosa); Kgotlamaswê (Kgatla); Mampuru (Pedi); Tshivhase (Venda); Tshosa (Ngwaketse); Sekgoma II (Ngwato).
[7] Ludvonga (Swazi); Thari (Kgatla).
[8] Phalo, Ndlambe (Xhosa); Dingane (Zulu); Mawewe (Shangana); Mathiba, Macheng, Sekgoma I (Ngwato); Davhana (Venda); Matume (Phalaborwa).
[9] LaMngangeni (Swazi); Tawana (Tawana); Dikotope (Pedi); Ramavhoya (Venda); Mawewe (Mthethwa).
[10] Shaka (Zulu); Motswasele II (Kwena); Letsêbê, Senwêlô, Motlotle (Kgatla); Malekutu (Pedi); Kherurubele, Kheapee (Letswalo); Tsoku (Mogôpa).

implication is that the institutions and practices mentioned above are by no means always an adequate safeguard against bloodshed between members of the royal family, let alone ordinary dissension. This the people themselves fully recognize. 'The king dies young', say the Swazi; 'princes die not of hunger but by the spear', say the Tswana; and a cynical Pedi proverb says, 'We pay homage to all the chief's sons, since which one of them will finally become chief is uncertain.'

It has recently been argued by Gluckman, referring primarily to Zulu and Swazi, that civil wars tend to strengthen rather than break tribal unity. 'I am tempted to go further', he says, 'and suggest that a periodic civil war was *necessary* to preserve that national unity: sections fought for the kingship and not for independence from it.' 'Territorial segments', he says elsewhere, 'developed, on the basis of local loyalties and cohesion, strong tendencies to break out of the national system and set up as independent. But in practice the leaders of these territorial segments often tended to struggle for the kingship, or for power around it, rather than for independence. Periodic civil wars thus strengthened the system by canalizing tendencies to segment, and by stating that the main goal of leaders was the sacred kingship itself.'[1]

The evidence, even for Zulu and Swazi, does not support Gluckman's main thesis. It is true that, both here and among other Bantu, rebels or conspirators usually aim at usurping the chieftainship, and not at breaking away to found tribes of their own. But, as shown by our examples, the outcome of their attempts almost always was the flight or secession of one section,[2] and there are even instances of men who seceded without making a bid for the chieftainship.[3] Indeed, of the eight tribes whose histories were summarized in the preceding section, five broke up into two or

[1] Gluckman (1954.a), p. 78; (1954.b), p. 25.
[2] Gwali, Ndlambe (Xhosa); Gququ, Mbulazi (Zulu); Mbilini, etc. (Swazi); Sekgoma I, Kgama III, Macheng, Sekgoma II (Ngwato); Mmakgotso, Kgotlamaswê (Kgatla); Mampuru (Pedi); Tsolobolo, Moshothi (Letswalo); Tshivhase, Davhana (Venda); Tshosa (Ngwaketse).
[3] Rarabe (Xhosa); Tawana, Moremi, Motswakhumo (Tawana); Phethu (Ngwato); Kgamanyane's brother Letsêbê (Kgatla); Kheitswadi (Letswalo).

more separate tribes each (Xhosa, Tawana, Pedi, Letswalo, Venda), and the three others (Zulu, Swazi, Kgatla) were all permanently deserted by groups whose descendants now belong to other tribes. This can hardly be regarded as valid ground for maintaining that civil war 'strengthened' tribal unity, let alone was 'necessary' for its preservation.

Conflicts of the kind that we have been discussing are not confined to the royal family, but are characteristic of the whole Bantu social system. In every local group of kin, from the household upwards, disputes often occur owing to arbitrary exercise of authority or rival claims to property or position; it is not fortuitous, for example, that most accusations of sorcery are made against relatives who are also close neighbours. The proximity in which they live, and the rules of patrilineal succession and inheritance complicated by the practice of polygamy, breed jealousies and rivalries that may prove stronger than the ties of mutual dependence and kinship solidarity. The usual outcome is that the group splits, some of the people moving away to establish their own household, lineage segment, etc. In the royal family the stakes are far more valuable and consequently far more tempting, but the underlying reasons for competition and strife are essentially the same.

Moreover, just as the head of an ordinary household allots to each of his wives cattle, fields and other property, so the chief allots to each of his wives not only property but also servants, who become the hereditary retainers of her eldest son and his line. The higher the rank of the wife, the more property and servants she tends to receive. Every senior prince (the heir of his mother's 'house') thus acquires a personal following, and by generous use of his cattle and other wealth he can also attract other dependants. Hence every successive chief finds that portions of his tribe are already attached to his brothers, uncles, cousins, etc., and he himself in due course provides similarly for his own sons. The system, as already noted, has one important consequence relevant to our present theme: it gives an ambitious prince the nucleus of popular support should he venture to aim either at the chieftainship or at independence.

The crucial factor in such cases is usually the attitude of the people generally. Here, as I have already emphasized, what matters most in the end is the conduct of the chief himself. So long as he satisfies his subjects, especially the commoners, they will tend to support him, even against the men to whom they are directly attached. As Ellenberger says of the Southern Sotho, 'At an early age every son of a chief of any importance had the nucleus of a following which increased according to his popularity, his father's favour, or other circumstances; and sometimes . . . younger sons have been in a position to secede from the parent tribe and form tribes of their own. That this did not happen oftener is probably due to the ties of blood which bound the young chief's mates to those of his elder brother. They had no chieftainship to quarrel about, and would lose, rather than gain, by separation from their relatives.'[1] But if the chief alienates his subjects by tyranny, injustice, or lack of generosity, they will abandon him and reinforce a more popular and open-handed ruler. Outstanding examples are the extent to which Rarabe and Ndlambe benefited at the expense of Gcaleka and Ngqika respectively (Xhosa), the growth of Mpande's following during Dingane's reign (Zulu), and the desertion of Matume in favour of Selwana (Phalaborwa). In such instances, if there is fighting many people may be involved and considerable bloodshed may result; the battles between Ndlambe and Ngqika (Xhosa, 1818), Cetshwayo and Mbulazi (Zulu, 1856), and Mzila and Mawewe (Shangana, 1856-62), are still remembered locally for the great destruction of life that they caused.

But, as our histories also show, struggles for the chieftainship are sometimes confined to a fairly small section of the tribe, and amount in effect to what may be termed 'palace conspiracies'. The murder of a chief, or his own killing of an uncle or brother, need not result from, or lead to, large-scale civil war, and may be accomplished before most of the people are aware that anything is amiss. The remarkable feature in such instances is how often a man who has killed or expelled his father or brother becomes accepted as chief with relatively little public opposition. The implication

[1] Ellenberger (1912), p. 264.

seems to be that, in general, the members of a tribe pay allegiance to their chief not as an individual but as the holder of an office; and so long as no attempt is made to extend the conflict by invoking the support of those not attached as personal retainers to the leading contestants, the affairs of the royal family may be regarded with comparative indifference, especially by 'foreign' (conquered or immigrant) sections. Here again the situation has its parallel in ordinary domestic life; as the proverb says, 'Outsiders should not intrude upon the affairs of the kin.'

VI

Problems similar to those we have been discussing also concern subordinate authorities, especially heads of local segments. In some respects such men are in a more difficult position than the chief, since they must rule to the satisfaction not only of their own followers but also of himself. This occasionally places them in a dilemma: they may have to side with their people against his policy, or run the risk of alienating them by carrying out his wishes. The conflict of loyalties tends to be most acute for heads of conquered or immigrant sections or of local groups of kin. On the other hand, so long as they serve him faithfully they can generally depend upon him for support and protection; their power is consequently strengthened by backing of a kind that he himself lacks in his own dealings with his subjects.

Like the chief, a local ruler often has trouble with his near relatives; for example, they may dispute the succession with him, or once he is in office they may find other reasons for challenging his authority. However, since sub-chiefs and headmen are either appointed or at least formally recognized by the chief, such disputes almost always result in his intervention. He may then decide in favour of the rightful heir or present incumbent. But, if at all possible and worth while, he may instead turn the opportunity to his own advantage by installing a rival claimant who is more dependable. Or, as sometimes happens among the Tswana, he may decide that to prevent future disorders the best solution would be to divide the group among the leaders of the different factions; as the relevant proverb says, 'troubles are cut with an axe', i.e. in case of dispute one of the parties moves away and with his axe cuts timber to build himself a new home. Thus, among the Ngwaketse, Kwelagobe ward is an offshoot from Maeakwena, Segwana from Manare, and Mhutsiwa from Logaba, and there are similar offshoots from Tsima, Sekokotla, Kgatleng, and several others. In each of these instances the division was due primarily to domestic quarrels about such matters as seniority of rank, inheritance or allocation of property, charges of sorcery, or unduly prolonged regency. It thus exemplifies, on a smaller scale, the process of fission that has so often led to the formation of new tribes. But it differs from major splits in two respects: with relatively few exceptions the seceding faction normally remains inside the tribe and, at least among the Tswana, the group cannot divide unless authorized by the chief.

The attitude both of himself and of the group's own members to such disputes depends largely upon the character and conduct of the men involved. Every local ruler should conform *mutatis mutandis* to the pattern of behaviour already described for the chief, and, like the chief, he is subject to controls of various kinds to ensure that he does. His own advisers and other assistants, in particular, are expected to keep him in check, and should he act wrongfully they must reprimand him and warn him to mend his ways. If this fails, other sanctions can be applied.

One of those sanctions is secession: a sub-chief or headman who is despotic, stingy, or otherwise unsatisfactory may be abandoned by such of his people as resent his behaviour. Among Tswana they cannot leave him without the chief's permission, seldom given except after public inquiry and unless good cause is shown; elsewhere, as among Nguni and Southern Sotho, there seems to be much more freedom of movement. Such desertions are not undertaken lightly, even if formal permission is not needed; at best the migrants will have to build new homes and clear new land for cultivation, perhaps among strangers, and sometimes, as among Mpondo and Swazi, they may also have to pay special fees to the appropriate rulers both before leaving and on arrival. Hence it is often only as a last resort, and if no other remedy is available, that people move away from their familiar neighbours and their existing plots of land. Nevertheless the likelihood of being thus deserted does help to restrain a local ruler from abusing his power or neglecting his subjects; their departure will deprive him of wealth and dignity and lessen his influence in the tribe, and once he has a bad reputation it is also highly improbable that people from elsewhere will come to live with him.

He himself may also be punished more directly. We have already seen that appeals can be made successfully to higher authorities against his judicial and other decisions, and, as among Tswana, he is then sometimes publicly rebuked or even fined if he has acted unjustly. Should he wrong one of his subjects or any other person (for example, by assault, adultery, damage to property, or failure to pay a debt), he can likewise be tried and sentenced at his own court, his deputy serving as judge. Usually, however, a case against him is taken to a higher court, especially if his conduct as ruler is in question; thus, among Tswana, ward-heads have been fined by the chief because of valid complaints from their people that they delayed unduly in trying cases, stayed away continuously from the council-place owing to drunkenness or preoccupation with private affairs, and refused to accept the advice of their councillors. A local ruler who is notoriously incompetent or persistently neglects his duties may even be deposed if his people say that they no longer wish to have him; his place is then taken by his nearest kinsman, unless the chief sees fit to appoint someone else.

Apart from thus alienating his own followers, a local ruler may fall foul of the chief. Often enough this may be due merely to incompetence or laziness, as when he fails to carry out his routine obligations; but his conduct may also take the form of deliberate defiance or even active opposition. The punishment he then receives depends upon the gravity of his offence. Among Tswana and Southern Sotho, for example, headmen have been fined and rebuked for failing to attend a meeting when summoned, pass on official messages, or report the presence of strangers. A ruler who persistently defies the chief's commands or is disloyal in other ways will be dealt with much more severely; he is not only deposed, but may have all his property confiscated, may be banished, or may even be put to death. Such penalties have for example been inflicted upon men who kept for themselves tribute due to the chief, organized ceremonies that are his prerogative, refused to take their adherents to tribal meetings or to war, and above all plotted against him or treacherously communicated with his foreign enemies. And if, as often happens in these cases, the culprit is supported by some or all of his people, they too are punished, though he as ringleader always suffers most.

The existence and application of such sanctions are one of the features immediately distinguishing the chief from all his subordinates. Although, as we have seen, he can be dealt with in other ways, in general he alone is immune from dismissal or other punishment by due process of law; in that sense he is a ruler independent of higher authority, whereas the heads of local segments are all subject to him.

It is apparently not often that local rulers who are commoners rebel against the chief. They have nothing special to gain by such action; unlike nobles, they cannot hope for the chieftainship, and unlike foreigners who have recently been incorporated they are not stimulated by the desire to regain independence or to return to their former homes. Hence it is only if they are provoked by his own conduct, or resent punishment however deserved, that they may wish to go against him; even then they usually tend to support or conspire with one of his rival kinsmen instead of attempting independent action.

He is much more apt to have trouble with the heads of immigrant or conquered groups. Once admitted into his territory, immigrants must submit to his authority, abide by the laws of his tribe, and pay tribute not to their own leaders but to himself. 'An elephant when it crosses a stream diminishes in size', says the proverb, i.e. no matter how important a person may have been at home he is always inferior in status to the chief whose subject he becomes.

However, immigrants do not always remain permanently attached to their new tribe. During the nineteenth century, for example, many Tswana tribes were scattered by invading enemies, sometimes more than once. Of the fugitives who reached other tribes, some are still represented locally by their descendants. But many returned to their former homes once the danger was past. Among them were the main body of the Ngwaketse, who lived with Rolong and Tlhaping (c. 1825-50); the Malete, who before recovering their identity as a separate tribe lived successively with Kwena, Ngwaketse, and Hurutshe (c. 1815-30); the Tshidi-Rolong under Montshiwa, who lived with the Ngwaketse from 1852 to 1877; and the Khurutshe, who lived with the Ngwato from 1864 to 1895. Sometimes, too, groups that had left home because of civil disputes afterwards became reconciled to their former chief or his successor and were then allowed to return. This happened, for example, with seceding or banished groups of Kgatla under Letsêbê (1863), Ngwato under Sekgoma I (1857, 1875) and Macheng (1872), and Kwena under Kgakge (1846) and Kgari (1894); all of these rejoined their own people after living for some time in other tribes.

The examples just given—and many others are known—show that neither banishment nor secession necessarily implies permanent loss of tribal membership: expatriates may be readmitted and restored to their former status if they express due repentance and promise to be loyal to the chief. It is for this reason, among others, that newcomers to a tribe are generally treated with reserve and excluded from its inner councils; there is, after all, no certainty that they will remain. As already mentioned, membership of a tribe is determined first by descent, and it is generally understood that people might wish in due course to return to their own kin. In such cases it rarely happens that the chief under whom they have been living will object to their departure with their live-stock and other property, provided of course that they observe the normal practice of seeking his consent.

Sometimes, however, immigrants leave not so much because they want to go back to their former homes as because they dislike the rule of their new chief or have other reasons for complaint. The Tlôkwa under Matlapeng attached themselves to Sechele's Kwena in 1853. They helped the Kwena in an expedition against the Ngwato (1858), but when Sechele again attacked the Ngwato (1872) they stayed behind. This led to their being accused of cowardice, and to ill-feeling and collisions between the young men on both sides. To avert bloodshed, Matlapeng therefore sought and obtained Sechele's permission to move away (1874). The Malete had also joined the Kwena in 1853. After some time Sechele asked them to pay tribute, but rather than do so and thus acknowledge him as paramount they preferred to go somewhere else (1875). The Kaa, a small tribe that had become subject to the Ngwato towards the end of the eighteenth century, quarrelled with them in 1848 and fled to the Kwena. In 1892, after the death of their headman, there was a dispute about the succession, and when the Kwena chief appointed a claimant who was not the senior son, most of the people moved away with the slighted heir and joined the Kgatla. In none of these instances, so far as the evidence indicates, was any attempt made to prevent the departure of those who wished to leave.

But should immigrants prove unruly or disobedient, they are sometimes ordered, and if necessary may be forced, to move away. For example, the Ngwato prince Kgari Macheng and a small group of adherents joined the Kgatla in 1878, but he was soon afterwards expelled when he was found to be communicating with the Kwena, with whom the Kgatla were then at war; in 1887 the Ngwato chief Kgama III attacked and after some fighting drove out an immigrant group of Seleka, whom he accused of inviting Boers into his country; and in 1934 Gobuamang, head of the Mmanaana, was banished by the Ngwaketse because for many years he had flouted the authority of their chiefs.

Such attempts at expulsion are not always successful. The Malete, after moving away from the Kwena in 1875, settled at a place called Ramoutsa. The Ngwaketse chief now intervened; he said that Ramoutsa belonged to him, and that the Malete must either pay him tribute or leave. They refused to do either, saying that they were in country inhabited long ago by their ancestors and never held by the Ngwaketse. An armed expedition sent to drive them out met with disastrous defeat (1881), and they have ever since remained at Ramoutsa as an independent tribe. The Kgatla, similarly, left the Transvaal in 1869 and settled at Mochudi, in what even they acknowledged to be the territory of the Kwena. Sechele duly claimed tribute, and when they not only refused to pay but began stealing his cattle and serfs, he sent a large force to expel them (1875). The attack was beaten off, and for several years afterwards there was intermittent warfare between the two tribes, the outcome being that the Kgatla remained masters of the land they had occupied.

Owing to the possibility of such conflicts, chiefs are not always willing to accept large groups of immigrants; several instances are known where they have in fact been deliberately excluded. Or, if admitted, they are sometimes broken up and dispersed among headmen of the ruling section, as happened to the Kubung who joined the Kwena early in the nineteenth century, and to a mixed group of Ngwato who joined the Tlôkwa soon after 1875. Alternatively, as among the Kgatla, a strong group of nobles or commoners may be settled beside or close to them, in order to ensure that they behave peacefully; this was done both for the Kaa who came in 1892 and for earlier accretions of Tlôkwa and Khurutshe.

Similar precautions are sometimes taken with newly-conquered peoples; we have already seen, for example, that the Western Tswana tribes, after occupying their present territories, appointed headmen of the ruling section as 'overseers' of the earlier inhabitants. Unlike immigrants, conquered groups are rarely allowed to leave the tribe peacefully, and any attempt to escape, or to regain their former independence, meets with immediate reprisal. The Kgwatlheng, for example, were invaded and subjugated by the Ngwaketse; they subsequently tried to break away (c. 1770), but were pursued and defeated, and those who failed to escape were distributed among several existing wards headed by nobles or commoners. Among the Ngwato, similarly, a Kgalagadi head-man named Mogolopolo managed through skill in hunting to acquire much wealth and a large following. His behaviour gave rise to suspicion that he was aiming to become independent. Kgama therefore attacked and killed him (c. 1880), burnt his village, confiscated all his property, and moved the survivors to another part of the tribal territory, where they could be controlled more directly.

As shown by several of our examples, the head of a subject group may be supported by all or most of his people if he seeks to leave the tribe; this seems to have happened when the Kgwatlheng broke away from the Ngwaketse (c. 1770), the Kaa from the Ngwato (1848), and the Tlôkwa from the Kwena (1874). But sometimes, if there is internal disagreement, some of them may refuse to go with him; thus when Gobuamang, after being banished by the Ngwaketse, found a home among the Kwena, he was soon joined by about half of his original following, but the others (including his own heir) preferred to stay behind, since they disapproved of the way in which he had been acting. Even those who accompany a migrating leader may afterwards break with him. Three years after the Kaa had settled among the Kgatla (1892) their headman quarrelled with one of his brothers, who moved away with a fairly large following to join the Ngwato, and soon afterwards a small group of alien servants, complaining of ill-treatment, were allowed by the Kgatla chief to establish a separate village under a headman of their own stock. Kgari Macheng, after being expelled by the Kgatla, settled among the Ngwaketse (1882); there some of his Khuruthse servants claimed that he was oppressing them, and the chief formed them into a separate ward; and when Kgari left again in 1898, they remained behind, as did some of his own relatives under one of his younger brothers. These and many similar instances illustrate once again the importance of the personal factor: whether or not people accompany the head of their group, and whether or not they remain with him afterwards, depends partly upon local conditions but partly also upon his own character and conduct.

Although all the examples so far given have been drawn from the Tswana, they can be matched in every other division. After Shaka's death several of the tribes that he had conquered, including the Qwabe, broke away from Zulu rule and escaped to the south; very many groups of Tsonga, including the Nkuna and Loyi, fled from Mozambique into the Transvaal because of ill-treatment by their Shangana conquerors; and many groups of Kalaka and other Rhodesian peoples fled into Bechuanaland to escape the oppressive rule of Mzilikazi's Ndebele. There were abortive attempts to regain independence, as when the Tau vainly rebelled on several occasions against their Pedi conquerors. There were also instances of immigrant groups subjecting and absorbing local tribes whose paramountcy they had had to acknowledge on arrival; the Pedi themselves did this to the Mongatane, and the Kekana-Ndebele overcame the Tlôkwa of Moletlane among whom they had settled, and drove out those unwilling to submit.

It should not be assumed from what has just been said that immigrant or conquered peoples always seek to become independent again. On the contrary, in very many instances they have remained part of the tribe ever since their absorption. Sometimes, as with the great majority of serf peoples among the Western Tswana, they lived in such small and weak groups that they had no option but to accept the rule of their conquerors; sometimes again, as with many of the tribes subdued by Shaka, they were so effectively broken up and scattered that they were unable to rebel afterwards. But often enough they were pleased with the treatment they received and became loyal subjects of their new rulers. This applies, for example, to most of the people now classed as 'commoners' among Kgatla, Ngwato, Kwena, and Ngwaketse; many, especially those of immigrant origin, speak of having been handled generously and justly, and in course of time their leaders gained the chief's favour and confidence and attained to positions of great responsibility. It applies also to such formerly independent tribes as the Kgwakgwa, Kgolokwe, Sia, and Taung, who became part of the 'Basuto nation' during the reign of Moshesh; to the various groups of Sotho, Nguni, and Tsonga, incorporated into the Swazi during the reigns of Sobhuza I and Mswati II; and to several groups of Southern Sotho who attached themselves to the Xhosa. With relatively few and sporadic exceptions, these peoples have seldom found much cause to complain against the rule of their alien overlords.

Nevertheless, it should by now be evident that a chief may have trouble not only with his own relatives but also with other sections of his tribe. Unlike himself, however, the rulers of such sections have authority over only part of the tribe, sometimes a very small part; and should they rise against him he can normally rely upon his far greater strength in order to cope with them. As I have already stressed, it is in fact largely through the division of the tribe into segments that he is able to control it as a whole; each segment is governed for him by an underling, and so long as most of them are loyal he can usually suppress local revolt with their aid. His main problem is to secure the loyalty of a sufficient majority; and that, sometimes unfortunately for himself but not necessarily for the people, depends not only upon his own character and conduct but also upon the readiness of others to forgo ambition or thoughts of independence.

VII

In contrast with the abundant information available for the Bantu, little is known about the Hottentot conception of a good chief. The quality mainly stressed in the literature is generosity: the worst that can be said of a chief, we are told, is that he is 'greatly left-handed', i.e. miserly. We are told also that such a man may be deposed in favour of someone more liberal, though no actual instances are cited.[1] However, it is recorded elsewhere that a younger son was once chosen to succeed to the chieftainship of the Rooinasie, because the elder 'had a bad character, being stingy and arrogant'.[2] There is also historical evidence about chiefs who

[1] Hahn (1881), p. 17; Wandres (1903), p. 322.
[2] Vedder (1934), p. 131.

were unsatisfactory in other ways, from which we can learn what else may be disliked about them.

On the whole, Hottentot chiefs seem unable to be as despotic as were some of their Bantu counterparts. As already mentioned, in the past they could not interfere in the internal affairs of any clan but their own, and in matters concerning the tribe as a whole they were and still are restricted in power both by the council and by the popular assembly. Their influence in the council depends not so much upon regard for their office as upon their own personality and the general state of the country. In times of war a forceful man can usually have his own way, especially if he is brave and enterprising, since common danger, or desire for plunder, will rally the people around him. But except when there is some such crisis he can seldom do much on his own, however ambitious he is. Almost all writers agree that should he attempt anything without first consulting his people and getting their consent, he is unlikely to meet with success. In 1853, for example, the Swartbooi chief Willem had to abandon a projected raiding expedition, the more sensible men refusing to accompany him 'because he had told no one, not even his councillors, what his actual plans were', and in 1844 the Rooinasie chief Oasib could not induce his people to move to another locality.[1]

Should a chief try to ignore his subjects' opinions, or should any of his other actions offend them, he may be dealt with more directly. Some writers state that he can be tried and punished by his own council, but apart from a casual remark that this was done to the Tsaib chief Jonathan (c. 1884), 'because of some incautious utterances',[2] no details are available. Some say also that a bad chief can be deposed, but others deny this, and in any event no instances have been recorded. Nor does it appear that chiefs have ever been assassinated or expelled because of misrule. The Rooinasie chief Petrus was killed by one of his own men while fighting against the Herero (1880), but this was due to rivalry for the chieftainship,

[1] Vedder (1934), p. 295; Moritz (1916), p. 191 (C. H. Hahn.)
[2] Schinz (1891), p. 39.

not to revolt against despotism.[1] A few other instances are known of a chief's relatives trying to usurp his position. But in contrast with those among the Bantu such dynastic conflicts are relatively uncommon, and they have apparently never led to large-scale civil wars. One reason may be that the chief's closest agnates normally form part of his entourage, and do not receive their own groups of retainers; possibly, also, the chieftainship itself is not always coveted, since there are records of men renouncing their claim to it.[2]

In practice, by far the most common reaction to a bad chief is secession. Tradition records that Haromab, an early Rooinasie chief, devoted himself mainly to managing his large herds of cattle, neglected the affairs of the tribe, and further antagonized people by his arrogance and brutality. Finally some of them left him. He sent for them, and when they did not return he attacked the chiefs to whom they had fled and seized both the fugitives and their protectors' cattle. We read also that many Orlam immigrants from the south, who had joined the Bondelswarts, left again because the chief would not let them till the soil (1807); that Chief Tsaib's 'wild and dissolute' behaviour caused his people to scatter until finally none but his own family remained with him (1844); and that when the chieftainship of the Rooinasie was, after the killing of Petrus, usurped by the instigator, 'a large portion' of the tribe, resenting what had happened, refused to acknowledge the new ruler and moved away.[3]

The chief himself is not always to blame, or at least not solely, for such desertions. The Bondelswarts say that they parted from the Rooinasie under a chief's son who had quarrelled with his elder brother, and the separation of both the Swartboois and the Tsaib from the Rooinasie is attributed mainly to their search for better pastures. There have been many other instances of families or individuals moving away owing to grazing conditions, local

[1] Vedder (1934), p. 598.

[2] *Ibid.*, p. 645.

[3] Vedder (1934), pp. 130 f., 645; Moritz (1916), p. 158 f. (Knudsen); Moritz (1918), p. 109 (Albrecht).

drought, the unsettled state of the country, inter-tribal marriage, fear of punishment for some offence, or simply because they preferred more freedom from control.

As shown by the example of Haromab, chiefs are occasionally able to force the return of absconding subjects. But in the main they seem powerless to prevent people from leaving. Certainly during much of the nineteenth century the frequent lack of respect for the chief and the common disregard of his authority were marked features of Hottentot public life. In 1814 one chief told a local missionary that 'some of his people, because of foolish talk, had caused trouble and left him; they had attacked other kraals and destroyed one; they had even attacked him, wounded many of his people, and stolen oxen and sheep; and were now under no authority'; and in 1820 the Rooinasie chief Gameb confessed to another missionary that to avoid paying him tribute his people 'often sneaked away to slaughter their cattle in secret'.[1] The Swartbooi chief Willem had by 1857 lost so much 'dignity and influence' that he himself moved away from his village and went to live with the Topnaars at Walfish Bay, whereupon his people said of him contemptuously, 'Our chief has become a Bushman'.[2]

But perhaps the best evidence is provided by the unavailing efforts of chiefs to deal with the situation. In 1854 Oasib and a colleague framed a joint regulation to check vagrancy, which was causing a good deal of public mischief. 'The idea was good', as Vedder says, but it came to nothing: Oasib lacked the power to enforce it, 'and in any event Nama vagrants roved about the land as before, and paid little attention to the haughty chiefs.'[3] In 1858, again, all the chiefs came together and under missionary guidance drew up a treaty to regulate inter-tribal relations in the future. The treaty was in fact soon broken, but in the present context one of its twelve clauses is of great significance. 'If the adherents of any chief in disobedience to him go on a raiding expedition against the Herero', it says, 'and he then imposes on them a punishment to

[1] Moritz (1915), pp. 212 (Schmelen), 217 (Kitchingman).
[2] Vedder (1934), p. 295.
[3] *Ibid.*, p. 335.

which they will not submit, the nearest chief must come to his aid and help him to enforce the punishment if he is too weak to do so himself.'[1]

There have, it is true, been chiefs who ruled with conspicuous success. One was Hab (c. 1720), the earliest known chief of the Rooinasie, of whom tradition relates that 'he made the Nama into one nation'; realizing the need for united effort to deal with the troublesome Bushman and Bergdama resistance and raids of those days, 'he took a firm hold upon his tribe, bent the individual clans to his will with a strong hand, and as head of the oldest and strongest tribe made the others acknowledge him as their overlord.' His grandson Gao-karib is also remembered as 'a friendly and peace-loving chief who did not oppress his subjects'.[2] But later chiefs of their line were less efficient, and during the rule of Oasib (c. 1835-67) the paramountcy of the Rooinasie finally came to an end.

The middle of the nineteenth century was admittedly a period of much warfare and unrest, and the intrusion of predatory immigrants from the south, and of European missionaries and traders, helped greatly to weaken tribal discipline. But the pastoral life of the Nama and their traditional dispersal over the land in small nomadic groups, also encouraged separatism and disregard for central authority. Except when the need for protection made them combine, there was in fact little to prevent people from wandering about as they wished; and although the creation of settled villages under missionary guidance tended to counteract this, it served incidentally to keep away those who disliked the new forms of control.

The chief's relations with his people suffered too from his lack of sanctions similar to those reinforcing the authority of his Bantu counterpart; as we have seen, he is neither ritual head of his tribe nor the source of wealth and reward, apart from his clansmen he has no personal adherents, and his office itself is not specially venerated. In the circumstances, his own character and conduct are factors of major importance. His tribe is so small that he is usually

[1] *Ibid.*, p. 306.
[2] *Ibid.*, p. 129 f.

well known to every one of his subjects, and should he forfeit their respect he has no means of compelling their obedience. Like Willem Swartbooi (c. 1860), he becomes a person of no consequence, and the council and popular assembly contrive to manage without him under the guidance of the abler and more conscientious men. Nevertheless it seems to be due largely to the basic weakness of chieftainship as an institution, and to the individual shortcomings of many chiefs, that so few of the Hottentot tribes still survive as cohesive entities.

VIII

We know even less than we do for the Hottentots about the actual working of the political system among Bergdama and Bushmen. No writer has given adequate attention to the subject, and there are very few case histories to indicate the kinds of problem that tend to arise. We may assume that because the band is so small and homogeneous there is not likely to be much scope for conflict between rulers and subjects: the few component families are all closely related to one another, their mode of subsistence does not create marked inequalities of wealth, there are no distinctive social classes, and the chief's power and privileges are on the whole too scanty to make the office a bone of contention. It is certainly not true of these peoples that the government represents the special interests of a small ruling section. On the contrary, we could more appropriately say that by its very nature it does away with the possibility of class exploitation, since decisions on matters of common concern are normally made by all the men in council.

Among Bushmen, especially, the chief is seldom able to be autocratic; even among Heikum and Kung, where his ritual functions distinguish him from all other men, he cannot do anything of importance without the general consent of the rest. The mere fact that he is recognized head of the community, and as such executive agent of the council, will generally ensure some respect for his wishes; but since he has no special means of enforcing them and no retainers or other assistants directly under his control, how much authority he can actually exercise depends largely upon his personal abilities. If capable and experienced, intelligent and sensible, he may be very influential in the council; and, as we have seen, an aggressive and successful warrior may in times of common danger also dominate over the people of neighbouring bands. If on the other hand he is dull and incompetent, or aged and feeble, the council's decisions will be determined by more able and energetic men, and he himself will tend to be ignored, as happened to the Auen chief who failed to retain the commanding position reached by his father.[1] There is no mention of a bad chief's being specially punished, nor of people leaving the band because they do not wish to continue living under him. But as he has so little personal power that his conduct can hardly injure the group as a whole, sanctions similar to those found among Bantu and Hottentots are perhaps not needed here.

The Bergdama chief is not only the patriarch and ritual head of his band, but, as his people themselves say, it is he who keeps them together and protects them from harm and misfortune. Consequently he tends to have more official authority than his Bushman counterpart, and although he discusses all matters of common concern with the other men his position always gives him distinctive influence. We are not told what happens if he is arbitrary or incompetent. But it is stated that when a chief dies his heir, if known to be avaricious and quarrelsome, may be driven out by the people, another son being chosen as successor instead; or, if they have 'neither inclination nor courage nor strength' to expel him, they may themselves move a little distance away 'and leave the unpopular man where he is'.[2] There is no other useful information bearing directly upon the problem of the chief's relations with his dependants.

IX

In the preceding sections I have tried to show that the way in

[1] See above, p. 133.
[2] Vedder (1923), i, p. 146.

which the affairs of a South African community are actually conducted depends largely upon the character of the men in positions of authority. The data for Bergdama and Bushmen are inadequate; but we know from historical evidence that the fortunes of Bantu and Hottentot tribes were often profoundly affected by the personal abilities and idiosyncrasies of their chiefs. That, after all, is what we should expect. All governmental tasks are performed either by the chief himself or by subordinates under his direction, and there is no toleration of deviant groups advocating policies of their own; he can thus influence the course of events more decisively than would be possible in systems characterized by separation of powers and by the existence of an accepted opposition party capable of providing an alternative government.

What effect a chief's behaviour can in fact have upon public life is determined also both by his official duties and by the power at his command; obviously he alone can accomplish little, whether for good or bad, unless he has some means of forcing or inducing people to comply with his wishes, nor can he rightly intervene in matters outside his recognized sphere of activity. The South African data suggest that the more comprehensive his duties, the greater the power that he wields; he is stronger among Bantu than Hottentots, and among Hottentots than Bergdama or Bushmen.

The data further suggest that the more comprehensive his duties and powers, the greater will be the public concern about the way in which he behaves; the more dependent his people are upon him, the more elaborate the precautions they take to ensure that he governs correctly. There are no constitutional arrangements anywhere in South Africa, similar to those found in modern Western states, by which unsatisfactory chiefs can be lawfully deprived of their office. Among Bantu, Hottentots, and Bergdama, an unsuitable heir may be passed over in favour of a more acceptable brother, and among Bantu, though apparently not elsewhere, the heir sometimes also receives special training for his future responsibilities. But although efforts may thus be made to secure the right kind of chief, once he is in office he normally remains there for life; he does not have to seek periodical re-election, nor must he resign if he forfeits public confidence. The principal methods of dealing with him are to limit his autocracy or to get rid of him if he behaves very badly.

Among Bergdama and Bushmen, the chief's lack of coercive power is apparently matched by the absence of special devices to keep him in check. The information on this point is very inadequate; but since he lives in direct and continuous contact with every other member of his band, and since important decisions are made by informal discussion among all the men around the camp fire, the indications are that public opinion is sufficient to prevent him from going astray and to counteract his deficiencies. Among Bantu and Hottentots he also rules with the advice of his people, whose views are intended to guide and correct him. This method of informing him about public reactions to his conduct is most fully developed among Hottentots and Tswana, where he must consult not only a relatively small council of notables but also an assembly of all the men. Among other Bantu the council is the only channel for the organized expression of public opinion. In either case the significant feature is that should he behave wrongfully the people are able to warn him of their disapproval. But if that fails, they may resort to various forms of obstruction or passive resistance. This too seems to be a device characteristic especially of Hottentots and Tswana, where it may be associated with the opportunity that the popular assembly provides for the exchange and diffusion of opinion.

Owing to the size and settlement patterns of Hottentot and Bantu tribes, the chief does not associate as intimately with all his subjects as does his Bergdama or Bushman counterpart; and owing to the relative infrequency of council meetings and assemblies, he is also not as continuously exposed to the direct pressure of public opinion. In any event his command of force, especially among Bantu, makes it possible for him, if he wishes, to ignore views with which he disagrees or to punish critics of whom he disapproves. But in the last resort he is not invulnerable. If sufficiently provoked, his people may kill or expel him, or they may withdraw from his jurisdiction.

Forcible revolt against a chief seems to be rare among Hottentots but relatively common among Bantu. Since its final aim is to instal someone more suitable, it is usually organized by, or round, one of his near kinsmen, who alone are entitled to take his place; and although it has sometimes led to widespread civil war, in most of the recorded instances it was confined to a fairly small group of men close to court. Other people generally choose to leave the tribe. Secession may occur at all levels and in varying proportions, from isolated individuals or families moving away surreptitiously to large groups openly accompanying a leader whom they prefer to the chief. Often enough it too has led to fighting, since the chief may try to stop the fugitives or to force their return; nevertheless almost every Hottentot or Bantu tribe whose history is adequately known seems to have lost members in this way, sometimes more than once.

It should again be emphasized that such methods of reaction to a bad chief never aim at changing the governmental system itself. A chief who is killed or expelled is always replaced by a close agnate; a group that secedes either joins another tribe or, if large enough to prefer independence, reproduces the old system by accepting its leader as chief. Nor, so far as one can tell, have either Bantu or Hottentots ever consciously sought to curtail the recognized powers of the chieftainship; and since there have also been very many good chiefs, of whom their people still speak with pride and affection, misrule is evidently not inherent in the system but results mainly from the personal characteristics of the ruler himself.

Revolt or secession are not always due to the chief's conduct alone. They are also the means by which ambitious or dissatisfied relatives try to usurp his position or to establish tribes of their own. Among Bantu dynastic quarrels are so common that certain institutional devices are employed to inhibit them or to protect the chief from the intrigues of his rivals. Among Hottentots, the evidence suggests, struggles for the chieftainship are relatively rare though by no means unknown, and apparently no special measures are taken to guard against them. One reason may be that since the chief's powers and privileges are much smaller than among the Bantu they are not so conspicuously enviable. I have suggested also that the household organization of the Bantu, where succession and inheritance are governed by an elaborate system of ranking wives, almost inevitably creates domestic rivalries and quarrels, and that the associated practice of giving personal retainers to every senior prince enables him to compete for the chieftainship by providing him with a ready-made nucleus of support. There is nothing to indicate that similar conflicts ever occur among Bergdama or Bushmen; this may be due partly, especially among Bergdama, to the chief's being the patriarch of his band, but the relatively slight material benefit derivable from taking his place probably also helps to account for their apparent absence.

Two features about attacks on Bantu chiefs need special notice. The one, already mentioned, is that such attacks are often confined to men of the inner circle. The mass of the people, especially those of alien stock, need not be directly involved, and historical evidence shows that they have usually acquiesced without marked reluctance in forced changes of chief. The implication seems to be that who actually holds the chieftainship is mainly the concern of the ruling section, and especially of the nobility, and that so long as ordinary tribesmen do not suffer by a change they are seldom prepared to react to it violently. The other feature is that even in those divisions where the chief's ritual attributes are highly stressed, as among Venda, Swazi, and North-Eastern Sotho, he is never so sacred a person that he cannot be killed, expelled, or abandoned; and since both usurpers and seceding founders of new tribes immediately acquire the same attributes, we must conclude that his 'sacredness' is a function of his office, and not of himself individually. Taken in conjunction with what has already been said, both features show that what the people respect is not so much the chief in person as the position that he occupies; and although he as incumbent derives considerable authority from their attitude, he may on the other hand suffer should he fall short of what they expect him to be.

Among Bantu and Hottentots the tribe is both larger and more dispersed than the Bergdama or Bushman band. In governing it the chief is therefore helped by local authorities, of whom, in most Bantu tribes, there are usually two or more different grades. Like himself, such men must answer to their own subjects for their behaviour, and may also have to deal with ambitious rivals; problems similar to his thus occur, though on a smaller scale, within separate portions of the tribe, where too they sometimes lead to fission. Among Bantu, local authorities can normally look to their superiors for support and protection, but among Hottentots the chief formerly could not interfere in the internal affairs of their group. The two peoples differ also in another respect. Among Hottentots, before developments due to European influence, clan-heads had considerable autonomy, and tribal splits usually took the form of a clan's breaking away to become completely independent. Among Bantu all local authorities are definitely subject to the chief, and it is mainly through their obligation to carry out his commands that he is able to control the tribe as a whole. They are so numerous, especially in the larger tribes, that few have enough followers to become a serious menace to his authority. But he himself cannot afford to alienate them, since without their assistance he cannot easily secure the services of their people, and if he does not treat them satisfactorily they too are apt to secede or to support one of his rivals.

Another problem found only among Bantu and Hottentots is the relationship between the ruling section and its alien subjects. Bergdama and Bushman chiefs do not have such subjects; the members of their band are as a rule all closely related to them by birth or by marriage, and do not include any conquered or immigrant strangers. Among Bantu, policy in regard to alien subjects varies according to their mode of absorption, their organization and numbers, and their culture: they may be allowed to retain corporate existence under their own leaders, they may have someone of the ruling section placed directly over them, they may be separated and dispersed throughout the tribe, or, as among Western Tswana and Rhodesian Ndebele, they may be made into serfs. Among Hottentots, immigrants either remain separate groups under their own leaders or, if few in number, are admitted as dependants into one of the clans; conquered peoples or captives, of whom the great majority are Bergdama, are usually attached to private households as hereditary servants.

Both conquered peoples and immigrants very often remain part of a tribe once they have been overcome or admitted, and it is indeed because of this that most tribes are nowadays so heterogeneous in composition. But both may also break away again or try to break away. Among Bantu attempts by conquered peoples to regain their independence are always resisted, but many succeed in fleeing elsewhere. Immigrants, on the other hand, are often allowed to depart peacefully; their reasons for wishing to leave are of various kinds, of which dissatisfaction with their treatment is not necessarily the most common or prominent. Among Hottentots, chiefs have sometimes had trouble with groups of immigrants, notably Orlams from the south; but conquered peoples, owing to their dispersion, are seldom able to unite for revolt or secession, though individuals sometimes run away from their masters.

I have stressed the incidence of secession among Bantu and Hottentots because it is an outstanding feature of their social systems. Tribes are often disrupted by conquest or invasion, but even in times of external peace they may be deserted by some of their members. The relative abundance of unoccupied or unclaimed land (in pre-European times), the possibility of subsisting *en route* not only upon live-stock but upon game and edible wild plants, and the readiness of chiefs to accept alien adherents, all facilitate movement and the creation of new tribes or transfer of allegiance from one to another.

Among Hottentots the process may be due partly to ecological conditions: the nomadic pastoral life of the people, and the aridity of the country they inhabit, make it difficult for very large groups to remain united for long, and such population figures as are available show that during the nineteenth century, for example, no tribe ever had more than about 2,500 members. Among Bantu there have also been instances of groups having to leave home owing to such natural causes as local drought. But the practice of agriculture, in addition to cattle-raising and hunting, normally permits much larger concentrations of population than are possible among Hottentots, especially as environmental conditions are on the whole far more favourable; there does not seem to' be what one might call an optimal size for the tribe, and indeed, as we have seen, even immediately adjoining tribes may vary markedly in size. The tendency for people to break away must accordingly be attributed mainly to factors inherent in the social system. There are several obvious lines of cleavage: splits may develop between a chief and his relatives, between him and his subjects generally, and between the ruling section and its alien dependants; and similar splits, sometimes leading to removal from the tribe, may likewise occur within component segments down to the smallest group. Social factors of such kinds also operate among Hottentots, where secession is by no means always due to population pressure alone.

We do not know how commonly Bergdama or Bushman bands are similarly disrupted. The very smallness of a band, the restriction of membership to near relatives, and the danger of entering other people's territory, all suggest that secession is likely to be rare. Nevertheless people do sometimes join other bands, especially at marriage. The mere fact that all bands are so very small suggests also that there is a limit beyond which they cannot expand, and for Bergdama we are explicitly told that when a band becomes too large for the area it occupies some of the people move away and establish a band of their own. We may therefore conclude that here too fission does occur, but mainly, though not exclusively, because of economic factors.

In view of the marked proclivity for social disruption among Bantu and Hottentots, as indicated by occasional civil wars and frequent secession, we have to ask how it is that tribes maintain any cohesion at all. Among Bantu there are many factors that serve to counteract fissiparous tendencies. From childhood upwards people learn to regard the chief with loyalty and devotion and to appreciate the work that he does for them, by means of his wealth and other systems of reward he can bind them more closely to himself, he administers the component sections of the tribe through a graded series of local rulers some of whom he appoints and all of whom are unmistakably subordinate to him, and he can use force if required to punish disaffection; through age-regiments, attachment to royal villages, and similar devices, people are also combined into units whose membership cuts across regional and kinship ties; and most of them, presumably, would prefer to remain peacefully settled where they are instead of being obliged to move away. Normally such factors are more than sufficient to keep them in the tribe, provided always that they are not alienated by the conduct of their rulers. Among Hottentots the chief has far less emotional appeal for his people, and owing to their nomadic way of life and the consequently greater autonomy of local groups he cannot control them as effectively as does his Bantu counterpart. The historical evidence for the pre-colonial period suggests that only in times of war are the members of a tribe at all disciplined, and that when not forced to unite for defence or aggression they show little regard for the authority of any ruler but the immediate head of their own clan. Hottentot tribes are therefore not nearly as well integrated as those of the Bantu, and because of the essentially federal nature of their government are more prone to break apart.

But if tribes lose by secession, they often also gain by conquest and immigration. Expansion by conquest is a feature more characteristic of Bantu than Hottentots. The very large states founded during the nineteenth century by such men as Mzilikazi (Ndebele), Soshangane (Shangana), Mswati (Swazi), Moshesh (Southern Sotho), and Sekwati (Pedi), were all due ultimately to the far-reaching repercussions of Shaka's campaigns in Zululand and Natal; but even before his time many tribes in other divisions, for example Tswana, Northern Sotho, and Venda, had grown by defeating their neighbours, or by seeking new homes and forcibly absorbing the local inhabitants. Among Hottentots the main form of warlike expansion has been the invasion and subjugation of areas occupied by Bergdama and Bushmen. Immigration has among both Bantu and Hottentots been the more persistent and widespread method of gaining new members, and it may be recalled in the present context that in choosing which tribe to join fugitives and secessionaries are often influenced largely by the reputation of its chief.

The general impression left by a study of Bantu tribal histories is that very few tribes have maintained a career of uninterrupted expansion. Apart from whatever disruption may have been due to external causes, the fortunes of any tribe have usually fluctuated according to the momentary state of its chieftainship. Under a good and strong ruler, at peace with his relatives, it gains new members by immigration and possibly also conquest; under a bad chief, or when members of the royal family are at variance, it loses members who either join other tribes or become independent. The two processes are thus complementary, and both have occurred repeatedly in many tribes. But the evidence suggests that on the whole fission is the more common of the two. Not only do people move from one tribe to another, but new tribes are continuously being created because of dynastic disputes; and although some may afterwards disappear through conquest, the dominant feature of Bantu political history has been the multiplication of tribes—and every new tribe means that another has divided. We must accordingly conclude that, in spite of the countervailing tendencies of conquest and immigration, the Bantu tribe is basically an unstable unit; and the most frequent causes of its breaking apart are the behaviour of the chief and the ambitions of his near kin. The same feature is characteristic of Hottentots, but here segmentation is perhaps due more to the dictates of their pastoral economy than to social disturbances.

VI

Forms of Tribal Government

I

Having reviewed the main aspects of tribal government in South Africa, we can now summarize the conclusions reached and make a final comparison of the systems described. I started with the assumption that in any comparative study of the kind here attempted the first essential is to identify the units to be discussed. Whatever may be the case elsewhere in primitive society—we are told, for example, that the Logoli of Kenya and the Tallensi of the Gold Coast 'have no clear spatially-defined political units'[1]—the problem is easy to solve for South Africa. The four peoples with whom we have been concerned are all divided into separate 'political communities', each claiming exclusive rights to a given territory and managing its affairs independently of external control. The members of a 'political community' (I use the term for want of something more suitable) share certain other rights and duties that do not extend to outsiders, and they all cooperate in certain activities. But that can also be said of such local segments as Hottentot clans or Bantu villages; hence I regard as the distinctive criterion of the community the fact that, unlike any of its subdivisions, it is not subject to the overriding authority of someone outside its own geographical boundaries.

Our data showed that in regard to size and residential patterns we must distinguish two major types of community. In the one, characteristic of Bergdama and Bushmen, the community is always very small and compact; it seldom has as many as a hundred members and often much fewer, especially among Bergdama, and they all live together in a single group either continuously or for the greater part of each year. In the other, found among Bantu

[1] Fortes and Evans-Pritchard (eds.), *African Political Systems* (1940), p. 6.

and Hottentots, the community is much larger and its population usually scattered. But it varies greatly in detail. Among Hotten-it has from 500 to 2,500 members, distributed over their territory in local groups of not more than 200–300 people each. (This refers to the traditional system, now replaced under European influence by a central village where most of the people have their homes.) Among Bantu some communities are no bigger than those of the Hottentots, but others have 100,000 members or more, and the majority lie in between. In addition, there are three main forms of local grouping: the isolated household (Nguni and Tsonga); the compact village embracing a number of different households (Venda and most Sotho); and the metropolitan type (Tswana and some Northern Sotho), where the capital (divided into 'wards') is always much larger than any of the other villages and sometimes contains more than half the total population.

Some of these differences can be related to differences in mode of subsistence and environmental conditions. Bergdama and Bush-men, as hunters and collectors, are obliged to live in small groups; Bushmen, indeed, practise both infanticide and abandonment of feeble old people because there is not always enough food for all. Hottentots as pastoralists and hunters have a more regular and de-pendable food supply, but owing to the grazing and water needs of their domestic animals they too cannot associate together con-stantly in large numbers. All three peoples, moreover, are neces-sarily nomadic, and since the regions that they inhabit are on the whole arid each community requires a relatively large territory for subsistence purposes. It is probably because of this that even Hottentot communities seem unable to expand beyond a certain limit without breaking apart. Bantu on the other hand not only keep cattle and hunt, but also grow crops of various kinds; in ad-dition, almost all of them live in comparatively fertile country. They are consequently both sedentary and more densely settled than any of the other peoples. Moreover, as shown by the varia-tions that they display, they are less rigorously affected by physical environment: owing to their superior resources and more ad-vanced techniques of food production, they are not restricted to communities of a given size or to any particular pattern of local grouping.

South African communities differ also in social composition. Here again we must distinguish two major types: kin-based (Bergdama and Bushmen), and heterogeneous (Bantu and Hottentots). In the former, membership is determined primarily by kinship ties, and (with but rare exceptions among Bergdama) everybody in the community is closely related to everybody else; in addition, there is uniformity of both language and custom. In the latter, membership may be acquired not only by descent but also by voluntary accession (e.g. immigration) or by means of force (e.g. conquest); hence the population, far from being a single body of kin, usually comprises several or even many separate stocks, sometimes differing in customs, language, and perhaps also race. Associated with this is a well-defined system of social classes. Hottentots distinguish between 'citizens', i.e. people of true Hottentot stock, and 'servants', who are mostly of Bergdama or other alien origin. Among Bantu three classes are usually recognized: 'nobles', who are of the same descent group as the chief; 'commoners', people of alien stocks long established in the community; and 'foreigners', people of alien stocks more recently absorbed by conquest or immigration.

It is thus obviously incorrect to say, as some sociologists still do, that political unity in primitive societies is always based solely on kinship ties. Even among Bergdama and Bushmen membership of the community is determined not by kinship as such, but by kinship of a certain kind, since owing to the rule of local exogamy a person's maternal relatives and affines will usually belong to groups other than his own. Nevertheless, kinship does feature far more prominently in the political systems of even our heterogeneous communities than it does in modern Western states. Among Hottentots, for example, the core of each local group is a patrilineal clan, and among Bantu the smaller local units are often also each composed of one or more well-defined bodies of agnatic kin; among Hottentots a person's nearest relatives formerly had to avenge his murder, and among Bantu they normally share responsibility for his wrongdoing (a principle that ensures payment of compensation or fines, and enables disputes to be settled by direct negotiation between the kin groups involved); among both peoples, too, political office is most often hereditary, and an office-bearer's brothers and uncles are his acknowledged advisers and assistants.

In South Africa differences in the social composition of the community coincide with differences in mode of subsistence: kin-based communities are characteristic of the food-gathering Bergdama and Bushmen, and heterogeneous communities of the food-producing Bantu and Hottentots. Comparison with primitive peoples elsewhere suggests that the coincidence is partly fortuitous; for example, the Andaman Islanders are also food-gatherers, but their communities are not composed exclusively of kin, and on the other hand kin-based communities are found among such cultivating peoples as the Hopi of Arizona and the Polynesians of Tikopia, though always much smaller in size than is usual among the Bantu. However, mode of subsistence does have some bearing on the situation. Bantu and Hottentot communities have expanded not only by natural increase of population, but also by the absorption of aliens; among Bantu, in fact, some communities that were at first fairly small have grown very considerably through both conquest and immigration. This has been possible only because of their comparatively superior economy. Bergdama and Bushman communities, owing to the precarious nature of their food supply, are far less able to enlarge and thus diversify their membership; absorption of aliens by conquest is virtually unknown, and immigration is in effect confined to residential changes at marriage. Normally, therefore, our food-gathering peoples will tend to retain their original kinship basis, whereas among food-producers the more a community expands by conquest or immigration the more mixed is its population likely to become. And where, as in Bechuanaland and the Transvaal, neighbouring peoples often differ in language and customs, an incidental further effect of expansion will be to increase cultural differentiation in the community.

It may be noted in this context that the view held by many sociologists about the origin of the class state is not wholly valid for South Africa. The class system found for example among Bantu is not always due to conquest, or to conquest alone, but has been shaped by such other factors as descent, local antiquity, and ethnic origins: the chief and his agnates constitute the nobility in every known community and not merely in those with a record of conquest, commoners often include people whose ancestors were conquered long ago, and on the other hand relatively recent immigrants always rank as foreigners and are denied certain rights shared by the two other classes. It is apparently only when incorporated peoples differ appreciably from those of the nuclear stock in language and culture, and above all race, that they are relegated to a position of marked social inferiority and economic exploitation. This may be seen in the different types of class structure found respectively among the Zulu and their offshoot the Rhodesian Ndebele, in the status of immigrant Tsonga among Venda and Swazi, and in the contrast between Western Tswana with their Bushman and other serfs and the Eastern Tswana who do not have such a class.

Expansion is by no means characteristic of all Bantu or Hottentot communities. Aliens absorbed by one community necessarily come from another; hence communities may also diminish in size, or through conquest by others may even disappear as separate entities. Moreover, communities are often deserted by sections seeking to become independent. The continuous emergence of new communities by secession has indeed been a dominant feature of political history in South Africa. Among Hottentots it seems to be due mainly to economic necessity resulting from pressure upon water-holes and pasture lands. Bergdama communities (information is not available for Bushmen) apparently also break apart when local food resources become inadequate. But among Bantu the primary cause is civil conflict, especially disputes about the chieftainship; these have occurred so widely and so repeatedly that fission must be regarded as a process made almost inevitable by the nature of the social system.

II

Whatever its size and social composition, there are in every South African community one or more persons whose recognized and regular duty it is to attend to the conduct of public affairs. Although such persons differ greatly from one people to another in powers and functions, they are everywhere the acknowledged officers of their community. It seems justifiable therefore to speak of them as its 'government', even if sometimes they have little in common with what is generally understood by the term when used in regard to more complex systems.

All South African forms of government share certain basic features that are by no means universally characteristic of primitive society. Every community, for example, has one official head (or 'chief'), and among Bantu and Hottentots, where communities are divided into local segments, every segment also has its own head. Throughout South Africa, therefore, government is based upon the principle of individual captaincy for every group. This contrasts markedly with some other primitive societies, which may have no official leaders at all (e.g. Andaman Islanders), a governing council of all fully initiated elders (as in parts of Australia and East Africa), a dual chieftainship (as in parts of Melanesia, where there is one leader for ritual and another for secular activities), or a federal council of 'fifty civil chiefs or lords, hereditary in certain maternal families, but elective in the limits of these families'[1] (Iroquois of North America).

Everywhere in South Africa, moreover, the chief is always in charge of all governmental activities (such as they are). Even if, as among Hottentots, he is merely *primus inter pares* in a council, it is still he who summons and presides over meetings and issues whatever instructions are needed; and even if, as among Bantu, he has special assistants for certain tasks, he nevertheless controls the whole apparatus of government and is usually himself supreme

[1] A. A. Goldenweiser, in *History of Political Theories: Recent Times* (ed. Merriam and Barnes, 1924), p. 450.

judge, military commander, economic director, and archpriest of his community. The head of every local segment has similar jurisdiction over his own group. This form of comprehensive personal rule, in which there is no 'separation of powers', is one of the reasons why seceding groups do not have to create special administrative machinery, and why conquered or immigrant groups can easily be absorbed by allowing their own leaders to continue directing internal affairs.

Chieftainship itself is everywhere hereditary in the senior line of descent from the founder (and first chief) of the community. Rules of succession vary considerably in detail, but with the dubious exception of certain Bushmen the office normally passes from father to son (or failing that to a brother), and once acquired is tenable for life. Formerly the heads of Hottentot local groups (who jointly constituted the tribal council) also inherited their posts. Among Bantu, local rulers and other dignitaries are sometimes appointed by the chief, but unless he intervenes they are automatically succeeded by their sons. Nowhere (except perhaps nowadays among Hottentots) are government officials habitually chosen by the people, though an unsuitable heir may be rejected in favour of a more acceptable brother. The hereditary principle also operates in another way: if any office-bearer (from the chief downwards) is ill or absent from home, or if he dies leaving an heir too young to rule, a senior relative acts in his place; in any event his nearest agnates always help him in his work and share in the benefits that accrue to him. Political office is thus the vested interest of a family group rather than the monopoly of an individual. It is because of this that succession disputes and attempts at usurpation are possible, since unless people have some sort of hereditary claim to an office they can hardly hope to secure widespread recognition and support.

Throughout South Africa there is usually also close personal contact between rulers and subjects in social life generally. That after all is what one would expect among Bergdama and Bushmen, where the chief always lives together with the other members of his very small community, all of whom are in any case also his near relatives and sometimes, as among Bergdama, his actual descendants. Hottentot clan-heads, and the heads of the smaller local groups among Bantu, are likewise in direct and continuous touch with all their adherents, with many of whom they too have kinship ties. Such regular intercourse with all his subjects is seldom possible among Bantu for the sub-chief of a large segment, especially if the group is widely dispersed, and still less for the chief, especially if the community is very large. Even here, however, he often meets many of them at feasts and on other social occasions, and he is expected also to be personally accessible to anybody wishing to speak with him. In consequence, rulers and subjects (especially at the local level) tend to know one another much more intimately, and to associate together far more extensively, than is customary in modern Western societies. This means that every ruler is constantly exposed to the influence of public opinion, and that he will be judged not merely by what he does in his official capacity.

In addition, South African forms of government all provide for special consultation between rulers and subjects. Among Bergdama and Bushmen this entails no separate organization, since all the men in a community foregather daily round the camp fire, and as the need arises the chief and others discuss what should be done. Among Bantu and Hottentots similar gatherings can be arranged fairly easily in the smaller local groups, where accordingly they feature prominently in public life. In other groups, and especially the whole community, it is obviously more difficult to get all or even most of the men together without much notice in advance, except where the people live in large compact settlements. Hence it is only among Sotho, and notably Tswana, that popular assemblies at the national level are held fairly often. Elsewhere they are summoned only for matters of critical importance (as in traditional Hottentot society), or tend to be restricted to great ceremonial occasions such as the annual first-fruits festival (Nguni). But among all Bantu, as among Hottentots, the chief has a formal council that includes the heads of all local groups; these men are the representatives of their followers, and through them the views of the whole community can be expressed. Among Bantu, more-over, any man can participate in the hearing of court cases and by his comments help to influence the verdict. Whatever the details, the essential point is that rulers everywhere are expected to ascertain public opinion before deciding matters of serious concern.

The extent to which a ruler can afford to ignore the views of his subjects will obviously depend in part upon the power at his command, and especially upon his control of armed force. But no-where, even among Bantu, is he always able to do just as he likes. He has to conform to well-known standards of conduct, and should he behave in a manner that gives offence there are various effective means of dealing with him, such as revolt or secession. As the proverb says, 'A chief is chief by grace of his people', and rarely has any chief been able to rule oppressively for long. If not democratic in the sense of being able to elect their rulers, South African communities can at least often restrain them and if sufficiently provoked get rid of them.

III

Despite the broad similarities just mentioned, South African governments are by no means alike in all respects. Initially we may distinguish two major forms. These coincide with the two major types of community already identified. Among Bergdama and Bushmen the chief is the only public officer. He is essentially a leader and not a ruler, and his primary function is to organize and direct such cooperative activities as hunting, moving camp, warfare, and trade with other communities. He has no legislative or judicial functions, and can neither compel personal obedience nor punish wrongdoers. We may accordingly, borrowing Lowie's term, designate this form of government 'titular chieftainship'.[1] Among Bantu and Hottentots the chief governs with the aid of

[1] 'By this I mean a condition with differentiation of one or more individuals as headmen, even though their actual power is circumscribed or even negligible.' ('Political Organization among the American Aborigines', *J. R. Anthrop. Inst.*, vol. 78 (1948), p. 14.)

special local authorities and other officers, all of whom have duties and powers that distinguish them from ordinary members of the community; they can use physical force to compel obedience to their commands and decisions; and their functions include the regular administration of justice in formal courts, occasional legislation, the conduct of warfare and other dealings with foreign communities, control of immigration, and the organization of various public enterprises. Here therefore we have what Lowie calls 'strong chieftainship', though for reasons that will soon appear I prefer to use other terms.

Within each major type we can distinguish certain varieties. The Bergdama chief is head of a patriarchal extended family, his functions always include certain ritual duties (in performing which he has a special assistant), and because of his age and position he exercises much influence in social life and enjoys various personal privileges. Heikum and Kung have a somewhat similar system. Among other Bushmen the chief is not necessarily patriarch of his community, he lacks ritual functions, and his office secures for him no particular influence or privilege.

Bantu and Hottentot systems differ more appreciably. In the traditional Hottentot system, matters affecting the whole community, such as warfare and inter-clan disputes, were dealt with by a council of all the clan-heads, the senior in hereditary status presiding as chief; but the head of each clan managed the internal affairs of his own group, and there was no appeal to the council from his judicial and other decisions. Now that most of the people live in one village, clans have far less autonomy (for example in the administration of justice), and any outlying settlements are under appointed headmen subject to the tribal council. The council itself has altered in composition; all members except the chief are specially chosen, and do not hold office by right of birth alone, and some of them also have separate executive or judicial functions. The agents of government usually also include some minor officials such as court messengers. Popular assemblies are as before confined to men of the citizen class, servants having no say at all in public life.

The Bantu system is much more complex. The chief heads a well-defined hierarchy of administrative officers including sub-chiefs of major segments and subordinate headmen of smaller units, both he and local rulers have special advisory and executive assistants of various kinds, and in most divisions there is a separate military and labour organization based on formal age-sets. Political office is often hereditary, but may be acquired by appointment through favour or personal merit. All major posts in the central government are with rare exceptions confined to nobles and commoners, but local rulers usually include men of every class, and popular assemblies are open to all (except serfs among Western Tswana). The government also has a far wider range of functions than among Hottentots: for example, it controls the allocation and use of land for residence, cultivation, and grazing; regulates the annual cycle of agricultural activity; levies tribute (in livestock, hunting spoils, crops, and other forms of produce); and organizes elaborate public rites (such as rainmaking, eating the first-fruits, and charming the army) for the welfare and protection of the community. The chief himself, and within his own group every local ruler, prays and sacrifices to the spirits of his ancestors on behalf of his subjects collectively. He also uses his wealth (including the tribute that he receives) to reward his assistants, entertain visitors, feed people at public gatherings, and help those in need.

The two peoples differ also in the personal status of the chief. Among Bantu he has far-reaching powers and can act on his own initiative in many matters. His authority is reinforced by such factors as the symbolic importance of his office, his mystical attributes, his use of wealth, and his command of patronage. He enjoys certain unique prerogatives in social and ritual life, his household is by far the largest and wealthiest in the community, his subjects treat him with marked deference and formal etiquette, his installation and death are signalized by great national ceremonies, and offences against him or other members of his family are punished with unusual severity. The Hottentot chief also has special protection in law, and like his Bantu counterpart only he can authorize the death penalty; but he is not particularly honoured in any other way, he has virtually no sanctions for his authority apart from command of force, and he cannot act independently of his council (in which, as already mentioned, he is merely *primus inter pares*). In view of these distinctions, and the others noted above, we may term the Bantu form of government 'paramount chieftainship', and the Hottentot form 'presidial chieftainship'.

Bantu themselves vary sufficiently in some respects to permit of our recognizing sub-types. Venda, North-Eastern Sotho, and Swazi stand apart from the rest in laying special stress on the sacred character of the chieftainship, and in using women either as rulers in their own right or as constitutional advisers of office-bearing male relatives. Among Cape Nguni and Southern Sotho the chief has comparatively little ritual significance; it is also in these two divisions alone that the army is based not on age-sets but on territorial segments. Other localized features include the maintenance of military villages or garrisons (Zulu, Swazi, and Ndebele), the outstanding importance of national assemblies in public life (Sotho, notably Tswana), the existence of a distinct servile class (Western Tswana and Ndebele), and the formalized opposition of nobles and commoners (certain Cape Nguni and Tswana).

We can readily relate some of the differences in form of government to differences in social structure and economic pursuits. For example, since Bergdama and Bushman communities have no territorial segments, they do not require special machinery for the administration of dependent local groups; as obviously it is only where age-sets exist that they can be used for military purposes, and only among Bantu (since none of our other peoples grow crops) that the government's functions can include control of arable land and regulation of agricultural activities. I have also previously suggested that organized judicial institutions are more likely to be found in the large heterogeneous communities of Bantu and Hottentots than in the very small kin-based communities of Bergdama and Bushmen; that the chief's powers and privileges are greatest among Bantu because there his duties are most numerous and varied; and that his role in ritual life necessarily depends upon the nature of the religious system generally. The clan autonomy formerly characteristic of Hottentots can be related to their nomadic life and to the wide separation of local groups; and the rule that members of the same clan should always live together helps to explain why clan-heads were the only local authorities. Among Bantu, in contrast, fixed homes and relatively dense settlement facilitate more intensive control from the centre, and with the scattering and intermingling of descent groups owing to warfare and migrations it has also been possible for the chief to send his own relatives and other nominees to administer different parts of his territory.

So, too, the major role of national assemblies among Tswana is obviously connected with the existence of large settlements, which makes it easy to call people together speedily and frequently. That is probably also one reason why Tswana do not need to maintain special military barracks, which among Zulu must have been developed partly in order to overcome the difficulty of mobilizing people normally resident in widely-scattered household groups. Hunter, incidentally, suggests that Zulu and Swazi differed in military organization from such Cape Nguni peoples as Mpondo and Mpondomise because they waged a different kind of warfare. They were, she says, aggressive peoples, and therefore used age-regiments as most efficient for the purpose; the others, however, fought mainly on the defensive, and therefore relied upon 'territorial regiments' (local divisions), which in case of sudden attack could be more quickly on the spot.[1] This explanation is hardly appropriate for say Venda and Tswana, who although not nearly as aggressive as the Zulu likewise fought in age-regiments; and, on the other hand, Cape Nguni peoples despite their military system often also took the initiative in attacking others. It is true that Zulu, Swazi, and Ndebele were more deliberately expansionist and predatory than most other divisions of Southern Bantu; but their military organization was distinguished less by the use of age-regiments than by the maintenance of standing armies, and

[1] Hunter (1949), p. 12.

that was dictated not by their policies alone but also by their settlement patterns.

Eisenstadt, similarly, has tried to correlate the presence or absence of age-sets with differences in the administrative system. Among such peoples as the Zulu, Swazi, and Tswana, he says, 'there exists a non-kinship organization of the political life of the chiefdom', whereas among others, such as Xhosa, Mpondo, and Southern Sotho, 'most of the political, ritual, etc. positions are vested in lineages, clans, or local descent groups. Among the first group we find highly organized age groups (regiments), while among the second no such groups are found. It is important to note that those functions—mainly military—which are fulfilled in the first group of tribes by the universal age-regiments, are organized in the second on a territorial-kinship basis; various contingents are organized according to loyalty [sic; locality?] and owe loyalty to their local kin-chief.'[1] The facts do not justify the conclusion that in communities having age-sets kinship is less important than elsewhere in the political organization. Among Zulu, Swazi, and Tswana, as among all other South African Bantu, most local rulers, many indunas, and certain ritual officers (such as 'tribal doctors'), hold office primarily because they belong to particular 'lineages, clans, or local descent groups'; among Tswana age-sets are internally segmented on a local basis, and the head of every segment, like the head of the whole set, owes his position solely to being senior by right of birth to all his followers; and among Cape Nguni (including Xhosa and Mpondo) and Southern Sotho, again as among all other Bantu, chiefs and even sub-chiefs sometimes appoint their own relatives or favourites to govern areas inhabited predominantly by members of other kin groups.

As shown by the examples just given, one can push correlations too far, especially when the comparative basis is not comprehensive enough. In some instances, at least, variations are the product of unique local events. We know for example that the Zulu military system was developed mainly by Shaka, and occurs among the Ndebele because they once formed part of his

[1] S. N. Eisenstadt, 'African Age Groups', *Africa*, vol. xxiv (1954), pp. 105, 106.

kingdom; that female chieftainship originated among the Lobedu, was retained by some seceding groups, and also spread to neighbouring tribes of kindred stock; that the Southern Sotho had formal age-sets as recently as the middle of last century, though (in marked contrast with Tswana and Northern Sotho) almost all trace of them has now disappeared; and that Western Tswana have serfs because, unlike Eastern Tswana, they migrated to regions where they found Bushmen and other peoples of inferior culture whom they could readily exploit. Certainly such variations could not have occurred unless social and economic conditions generally had favoured their development; but the very fact that they are so localized suggests that to explain them we must allow also for the influence of individual personalities and historical accident.

IV

Our data prompt several comments of a more general nature. They show that in primitive societies the functions of government may well be what MacIver terms 'minimal', but may on the other hand also be very comprehensive indeed and include some, such as priesthood, that are not nowadays usually characteristic of more advanced systems. They show also that apart from maintaining territorial boundaries and resisting external agression the only function common to all forms of government is the organization and direction of cooperative enterprises often involving the whole community. The enforcement of law and order—what MacIver calls 'the police function and the administration of justice'—is not, as he maintains, one of the functions 'that all governments always fulfill, on whatever scale'.[1] Communities such as those of the Bergdama and Bushmen are able to lead an orderly existence despite their lack of courts and despite the inability of their chiefs to punish offenders in other ways.

It therefore seems inappropriate to say, as Radcliffe-Brown does, that 'The political organization of a society is that aspect of

[1] R. M. MacIver, *The Web of Government* (1947), pp. 156, 316.

the total organization which is concerned with the control and regulation of the use of physical force.'[1] The presence or absence of coercive institutions, and their nature where they exist, may be useful as a basis for classifying types of polity. But organized force is only one of the mechanisms making for orderly life in any community, and to adopt it as the distinctive criterion of political organization would mean neglecting unduly the various others that help to unite people into self-governing groups. It is more useful, I think, to base our definition on function and not on means, and to regard political organization as 'that aspect of the total organization which is concerned with the establishment and maintenance of internal cooperation and external independence.' Cooperation necessarily implies some form of social control, some system of regulating relations between members of the community. As among Bergdama and Bushmen, however, violation of accepted norms may be dealt with solely or largely by institutions such as self-help, which although publicly approved are exercised at the discretion, and according to the ability, of the persons injured. The basic, indeed almost the only, tasks of the official authorities here are organization and leadership: but it is these that serve above all, as they do everywhere else, to coordinate people's activities and to bind together the members of the community.

Independence of external control and cooperation in domestic affairs are the essential characteristics of the community. In studying political organization we therefore have to study more than merely 'the maintenance or establishment of social order, within a territorial framework, by the organized exercise of coercive authority through the use, or the possibility of use, of physical force.'[2] We have to study, in fact, the whole system of communal leadership and all the functions (as well as the powers) of the leaders; and in this context such activities as the organization of religious ceremonies or collective hunts, or the concentration and

[1] Preface to *African Political Systems* (ed. Fortes and Evans-Pritchard, 1940), p. xxiii.
[2] Radcliffe-Brown, *op. cit.*, p. xiv.

redistribution of wealth, are as relevant as the administration of justice and similarly significant for comparative purposes.

Our data suggest also that there is a broad correlation between the political system and mode of subsistence. This does not imply that economic factors necessarily determine the precise form of a government. As we have seen, chieftainship among Heikum and Kung differs in certain respects from chieftainship among other Bushmen, and among Bantu there are striking local variations in such features as rules of succession, the sacredness of the chief, and the recognition of female authorities; these almost certainly are associated with specific socio-historical conditions, and not with differences in material progress generally. But increased efficiency in methods of food production does seem to render possible certain developments that otherwise could not occur. In South Africa, judging by the contrast between Bushman hunters and collectors and Bantu cultivators and pastoralists, the following are some of the apparent trends.

(a). The community tends to become much larger and more heterogeneous in composition, and ceases to be a simple face-to-face group. Kinship recedes in importance as the basis of political attachment, and outsiders can become members of a community through such non-hereditary processes as immigration and conquest. With increased diversity of population we tend also to get distinct social classes, in which the chief and his descent group constitute a dominant aristocracy.

(b). The functions of the government become more numerous and varied. Instead of being confined to the organization and direction of cooperative enterprises they come to include, for example, the administration of justice, the institution and control of private rights in land, and the beginnings of systematic taxation (in the form of compulsory tribute) for the upkeep of public services. Warfare ceases to consist mainly of sporadic inter-communal fights arising out of trespass and homicide, and is often undertaken either for plunder (e.g. cattle-lifting raids) or as a deliberate instrument of expansionist policy (e.g. conquest of territory and subjugation of other communities).

(c). The government itself becomes more complex and specialized. Instead of a chief who is the only political officer, we get a hierarchy of regional authorities subject to a paramount authority, formal advisory councils of limited membership, regular courts of law, and a separate organization for warfare and communal labour. Central and local rulers are helped by a special staff, whose members sometimes differ in function. Political office is no longer exclusively hereditary, but may also be acquired by formal appointment; this provides opportunity for promotion through personal merit or faithful service, and at the same time strengthens the chief's control over his subordinates.

(d). With increasing range of activity and complexity of organization, the government becomes more powerful and privileged. From having no command of force at all, it acquires the right and the means to deprive people of property and to inflict corporal punishment or even death; and from being treated with bare respect the chief comes to be a very exalted personage with many unique and outstanding prerogatives. But increased power is always checked and balanced by increased responsibility: the more powerful a government becomes, the more numerous and elaborate are the devices by means of which subjects can protect themselves against misrule and oppression.

(e). As the powers and privileges of the government increase, struggles for their control or for access to the perquisites of office tend to become more common and vehement. Where little is to be gained by being chief, there is seldom if ever competition for the office; but where it carries great material advantage and prestige, disputes about succession and conspiracies against an incumbent often occur. In heterogeneous communities where the central government is dominated by a hereditary aristocracy, there are likely also to be revolts by subject groups resenting ill-treatment or economic exploitation. Civil wars aiming at change of ruler, or attempts to break away and become independent, are accordingly characteristic features of the political system. To counteract such disruptive tendencies, special techniques of control may develop that are not needed in the simpler communities.

(f). The fundamental condition for developments such as those listed seems to be the growth of the community beyond the stage at which it consists of a few closely related families living together in a single settlement. It is only in large, heterogeneous, and scattered communities that government tends to become an institution with specialized personnel and distinctive powers; and the existence of such communities is possible only where people do not depend for their livelihood solely upon the natural resources of their environment.

LIST OF MAIN SOURCES

This list includes all publications on South African peoples cited in the foot-notes, and various others that contain useful information on the indigenous political systems.

Alexander, J. E.

> 1838. *An Expedition of Discovery into the Interior of Africa*. 2 vols. London. [Hottentots]

Ashton, E. H.

> 1937. Notes on the political and judicial organization of the Tawana. *Bantu Studies*, 11: 67–83.

> 1938. Political organisation of the Southern Sotho. *Bantu Studies*, 12: 287–320.

> 1952. *The Basuto*. London.

Beemer, Hilda, *see* Kuper.

Bennie, W. G.

> 1939. *The Ciskei and Southern Transkei Tribes (Xhosa and Thembu)*. (Reproductions of photographic studies by A. M. Duggan-Cronin, vol. III, sect. I.) Cambridge.

Bleek, Dorothea F.

> 1928.a. *The Naron: a Bushman Tribe of the Central Kalahari*. Cambridge.
> 1928.b. Bushmen of Central Angola. *Bantu Studies*, 3: 105–25.

Breutz, P. L.

> 1941. *Die politischen und gesellschaftlichen Verhältnisse der Sotho-Tswana*. Hamburg.

> 1953.a. *The Tribes of Rustenburg and Pilansberg Districts*. Pretoria.

> 1953.b. *The Tribes of Marico District*. Pretoria.

Brownlee, F.

> 1923. *The Transkeian Native Territories: historical records*. Lovedale.

> 1943. The social organization of the Kung (!Un) Bushmen of the North-Western Kalahari. *Africa*, 14: 124–9.

Bryant, A. T.

> 1905. *A Zulu-English Dictionary*. Marianhill, Natal.

> 1929. *Olden Times in Zululand and Natal*. London.

> 1949. *The Zulu People*. Pietermaritzburg.

Callaway, H.

> 1870. *The Religious System of the Amazulu*. London.

Cape of Good Hope Government.
1883. *Report and proceedings . . . of the Commission on Native Laws and Customs*. (G.4.–1883). Cape Town.

Casalis, E.
1861. *The Basutos*. London.

Cook, P. A. W.
1931. *Social Organisation and Ceremonial Institutions of the Bomvana*. Cape Town.

Döhne, J. L.
1857. *A Zulu-Kafir Dictionary*. Cape Town.

Doke, C. M., and Vilakazi, B. W.
1953. *Zulu-English Dictionary*, 2nd. ed. Johannesburg.

Eiselen, W.
1932. Ueber die Häuptlingswürde bei den BaPedi. *Africa*, 5: 297–306.

Ellenberger, D. F.
1912. *History of the Basuto*. London.

Fourie, H. C. M.
1921. *Amandebele van Fene Mahlangu*. Zwolle.

Fourie, L.
1928. The Bushmen of South West Africa. *The Native Tribes of South West Africa* (Hahn *et al.*): 79–105. Cape Town.

François, H. von.
1896. *Nama und Damara*. Magdeburg.

Fynn, H. F.
1853. [Evidence on Zulu tribes and customs]. *Natal Government Commission . . . (on) the Kafirs, Proceedings*, Part V: 44–85.
1950. *The Diary of Henry Francis Fynn*. Pietermaritzburg.

Galton, F.
1853. *The Narrative of an Explorer in Tropical South Africa*. London. [Hottentots]

Gluckman, M.
1940.a. The kingdom of the Zulu. *African Political Systems* (ed. M. Fortes and E. E. Evans-Pritchard): 25–55. London.

1940.b. Analysis of a social situation in modern Zululand. *Bantu Studies*, 14: 1–30, 147–74.

1954.a. Political Institutions. *The Institutions of Primitive Society* (Evans-Pritchard *et al.*): 66–80. Oxford.

1954.b. *Rituals of Rebellion in South-East Africa.* (Frazer Lecture). Manchester.

Hahn, T.

1883. [Memorandum on Nama laws and customs]. *Report of Cape Government Commission on Native Laws and Customs* (G.4.–1883), Appendix C: 248–58. Cape Town.

Harries, C. H. L.

1929. *The Laws and Customs of the Bapedi and Cognate Tribes.* Johannesburg.

Hoernlé, Agnes W.

1925. The social organization of the Nama Hottentots. *Amer. Anthrop.*, 27: 1–24.

Hoffmann, C.

1934. Sotho-Texte . . . Rechtsgebräuche der Basutho. *Z. Eingeb. Spr.*, 24; 58–76, 122–50, 201–30, 282–303.

1938. Sotho-Texte . . . Politische Organisation. *Z. Eingeb. Spr.*, 28: 29–66, 123–38, 174–98.

Hughes, A. J. B., and van Velsen, J.

1955. *The Ndebele.* London. (International African Institute: Ethnographic Survey of . . . Southern Africa, Part IV.)

Hunt, D. R.

1931. An account of the Bapedi. *Bantu Studies*, 5: 275–326.

Hunter, Monica.

1936. *Reaction to Conquest.* London. [Mpondo]

1949. *The Mpondo and Mpondomise.* Cambridge. (Reproductions of photographic studies by A. M. Duggan-Cronin, vol. III, sect. II.)

Isaacs, N.

1836. *Travels and Adventures in Eastern Africa.* 2 vols. London. [Zulu]

Junod, H. A.

1927. *The Life of a South African Tribe.* 2nd. ed. 2 vols. London. [Tsonga]

Junod, H. P., and Jacques, A. A.

1936. *The Wisdom of the Tonga-Shangaan People.* Cleveland, Transvaal.

Kaufmann, H.
  1910. Die Auin: ein Beitrag zur Buschmannforschung. *Mitt. dtsch. Schutzgeb.*, 23: 135–60.
Krige, Eileen J.
  1936. *The Social System of the Zulus.* London.
  1937. Notes on the Phalaborwa. *Bantu Studies*, 11: 357–66.
  1938. The place of the North-Eastern Transvaal Sotho in the South Bantu complex. *Africa*, 11: 265–93.
Krige, Eileen J. and J. D.
  1943. *The Realm of a Rain-Queen.* London. [Lobedu]
Krige, J. D.
  1937. Traditional origins and tribal relationships of the Sotho of the Northern Transvaal. *Bantu Studies*, 11: 321–56.
Krige, J. D., and Eileen J.
  1954. The Lovedu of the Transvaal. *African Worlds* (ed. C. D. Forde): 55–82. London.
Kropf, A.
  1889. *Das Volk der Xosa-Kaffern.* Berlin.
Krüger, F.
  1935. Das Recht der Sotho-Chuana-Gruppe. *Mitt. Sem. Orient. Spr.* (Berlin), 38. iii: 53–144.
  1936.a. Ueberlieferungen der Letsoalo. *Mitt. Auslands-Hochschule* (Berlin), 39.iii: 176–227.
  1936.b. The Lovedu. *Bantu Studies*, 10: 89–105.
Kuper, Hilda.
  1937. The development of the military organisation in Swaziland. *Africa*, 10: 55–74, 176–205.
  1941. *The Swazi.* Cambridge. (Reproductions of photographic studies by A. M. Duggan-Cronin, vol. III, sect. IV.)
  1947. *An African Aristocracy.* London. [Swazi]
  1952. *The Swazi.* London. (International African Institute: Ethnographic Survey of . . . Southern Africa, Part I.)

Language, F. J.
  1943.a. *Stamregering by die Tlhaping.* Stellenbosch.
  1943.b. Die verkryging en verlies van lidmaatskap tot die stam by die Tlhaping. *African Studies*, 2: 77–92.
Lebzelter, V.
  1934. *Eingeborenenkulturen in Südwest- und Südafrika.* Leipzig.

Lestrade, G. P.

    1928. Some notes on the political organization of the BeChwana. *S. Afr. J. Sci.*, 25: 427–32.

    1930. Some notes on the political organization of the Venda-speaking tribes. *Africa*, 3: 306–22.

    1937. Some notes on the political organisation of certain Xhosa-speaking tribes. *Trans. roy. Soc. S. Afr.*, 24: 281–301.

Liengme, G.

    1901. Un potentat africain: Goungounyane et son règne. *Bull. Soc. neuchâtel. Géogr.*, 13: 99–135.

Mackenzie, J.

    1871. *Ten Years North of the Orange River*. Edinburgh.

MacLean, J. (ed.)

    1858. *Compendium of Kafir Laws and Customs*. Mount Coke.

Merensky, A.

    1890. *Erinnerungen aus dem Missionsleben in Transvaal*. Berlin. [Pedi]

Metzger, F.

    1950. *Narro and his Clan*. Windhoek. [Bushmen]

Moritz, E. (ed.)

    1915–18. Die ältesten Reiseberichte über Deutsch-Südwest-afrika. *Mitt. dtsch. Schutzgeb.*, 28: 161–268; 29: 135–253; 31: 17–143.

Myburgh, A. C.

    1949. *The Tribes of Barberton District*. Pretoria.

Nettelton, G. E.

    1934. History of the Ngamiland tribes. *Bantu Studies*, 8: 343–60.

Olpp, J.

    1896. Die rechtlichen und wirtschaftlichen Verhältnisse des Kowesi-Stammes im Gross-Namaland. *Mitt. Ges. vergl. Rechts-u. Staatswiss.* (Berlin), 1: 162–88.

Passarge, S.

    1907. *Die Buschmanner der Kalahari*. Berlin.

Ridsdale, B.

    1883. *Scenes and Adventures in Great Namaqualand*. London.

Schapera, I.

> 1930. *The Khoisan Peoples of South Africa: Bushmen and Hottentots*.London.
>
> 1938. *A Handbook of Tswana Law and Custom*. London.
>
> 1940. The political organization of the Ngwato. *African Political Systems* (ed. M. Fortes and E. E. Evans-Pritchard): 56–82. London.
>
> 1942.a. *A Short History of the BaKgatla-bagaKgaféla*. Cape Town.
>
> 1942.b. A short history of the BaNgwaketse. *African Studies*, 1: 1–26.
>
> 1943.a. *Native Land Tenure in the Bechuanaland Protectorate*. Lovedale.
>
> 1943.b. The work of tribal courts in the Bechuanaland Protectorate. *African Studies*, 2: 27–40.
>
> 1943.c. *Tribal Legislation among the Tswana*. London.
>
> 1947. *The Political Annals of a Tswana Tribe*. Cape Town.
>
> 1952. *The Ethnic Composition of Tswana Tribes*. London.
>
> 1953. *The Tswana*. London. (International African Institute: Ethnographic Survey of . . . Southern Africa, Part III.)

Schapera, I. (ed.)

> 1937. *The Bantu-Speaking Tribes of South Africa*. London.
>
> 1938. *Mekgwa le Melaô ya BaTswana*. Lovedale. [Vernacular texts on Tswana law and custom.]
>
> 1940. *Ditirafalô tsa Merafe ya BaTswana*. Lovedale. [Vernacular histories of Tswana tribes.]
>
> 1951. *Apprenticeship at Kuruman*. London. [Journals and letters of Robert and Mary Moffat.]

Schinz, H.

> 1891. *Deutsch-Südwest-Afrika*. Oldenburg and Leipzig.

Sheddick, V. G. J.

> 1953. *The Southern Sotho*. London. (International African Institute: Ethnographic Survey of . . . Southern Africa, Part II.)

Shepstone, T.

> 1883. [Evidence on Zulu laws and customs] *Report of Cape Government Commission on Native Laws and Customs* (G.4.–1883), Minutes of Evidence: 1–68. Cape Town.

Sillery, A.

> 1952. *The Bechuanaland Protectorate*. London.

Soga, J. H.

> 1930. *The South-Eastern Bantu*. Johannesburg. [Historical.]
>
> 1932. *The Ama-Xosa: Life and Customs*. Lovedale.

Stayt, H. A.

> 1931. *The BaVenda*. London.

Stuart, J.

   1913. *History of the Zulu Rebellion, 1906.* London. [Zulu military system]

Transvaal Native Affairs Department.

   1905. *Short History of the Native Tribes of the Transvaal.* Pretoria.

van Warmelo, N. J.

   1932. *Contributions towards Venda History, Religion, and Tribal Ritual.* Pretoria.

   1935. *A Preliminary Survey of the Bantu Tribes of South Africa.* Pretoria. [Tribes and their distribution]

   1937. *Tshivenda-English Dictionary.* Pretoria.

   1938. *History of Matiwane and the Amangwane Tribe.* Pretoia.

   1940. *The Copper Miners of Musina.* Pretoria.

   1944.a. *The Ba Letswalo or Banarene* [etc.].Pretoria.

   1944.b. *The Bakgatla ba ga Mosêtlha* [etc.].Pretoria.

   1951. *Notes on the Kaokoveld (South West Africa) and its people.* Pretoria.

   1952. *Language Map of South Africa.* Pretoria.

   1953. *Die Tlôkwa en Birwa van Noord Transvaal.* Pretoria.

van Warmelo, N. J.,and Phophi, W. M. D.

   1948–9. *Venda Law.* 4 vols. Pretoria.

Vedder, H.

   1923. *Die Bergdama.* 2 vols. Hamburg.

   1934. *Das alte Südwestafrika.* Berlin.

Wandres, C.

   1903. Die Khoi-Khoin oder Naman. *Rechtsverhältnisse von Eingeborenen Völkern* (ed. S. R. Steinmetz): 313–25. Berlin.

   1909. Ueber das Recht der Naman und Bergdaman. *Z. Kol. Pol.,* 11: 657–86.

   1910. Ueber Rechtsbewusstsein und Recht . . . der Hottentotten. *Z. Kol. Pol.,* 12: 269–81.

Wikar, H. J.

   1779. [Report of a Journey along the Orange River.] *Publications of the van Riebeeck Society,* No. 15 (1935): 20–219. Cape Town.

Wilhelm, J. H.

   1953. Die Kung-Buschleute. *Jb. Mus. Völkerkunde* (Leipzig), 12: 91–189.

Zastrow, B. von, and Vedder, H.

   1930. Die Buschmänner. *Das Eingeborenenrecht* (ed. E. Schultz-Ewerth and L. Adam), ii: 399–435. Stuttgart.

INDEX

Advisers and officers, political:
  Bantu, 42 ff., 46 ff., 57 f., 60, 61,
    109, 140 ff., 143, 144 ff., 150.
  Bergdama and Bushmen, 46, 49,
    62 f., 86.
  Hottentots, 45 f., 49, 61 f., 83, 117.
  Cf. Food-master, indunas
Age and political influence:
  Bantu, 60 f.
  Bergdama and Bushmen, 62 f.
  Hottentots, 62.
Age-groups (Bergdama), 63
Age-sets (Bantu):
  distribution, 65
  creation, 47, 70
  organization, 55, 59, 76, 77, 108,
    216
  functions, 47, 48, 61, 72, 123,
    215 f.
  attachment to leaders, 27, 61
Agricultural cycle (Bantu), 71 f., 99
Ancestor worship, 73, 86, 125
Andaman Islanders, 4, 38, 39, 206,
  208
Andersson, C. J., 84
Army. See Military Organization
Assemblies, popular:
  Bantu, 43 ff., 59 f., 65, 75, 150 ff.
  Hottentots, 46, 53, 62, 82, 192
Auen. See Bushmen
Australian aborigines, 4 f., 18, 38,
  208
Band (Bergdama and Bushmen):
  origin, 26, 207
  size, 9, 34, 203, 204
  territory, 11 f.
  social composition, 16 f., 24, 33 f.,
    36, 205
  membership, 20, 21, 25, 206
  integration, 119 f.

Banishment, 25, 79
Bantu:
  subdivisions, 7 f.
  mode of subsistence, 8, 204
  political communities, 10
  settlement patterns, 15, 204
  local variations, 64 f., 214
  common features, 65
    Cf. advisers, age, age-sets, agri-
    cultural cycle, ancestor worship,
    assemblies, chief, clans, class dis-
    tinctions, commoners, conquest,
    councils, crime, dynastic disputes,
    first-fruits ceremony, homicide,
    immigrants, judicial system, kin-
    ship, labour, land tenure, law,
    legislation, local authorities, local
    units, magicians, military organi-
    zation, natural products, Nguni,
    nobles, regency, secession, serfs,
    settlement patterns, social mobi-
    lity, Sotho, subsistence, succes-
    sion, Swazi, tribe, tribute, Tsonga,
    Tswana, Venda, women, Xhosa,
    Zulu
Barnes, H. E., 127
'Basuto'. See Sotho (Southern)
Beals, R. L., and Hoijer, H., 127
Bergdama, 6 f.
  mode of subsistence, 7
  settlements, 12
  political communities, 9, 133 f.
    Cf. advisers, age, age-groups,
    band, chief, councils, crime, fire,
    food-master, homicide, immi-
    grants, kinship, land tenure, magi-
    cians, natural products, rainmak-
    ing, religion, settlement patterns,
    social control, subsistence, suc-
    cession, tribute
Blood-feuds (Hottentots), 84, **116**

Khurutshe, 10; history, 23, 182
Kinship:
Bantu, 18 f., 30 ff., 114 f., 176
Bergdama and Bushmen, 16 f.,
32 f.
Hottentots, 18 f., 30, 31, 32
and political organization, 2, 4 f.,
16, 29 ff., 60, 108, 112 f., 123,
124, 205 f., 209, 219
Cf. Band, blood-feuds, clans,
dynastic disputes, lineages, nobles,
regency, succession
Kung. *See* Bushmen
Kuper, Hilda, 169, 171
Kwena, 10, 14
history, 23, 27, 149, 154, 182 ff.
local authorities, 59
chief's fields, 99
Cf. Motswasele

Labour, communal:
Bantu, 48, 49, 72, 76
Hottentots, 82
Cf. age-sets, tribute
Land tenure:
Bantu, 14 f., 24, 71, 75, 90, 96 f.,
121
Bergdama and Bushmen, 12
Hottentots, 12 f.
Cf. Territory
Laski, H. J., 39 n., 89 n.
Law (Bantu), 28 f., 69 f., 77 f.
Cf. Crime, judicial system,
legislation
Legislation:
Bantu, 69 f., 89, 141 ff., 144, 147
Hottentots, 49, 83, 89, 190 f.
Lentswe (Kgatla chief), 156, 170
Lineages:
Bantu, 30 ff.
Hottentots, 30
Cf. Clans, kinship

Linton, R., 127
Lobedu, 71, 101, 152
tribal population, 18, 36
female chieftainship 51, 166, 217
chieftainship and rainmaking, 74
sacredness of chief, 107
Local authorities (Bantu), 32, 41 f.,
64, 76 f., 122 f., 171 f.
acquisition of office, 55, 58 f., 60,
171 f.
duties and powers, 43, 71, 75 ff.,
79, 96, 113 f.
advisers and officers, 32, 45, 49,
59, 179
relations with chief, 76, 178,
180 ff., 187
relations with subjects, 76,
178 ff., 185
Local authorities (Hottentots), 41,
46, 49, 61, 62, 84 f., 122
Local units:
Bantu, 15, 30 ff., 32, 41, 48 f.,
76 f., 179 f.
Hottentots, 12 f., 30
Lowie, R. H., 3, 50 n., 95, 127,
211, 212
Mabbott, J. D., 88 n.
MacIver, R. M., 3, 4, 11, 38, 39 n.,
67 n., 68, 88, 89, 94, 217
Mackenzie, J., 129
MacLeod, W. C., 38, 39, 217
Magicians, role in public life, 47, 49,
57, 74, 87
Maine, H. S., 2, 16, 18, 20, 29, 32,
33, 37, 38
Malete, 10, 21
local authorities, 59
history, 182, 183 f.
Malinowski, B., 3 f., 19, 38, 39, 95
Military organization:
Bantu, 48 f., 72, 76, 215 f.